Wisdom
from Above

Wisdom from Above

God's Wisdom
from the Book of Proverbs

Campbell McAlpine

New Wine Press

New Wine Ministries
PO Box 17
Chichester
West Sussex
United Kingdom
PO19 2AW

Unless otherwise stated, Scripture quotations are taken from The Holy Bible,
New King James Version. Copyright © 1982 by Thomas Nelson Inc.

Other versions used are:

NIV – New International Version. Copyright © 1973, 1978, 1984 by International
Bible Society.

KJV – King James Version. Crown copyright.

ISBN: 978–1–903725–94–8

Typeset by CRB Associates, Reepham, Norfolk
Cover design by CCD, www.ccdgroup.co.uk
Printed in Malta

I dedicate this book to the memory
of my late wife Shelagh.

"A woman who fears the LORD
she shall be praised."
(Proverbs 31:30)

Contents

Foreword

Life is a one-way ticket. It is likened to a voyage on the sea of time; like a race to be run; like a journey with a destination. Although at times it may seem long, it is, to quote a line from an old hymn, "Life at best is very brief, like the falling of a leaf." Its brevity is described as a "vapor that appears for a little time and is gone"; like a "flower that blooms, then quickly withers." Life is punctuated by such a variety of experiences, and is governed mainly by our own choices. We can be the victims of wrong choices either by ourselves or others, and are sometimes affected by circumstances beyond our control. There is one thing that every honest person will admit – we need help. That help is required from the cradle to the grave. Proper instruction is required, good examples need to he shown, and warnings need to be given. We need to have goals with the right ability to achieve them.

Many years ago a helpful book was written with the title of *Proverbs*. It was written by King Solomon, the son of King David. Solomon had the reputation of being the wisest of men, and his fame spread throughout the known world. He spoke three thousand proverbs, not all of which are recorded, but what we do have contain the finest counsel, encouragement and advice. Many people read a chapter of Proverbs every day which is a recommended practice, for every day we need assistance.

Solomon had a happy childhood, being greatly loved by his mother Bathsheba, and his father David. From a child he was taught the things of God, and the book contains much of what his parents had said. Although he was not the oldest of David's sons, he was the one chosen to succeed him. Solomon's reign has been called "the golden age of Israel." The splendor of his court was unrivaled, and his wisdom and activities unprecedented. He built the Temple with all its magnificence, as well as many other buildings. He reigned for forty years, and his successes were because, he "loved the LORD, walking in the statutes of his father David" (1 Kings 3:3). His wisdom was the result of an answer to prayer in a dramatic encounter with God.

I had a dream

One night while staying in a place called Gibeon, about six miles from Jerusalem, Solomon had a dream. During the day he had been offering sacrifices to God, and God appeared to him and gave him an offer: "Ask! What shall I give you?" (2 Chronicles 1:7).

Knowing that it was God who had placed him on the throne, and realizing the enormity of the task, he replied:

> "Give me wisdom and knowledge, that I may go out and come in before this people; for who can judge this great people of Yours?"
>
> (2 Chronicles 1:10)

God was so pleased with his response in that he had not asked riches, wealth, or honor for himself, or the defeat of his enemies, that He said:

> "Wisdom and knowledge are granted to you; and I will give you riches and wealth and honor, such as none of the kings have had who were before you, nor shall any after you have the like."
>
> (2 Chronicles 1:12)

It is God-given wisdom which marks people as being different. The book of Proverbs is God-given wisdom. It is inspired by God. It contains not only good advice but the very best advice. What would your response be to God's offer, "Ask! What shall I give you?" Actually, God does give us that offer, and promise. It is found in the epistle of James 1:5–6:

> "If any of you lacks wisdom, let him ask of God, who gives to all liberally and without reproach, and it *will* be given to him. But let

him ask in faith, with no doubting, for he who doubts is like a wave of the sea driven and tossed by the wind." (emphasis added)

This God given wisdom is described as:

" ... the wisdom that is from above is first pure, then peaceable, gentle, willing to yield, full of mercy and good fruits, without partiality and without hypocrisy." (James 3:17)

As we go into this wonderful book, let us follow Solomon's example to love and obey God. Proverbs follows the book of Psalms and has been described as coming from the sanctuary to the market-place; from our devotions to our everyday duties. If we obey its teachings, our lives will be changed and blessed, and others will be blessed too.

It is recommended that you read one chapter a day, and read meditatively, then at the end of each chapter apply the truths, receive the encouragement, heed the warnings, and pray for help to be given to receive the Word of God. The application of these truths will affect your life as an individual, as a young person, as a husband or wife, as a parent, as a business person, as a leader, or whatever your calling in life may be. The book of Proverbs is life changing, not only affecting yourself, but also those with whom you come in contact.

Chapter 1

The beginning of knowledge

1. The proverbs of Solomon the son of David, king of Israel:
2. To know wisdom and instruction, to perceive the words of understanding,
3. To receive the instruction of wisdom, justice, judgment, and equity;
4. To give prudence to the simple, to the young man knowledge and discretion –
5. A wise man will hear and increase learning, and a man of understanding will attain wise counsel,
6. To understand a proverb and an enigma, the words of the wise and their riddles.
7. The fear of the Lord is the beginning of knowledge, but fools despise wisdom and instruction.

Shun evil counsel

8. My son, hear the instruction of your father, and do not forsake the law of your mother;
9. For they will be a graceful ornament on your head, and chains about your neck.
10. My son, if sinners entice you, do not consent.
11. If they say, "Come with us, let us lie in wait to shed blood; let us lurk secretly for the innocent without cause;
12. Let us swallow them alive like Sheol, and whole, like those who go down to the Pit;
13. We shall find all kinds of precious possessions, we shall fill our houses with spoil;
14. Cast in your lot among us, let us all have one purse" –
15. My son, do not walk in the way with them, keep your foot from their path;
16. For their feet run to evil, and they make haste to shed blood.
17. Surely, in vain the net is spread in the sight of any bird;

18. But they lie in wait for their own blood, they lurk secretly for their own lives.
19. So are the ways of everyone who is greedy for gain; it takes away the life of its owners.

The call of wisdom

20. Wisdom calls aloud outside; she raises her voice in the open squares.
21. She cries out in the chief concourses, at the openings of the gates in the city she speaks her words:
22. "How long, you simple ones, will you love simplicity? For scorners delight in their scorning, and fools hate knowledge.
23. Turn at my rebuke; surely I will pour out my spirit on you; I will make my words known to you.
24. Because I have called and you refused, I have stretched out my hand and no one regarded,
25. Because you disdained all my counsel, and would have none of my rebuke,
26. I also will laugh at your calamity; I will mock when your terror comes,
27. When your terror comes like a storm, and your destruction comes like a whirlwind, when distress and anguish come upon you.
28. Then they will call on me, but I will not answer; They will seek me diligently, but they will not find me.
29. Because they hated knowledge and did not choose the fear of the LORD,
30. They would have none of my counsel and despised my every rebuke.
31. Therefore they shall eat the fruit of their own way, and be filled to the full with their own fancies.
32. For the turning away of the simple will slay them, and the complacency of fools will destroy them;
33. But whoever listens to me will dwell safely, and will be secure, without fear of evil."

Please first read Proverbs chapter 1. The most important part of this book is the scriptures themselves. Proverbs has rightly been called, "the Book of Wisdom." We require wisdom to live a successful and fulfilling life. There are snares, attractions, dangers, choices to be made, and great wisdom is needed to make the right decisions. The book is so practical, so "nitty gritty" with no frills, just straight talking. The application of its truths will require discipline of life, and the person who refuses to take heed to it, is, in the language of these scriptures "a fool."

The purpose of Proverbs (vv. 2–4)

With an economy of words Solomon gives us the main purposes of this book:

- To know wisdom and instruction.
- To perceive the words of understanding.
- To receive instruction about wisdom, justice, judgment and fairness.
- To give prudence.
- To give young men knowledge and sense.

What an encouragement at the very beginning. If we will personally apply the truths of this book, we will be people of wisdom, understanding, and knowledge. This will enable us to assess circumstances fairly and intelligently, leading us to the right conclusions and actions.

The prerequisites for wisdom

"A wise man will hear." (v. 5). A wise person will be a good listener. Many times we are more prone to speak than to listen. I like the story of the linguist who could be silent in ten different languages! Later in the book Solomon makes the observation,

> "Even a fool is counted wise when he holds his peace;
> When he shuts his lips, he is considered perceptive."   (17:28)

James in his epistle exhorts us to "be swift to hear, slow to speak" (James 1:19).

The other requirement is to "increase learning" (v. 5). We should continually be in the pursuit of God. There is no graduation certificate as there is a great ocean of unexplored knowledge still to be discovered. It is always important to notice two things when we read promises in the Bible: firstly what God tells us to do, and secondly what God promises He will do – the "ifs" and the "thens."

If we fulfill the conditions He will fulfill His promise. Here we are

promised that if we will hear, increase in learning, we will understand the proverbs, the words of the wise.

The primary principle

Lesson number one in the school of wisdom and knowledge is to
fear God. "The fear of the LORD is the beginning of knowledge"
(v. 7). In another chapter we read, "the fear of the LORD is the
beginning of wisdom" (9:10). We are going to be reminded
throughout the whole of Proverbs of the importance and results
of fearing God. What is it to fear God? It is a reverential respect and
love for God. It is an awe of God because of who He is in the
perfection of His character, His holiness, purity, power, glory,
justice, love, grace, mercy, compassion etc. It is a love for God
which does not want to grieve Him. The first instruction that
God gave to Israel was not to serve Him, but to fear Him. What is
the main problem in the lives of those who have no place for God?
Paul gives the answer: "There is no fear of God before their eyes"
(Romans 3:18). They live as if there is no God, no death, no eternity,
no heaven, no hell, no judgment day. The evidence of fearing God
is obeying Him. The description of the early Church was that they
were "walking in the fear of the Lord, and in the comfort of the
Holy Spirit" (Acts 9:31). Verse 7 in this first chapter says:

> "The fear of the LORD is the beginning of knowledge,
> But fools despise wisdom and instruction."

Parental influence

What responsibilities and privileges parents have in bringing up
children. Are you a parent? How are you bringing up your family?
Solomon exhorts his son,

> "My son, hear the instruction of your father,
> And do not forsake the law of your mother."   (v. 8)

Solomon had been well taught by his parents, and much that he
learned from them he is passing on to another generation. How

many have been influenced by godly parents such as Jacob, Joseph, Moses, Samuel, John the Baptist, etc. In a later chapter Solomon writes:

> "Train up a child in the way he should go,
> And when he is old he will not depart from it." (22:6)

How many, including myself, are so grateful for godly parents who instructed us in the ways of God?

Plotters and parasites

Included in his instructions to his son is the warning of the dangers of bad company. He foresees those who would tempt him to join their company in some get-rich quick scheme. He portrays a dramatic plan of theft and bloodshed, and pleads not to get involved in their plans or walk with them. He shows that they will suffer self-inflicted wounds, and in seeking to trap others will themselves be trapped. He adds:

> "So are the ways of everyone who is greedy of gain.
> It takes away the life of its owners." (v. 19)

The pleading of wisdom

Wisdom is personified as a lady, raising her voice, and pleading with people to listen. She desires the best for the inhabitants of the town, "in the open squares," for those "in the chief concourses" – the market-place, and for those in authority "at . . . the gates of the city" (vv. 20–21). She is grieved because of their naivete, and self-confident mocking. She pleads with them to repent and take heed to the warnings, with the promise of God's Spirit being outpoured. They refused the call, and would not choose the fear of the Lord. The chapter closes with a wonderful promise:

> "But whoever listens to me will dwell safely,
> And will be secure, without fear of evil." (v. 33)

Personal application

Obey the instructions

- Hear and increase in learning (v. 5).
- Attain wise counsel (v. 5).
- Fear God (v. 7).
- Listen to your parents' good instructions (v. 8).
- If sinners entice, do not consent (v. 10).
- Do not walk in the way with them (v. 15).
- Turn at reproof (v. 23).

Promises

- A wise man will increase in learning (v. 5).
- A man of understating will attain wise counsel (v. 5).
- Surely I will pour out My Spirit on you, I will make My words known to you (v. 23).
- Whoever listens to Me will dwell safely, and will be secure, without fear of evil (v. 33).

Your own personal response to God:

---

*If any of you lacks wisdom, let him ask of God, who gives to all liberally and without reproach, and it **will** be given to him (James 1:5).*

Chapter 2

The value of wisdom

1. My son, *if* you receive my words, and treasure my commands within you,
2. So that you incline your ear to wisdom, and apply your heart to understanding;
3. Yes, *if* you cry out for discernment, and lift up your voice for understanding,
4. *If* you seek her as silver, and search for her as for hidden treasures;
5. *Then* you will understand the fear of the LORD, and find the knowledge of God.
6. For the LORD gives wisdom; from His mouth come knowledge and understanding;
7. He stores up sound wisdom for the upright; He is a shield to those who walk uprightly;
8. He guards the paths of justice, and preserves the way of His saints.
9. Then you will understand righteousness and justice, equity and every good path.
10. When wisdom enters your heart, and knowledge is pleasant to your soul,
11. Discretion will preserve you; understanding will keep you,
12. To deliver you from the way of evil, from the man who speaks perverse things,
13. From those who leave the paths of uprightness to walk in the ways of darkness;
14. Who rejoice in doing evil, and delight in the perversity of the wicked;
15. Whose ways are crooked, and who are devious in their paths;
16. To deliver you from the immoral woman, from the seductress who flatters with her words,
17. Who forsakes the companion of her youth, and forgets the covenant of her God.
18. For her house leads down to death, and her paths to the dead;

19. None who go to her return, nor do they regain the paths of life –
20. So you may walk in the way of goodness, and keep to the paths of righteousness.
21. For the upright will dwell in the land, and the blameless will remain in it;
22. But the wicked will be cut off from the earth, and the unfaithful will be uprooted from it.

We continue in the university of wisdom. This chapter contains some of the most important teaching in the Bible. Three things are essential for the benefits of God's Word: knowledge, understanding and wisdom. By knowledge we obtain the facts, the truth. By understanding we have insight, knowing what the facts mean. By wisdom we apply what we know and understand to our lives and circumstances.

God loves you

The chapter starts with "My son." Behind these words is the loving heart of the father. Solomon may have been repeating some things his father David had shared with him, or he may have been thinking of his own family. We can be assured of the great love God has for us. It is His love that desires us to be wise. "My son ... My daughter..."

> "Behold what manner of love the Father has bestowed on us, that we should be called children of God!"   (1 John 3:1)

God had promised David that He would be a Father to his son, Solomon: "I will be his Father, and he shall be My son" (2 Samuel 7:14). How wonderful that the Lord Jesus came, lived, died, rose again so that we might have "fellowship ... with the Father and with His Son Jesus Christ" (1 John 1:3). All the instructions, teachings, warnings, encouragements in the book of Proverbs are evidence that He loves and cares. The evidence of our love to Him is that we receive and obey His Word. Jesus said, "He who has My command-ments and keeps them, it is he who loves Me" (John 14:21) and again,

"You are My friends if you do whatever I command you" (John 15:14).

A key to the knowledge of God

A great promise is given to us in verse 5:

> "*Then* you will understand the fear of the LORD,
> And find the knowledge of God." (emphasis added)

As we saw in the last chapter the importance of the "ifs" and the "thens" . . . God's promises and His conditions for their fulfillment. Here are the conditions for understanding the fear of the Lord and finding the knowledge of God:

If you receive My words (v. 1)
Not merely reading the Word, but receiving it. Receiving involves agreeing with the Word; obeying the Word; responding to it.

If you treasure My commands within you (v. 1)
That is, we put great value on what God tells us to do. His Word is "better than gold and riches." As we read and receive we are storing up great wealth within us. David said,

> "Your word have I *hidden* in my heart,
> That I may not sin against You." (Psalm 119:11, emphasis added)

The value we put on God's Word will be measured by the priority we give to it.

If you listen, apply, cry out, lift up your voice, seek and search (vv. 2–4)
What language! This is not a casual reading of God's Word, a few verses with breakfast, but the longing, thirsting, praying, hungering to know God with a seeking heart.

If you seek her as silver, and search for her as for hidden treasure (v. 4)
The Word of God is like a gold mine. The treasure is not only on the

surface, we have to dig. Thank God we have the greatest Teacher with us wherever we are, the Holy Spirit. Jesus said, "He will guide you into all truth" (John 16:13).

Then you will understand the fear of the LORD and find the knowledge of God" (v. 5)

We have already seen that the essential starting point in the school of wisdom and knowledge is the fear of the Lord. The promise is that if we obey the instructions we will understand the fear of the Lord, and find the knowledge of God. Let us be convinced that there is no greater knowledge than the knowledge of God. Hear the expressed desire of, or through, some of the great saints:

Moses:

> "Show me now Your way, that I may *know You*."
>
> (Exodus 33:13, emphasis added)

David:

> "As the deer pants for the water brooks,
> So pants my soul for You, O God."   (Psalm 42:1)

Jeremiah:

> " 'Let not the wise man glory in his wisdom,
> Let not the mighty man glory in his might,
> Nor let the rich man glory in his riches;
> But let him who glories glory in this,
> That he understands and *knows Me*,
> That I am the LORD, exercising lovingkindness,
>   judgment and righteousness in the earth,
> For in these I delight,' says the LORD."
>
> (Jeremiah 9:23–24, emphasis added)

Paul:

> "That I may *know Him* and the power of His resurrection, and the fellowship of His sufferings, being conformed to His death."
>
> (Philippians 3:10, emphasis added)

Peter:

> "Grow in the grace and *knowledge of our Lord and Saviour Jesus Christ*. To Him be the glory both now and forever."
>
> (2 Peter 3:18, emphasis added)

The fear of the Lord

How precious is the promise that we will understand the fear of the Lord. How very, very important this is. Let's ask some questions and discover the answers:

- Do you want knowledge?
  "The fear of the LORD is the beginning of knowledge."   (1:7)
- Do you want wisdom?
  "The fear of the LORD is the beginning of wisdom."   (9:10)
- Do you want to hate evil?
  "The fear of the LORD is to hate evil."   (8:13)
- Do you want long life?
  "The fear of the LORD prolongs days."   (10:27)
- Do you want to be confident?
  "In the fear of the LORD there is strong confidence."   (14:26)
- Do you want riches and honor?
  "By humility and the fear of the LORD
  Are riches and honor and life."   (22:4)
- Do you want happiness?
  "Happy is the man who is always reverent."   (28:14)

Promises in this chapter to those who fear God and find the knowledge of God

Protection

- God is a shield to those who walk uprightly (v. 7).
- He guards the path . . . and preserves the way of His saints (v. 8).
- He delivers from the evil man and the evil woman (vv. 12, 16).

Provision

- You will understand righteousness, justice, equity and every good work (v. 9)
- Discretion will preserve you (v. 11).

The description of evil people

We live in an evil world in which there are evil men and women from whom we need deliverance. Here is the description of evil men:

- They walk in the way of evil (v. 12).
- They speak perverse things (v. 12).
- They leave the paths of righteousness (v. 13).
- They walk in darkness (v. 13).
- They rejoice and delight in doing evil (v. 14).
- Their ways are crooked (v. 15).
- They are devious, unscrupulous (v. 15).

Here is the description of the "evil woman":

- She is immoral (v. 16). '
- She is a seductress (v. 16).
- She is a flatterer (v. 16).
- She forsakes her husband (v. 17).
- She breaks her marriage vows (v. 17).
- Her house leads to death (v. 18).

Personal application

Thank and worship God for who He is

- Your Father who loves you (v. 1).
- The giver of wisdom, knowledge and understanding (v. 6).
- Your shield, protector, provider (vv. 7, 8).
- Your deliverer (vv. 12, 16).
- For Jesus who made it possible for us to know God.

Obey the instructions

- Receive His words; treasure them (v. 1).
- Listen and apply truth (v. 2).
- Cry out for discernment and understanding (v. 3).
- Seek and search (v. 4).

Receive the promises

- You will understand the fear of the Lord (v. 5).
- You will find the knowledge of God (v. 5).
- The Lord gives wisdom, knowledge and understanding (v. 6).
- You will understand righteousness, justice, equity and every good path (v. 9).
- Discretion will preserve you; understanding will keep you (v. 11).
- You will be delivered from the evil man and woman (vv. 12, 16).
- You will walk in the way of goodness and keep the paths of righteousness (v. 20).
- You will dwell in the land (v. 22).

Other things God has said to you in this chapter

Things and people to pray for

*If any of you lacks wisdom, let him ask of God, who gives to all liberally and without reproach, and it **will** be given to him (James 1:5).*

Chapter 3

Guidance for the young

1. My son, do not forget my law, but let your heart keep my commands;
2. For length of days and long life and peace they will add to you.
3. Let not mercy and truth forsake you; bind them around your neck, write them on the tablet of your heart,
4. And so find favor and high esteem in the sight of God and man.
5. Trust in the LORD with all your heart, and lean not on your own understanding;
6. In all your ways acknowledge Him, and He shall direct your paths.
7. Do not be wise in your own eyes; fear the LORD and depart from evil.
8. It will be health to your flesh, and strength to your bones.
9. Honor the LORD with your possessions, and with the firstfruits of all your increase;
10. So your barns will be filled with plenty, and your vats will overflow with new wine.
11. My son, do not despise the chastening of the LORD, nor detest His correction;
12. For whom the LORD loves He corrects, just as a father the son in whom he delights.
13. Happy is the man who finds wisdom, and the man who gains understanding;
14. For her proceeds are better than the profits of silver, and her gain than fine gold.
15. She is more precious than rubies, and all the things you may desire cannot compare with her.
16. Length of days is in her right hand, in her left hand riches and honor.
17. Her ways are ways of pleasantness, and all her paths are peace.
18. She is a tree of life to those who take hold of her, and happy are all who retain her.
19. The LORD by wisdom founded the earth; by understanding He established the heavens;

20. By His knowledge the depths were broken up, and clouds drop down the dew.
21. My son, let them not depart from your eyes – keep sound wisdom and discretion;
22. So they will be life to your soul and grace to your neck.
23. Then you will walk safely in your way, and your foot will not stumble.
24. When you lie down, you will not be afraid; yes, you will lie down and your sleep will be sweet.
25. Do not be afraid of sudden terror, nor of trouble from the wicked when it comes;
26. For the LORD will be your confidence, and will keep your foot from being caught.
27. Do not withhold good from those to whom it is due, when it is in the power of your hand to do so.
28. Do not say to your neighbor, "Go, and come back, and tomorrow I will give it," when you have it with you.
29. Do not devise evil against your neighbor, for he dwells by you for safety's sake.
30. Do not strive with a man without cause, if he has done you no harm.
31. Do not envy the oppressor, and choose none of his ways;
32. For the perverse person is an abomination to the LORD, but His secret counsel is with the upright.
33. The curse of the LORD is on the house of the wicked, but He blesses the home of the just.
34. Surely He scorns the scornful, but gives grace to the humble.
35. The wise shall inherit glory, but shame shall be the legacy of fools.

In this chapter we are reminded of the greatness and value of God given wisdom, and how it can be practically applied to our lives. The mention of "dos" and "don'ts" is not a mere legalistic formula, but instructions and demonstrations of how wise people live, and how they act. Again we are addressed as children, "My son . . ." We are in His family and also in His school. God, like any good parent, wishes the very best for His children – for you. He wants us to really understand and appreciate the true value of wisdom.

The greatness and value of wisdom

God created the universe by wisdom, understanding and knowledge:

> "The LORD by wisdom founded the earth;
> By understanding He established the heavens;
> By His knowledge the depths were broken up,
> And clouds drop down the dew."   (vv. 19–20)

His wisdom is creative:

> "The heavens declare the glory of God;
> And the firmament shows His handiwork."   (Psalm 19:1)

No wonder Paul cries out, "Oh, the depth of the riches of the wisdom and knowledge of God" (Romans 11:33). Speaking of the Lord Jesus, he writes, "in whom are hidden all the treasures of wisdom and knowledge" (Colossians 2:3).

Wisdom is more valuable than silver, gold and the finest jewels.

> "Her proceeds are better than the profits of silver,
> And her gain than fine gold.
> She is more precious than rubies,
> And all the things you may desire cannot be compared with her."
>   (vv. 14–15)

The blessings of wisdom and obedience

Longevity

- Length of days and long life and peace they will add to you (v. 2).
- Length of days is in her right hand, in her left hand riches and honor (v. 16).

Life and happiness

- Happy is the man who finds wisdom, and the man who gains understanding (v. 13).

- She is a tree of life to those who take hold of her, and happy are all who retain her (v. 18).
- They will be life to your soul and grace to your neck (v. 22).
- It will be health to your flesh, and strength to your bones (v. 8).

Honor

- So find favor and high esteem in the sight of God and man. (v. 4).
- The wise shall inherit glory = honour (v. 35).

Safety

- You will walk safely in your way, and your foot will not stumble (v. 23).
- When you lie down you will not be afraid; yes, you will lie down and your sleep shall be sweet (v. 24).
- For the LORD will be your confidence, and will keep your foot from being caught (v. 26).
- He blesses the habitation of the just (v. 33).

Grace

- He gives grace to the humble (v. 34).

Direction

- He shall direct your paths (v. 6).

Loved by God

- For whom the LORD loves He corrects, just as a father the son in whom he delights (v. 12).

Counsel

- His secret counsel is with the upright (v. 32).

Conditions for the blessings of wisdom

Do . . .

- Let your heart keep my commands (v. 1).
- Bind them – mercy and truth – around your neck, write them on the tablet of your heart (v. 3).
- *Trust* in the LORD with all your heart (v. 5).
- In *all* your ways acknowledge Him (v. 6).
- Fear the LORD and depart from evil (v. 7).
- Honor the LORD with your possessions and with the firstfruits of all your increase (v. 9).

Do not . . .

- Forget my law (v. 1).
- Let not mercy and truth forsake you (v. 3).
- Lean to your own understanding (v. 5).
- Be wise in your own eyes (v. 7).
- Despise the chastening of the LORD, nor detest His correction (v. 11).
- Be afraid of sudden terror, nor of trouble from the wicked when it comes (v. 25).
- Withhold good from those to whom it is due, when it is in the power of your hand to do so (v. 27).
- Say to your neighbor, "Go, and come back, and tomorrow I will give it," when you have it with you (v. 28).
- Devise evil against your neighbor, for he dwells by you for safety's sake (v. 29).
- Strive with a man without cause, if he has done you no harm (v. 30).
- Envy the oppressor, and choose none of his ways (v. 31).

Application

- Go though the list of God's promised blessings to the wise and obedient. Tell the Lord you desire His blessings. Ask Him to show you if there is any realm of disobedience in your life. If

so, confess, repent – receive His forgiveness with the promise of making any restitution necessary.
- Praise Him for all past blessings.
- Go through the "dos" and "don'ts." Pray them in.
- Pray for anything in the chapter that has quickened a need or desire for yourself or others.
- Acknowledge Him in all your ways.

If any of you lacks wisdom, let him ask of God, who gives to all liberally and without reproach, and it **will** *be given to him* (James 1:5).

Chapter 4

Security in wisdom

1. Hear, my children, the instruction of a father, and give attention to know understanding;
2. For I give you good doctrine: do not forsake my law.
3. When I was my father's son, tender and the only one in the sight of my mother,
4. He also taught me, and said to me: "Let your heart retain my words; keep my commands, and live.
5. Get wisdom! Get understanding! Do not forget, nor turn away from the words of my mouth.
6. Do not forsake her, and she will preserve you; love her, and she will keep you.
7. Wisdom is the principal thing; therefore get wisdom. And in all your getting, get understanding.
8. Exalt her, and she will promote you; she will bring you honor, when you embrace her.
9. She will place on your head an ornament of grace; A crown of glory she will deliver to you."
10. Hear, my son, and receive my sayings, and the years of your life will be many.
11. I have taught you in the way of wisdom; I have led you in right paths.
12. When you walk, your steps will not be hindered, and when you run, you will not stumble.
13. Take firm hold of instruction, do not let go; keep her, for she is your life.
14. Do not enter the path of the wicked, and do not walk in the way of evil.
15. Avoid it, do not travel on it; turn away from it and pass on.
16. For they do not sleep unless they have done evil; and their sleep is taken away unless they make someone fall.
17. For they eat the bread of wickedness, and drink the wine of violence.
18. But the path of the just is like the shining sun, that shines ever brighter unto the perfect day.

19. The way of the wicked is like darkness; they do not know what makes them stumble.
20. My son, give attention to my words; incline your ear to my sayings.
21. Do not let them depart from your eyes; keep them in the midst of your heart;
22. For they are life to those who find them, and health to all their flesh.
23. Keep your heart with all diligence, for out of it spring the issues of life.
24. Put away from you a deceitful mouth, and put perverse lips far from you.
25. Let your eyes look straight ahead, and your eyelids look right before you.
26. Ponder the path of your feet, and let all your ways be established.
27. Do not turn to the right or the left; remove your foot from evil.

The importance of parental influence

How very important it is to bring up children in the right way, and teach them the right things. Solomon had good memories of his childhood, being greatly loved by both his parents. Having been so influenced by the instructions he received as a child, he now encourages his own to listen to instructions and obey them. He assures them he is giving them good teaching, "I give you good doctrine" (v. 2). The Bible speaks of different doctrines: "the doctrine of men," "the doctrine of demons," "the doctrine of God," and "the doctrine of Christ." How wonderful that we can wholly rely on the teachings of the Bible.

> "All scripture is given by inspiration of God, and is profitable for doctrine, for reproof, for correction, for instruction in righteousness, that the man of God may be complete, thoroughly equipped for every good work." (2 Timothy 3:16–17)

So Solomon is teaching what he was taught as a child. Sometimes in conversation we hear people say, or say ourselves, "as my father used to say," or "as my mother used to say." David had brought Solomon up in the right way, and he continually quotes his Dad. One of the great and concise teachings David gave to him was:

> "As for you my son Solomon, *know the God* of your father, and *serve Him* with a loyal heart, and with a willing mind; for the LORD searches all hearts and understands all the intent of the thoughts. If you seek Him, He will he found by you; but if you forsake Him. He will cast you off forever." (1 Chronicles 28:9, emphasis added)

What great teaching. What are you teaching your children? What advice are they receiving which one day they will quote to their own children? Solomon quotes something his father said:

> "Let your heart retain my words;
> Keep my commands, and live.
> Get wisdom! Get understanding!
> Do not forget, nor turn away from the words of my mouth.
> Do not forsake her, and she will preserve you;
> Love her, and she will keep you.
> Wisdom is the principal thing;
> Therefore get wisdom.
> And in all your getting, get understanding.
> Exalt her, and she will promote you;
> She will being you honor, when you embrace her.
> She will place on your head an ornament of grace;
> A crown of glory she will deliver to you." (vv. 4–9)

Promises to those who choose wisdom

- *Preservation* – she will preserve you (v. 6).
- *Protection* – she will keep you (v. 6).
- *Promotion* – she will promote you (v. 8).
- *Position*– she will honor you (v. 8).
- *Graciousness* – she will place on your head an ornament of grace (v. 9).
- *Glory* – a crown of glory she will deliver to you (v. 9).
- *Long life* – the years of your life will be many (v. 10).
- *Safety* – your steps will not he hindered . . . when you run you will not stumble (v. 12).
- *Life* – she is your life (v. 13).

The conditions for the fulfillment of the promises

Once agan we must note the conditions that are given for the fulfillment of these glorious promises:

- Hear instruction (v. 1).
- Give attention to understanding (v. 1).
- Do not forsake the law (v. 2).
- Let your heart retain my words (v. 4).
- Keep my commands (v. 4).
- Get wisdom (v. 5).
- Get understanding (v. 5).
- Do not forget it (v. 5).
- Do not turn away from it (v. 5).
- Do not forsake her (v. 6).
- Get wisdom (v. 6).
- Get understanding (v. 7).
- Exalt wisdom (v. 8).
- Hear and receive my sayings (v. 10).
- Take firm hold of instruction (v. 13).
- Keep her, don't let her go (v. 13).
- Do not enter the path of the wicked (v. 14).
- Do not walk in the way of evil (v. 14).
- Avoid the way of evil, do not travel on it, turn away from it, pass on (v. 15).
- Give attention to my words (v. 20).
- Incline your ears to my sayings (v. 20).
- Don't let them depart from your eyes (v. 21).
- Keep them in the midst of your heart (v. 21).
- Keep your heart with all diligence (v. 23).
- Put away a deceitful mouth (v. 24).
- Put perverse lips far from you (v. 24).
- Let your eyes look straight ahead (v. 25).
- Let your eyelids look right before you (v. 25).
- Ponder the path of your feet (v. 26).
- Let all your ways be established (v. 26).
- Do not turn to the right or to the left (v. 27).
- Remove your foot from evil (v. 27).

God can give us the wisdom, the ability to do His will when we choose to obey Him.

Life is governed and determined by choices

In this chapter we are reminded that there are two paths on which people can travel: the path of the wicked and the path of the just. Jesus taught that there are two ways: a broad way that leads to destruction, and a narrow way that leads to life. Wise people choose the way of the just; foolish people choose the way of the wicked. Thank God that Jesus came to show us the right way. He said of Himself, "I am the way, the truth, and the life. No one comes to the Father except through Me" (John 14:6). When we come to Him who is the only way to the Father, we join the ranks of the just – those who have been justified: "not by works of righteousness which we have done, but according to His mercy He saved us" (Titus 3:5). The righteousness of God, which is available to all through faith in Jesus Christ, is on all who believe. Because Jesus died for our sins when we believe in Him, His righteousness is imputed to us. What a miracle salvation is! We are delivered from the way of the wicked to the way of the just.

> "He has delivered us from the power of darkness and conveyed us into the kingdom of the Son of His love."   (Colossians 1:13)

Pause and thank Him. Notice how Solomon describes the two ways.

The path of the wicked

- It is an evil way (v. 14).
- It is to be avoided at all cost (v. 15).
- The wicked don't rest unless they have done evil – it's part of their nature, their life (v. 16).
- They are not only wicked themselves, but they cause others to do evil (v. 16).
- Their way is the way of violence and darkness (v. 19).

The path of the just

What a contrast: light instead of darkness; goodness instead of evil; things getting better instead of getting worse – "the path of the just is like the shining sun" (v. 18). Solomon doesn't say or imply that the path of the just is easy, but that it is best. Christians are persecuted for righteousness' sake. Darkness hates light. Jesus made it clear that the just, the righteous, would be misunderstood, persecuted, hated, and many would die ... but it is still the best way. It is like the shining sun. John writes about walking "in the light as He is in the light" (1 John 1:7). In Job we read:

> "And your life would be brighter than noonday.
> Though you were dark, you would be like the morning.
> And you would be secure, because there is hope."
>
> (Job 11:17–18)

The wicked have no hope, but the just do. When David came to end of his life he described the person who would live in the fear of the Lord, loving reverence for Him. He said:

> " ... he shall be like the light of the morning when the sun rises,
> A morning without clouds,
> Like the tender grass springing out of the earth,
> By clear shining after rain." (2 Samuel 23:4)

The path of the just is like the shining sun, because Jesus is the Light of the world. He is perfect light. Remember Saul of Tarsus's encounter with Him on the Damascus road – "a light shone around him from heaven" (Acts 9:3). When he described his experience to King Agrippa he said: "I saw a light from heaven, brighter than the sun, shining around me" (Acts 26:13).

Jesus said, "I am the light of the world. He who follows Me shall not walk in darkness, but have the light of life" (John 8:12). What an encouragement for the just; things are going to get brighter. The best is yet to come.

Are you going through times of difficulty; times of unanswered questions; times of sorrow and disappointment; times of doubt? Look up – the best is yet to come! A perfect day is coming.

Remember the Lord Jesus. He knows what it is like to live down here. He was criticized, mocked, rejected, scorned, scourged, crucified, but He knew there was a perfect day in the future. The writer to the Hebrews exhorts us to be

> "looking into Jesus, the author and finisher of our faith, who for *the joy that was set before Him* endured the cross, despising the shame, and has sat down at the right hand of the throne of God."
>
> (Hebrews 12:2, emphasis added)

The Cross was in the foreground, and eternity in the background. For all the saints who have followed Jesus the most important thing is not the "here" but the "hereafter." The heroes of Hebrews 11 desired "a better, that is, a heavenly country." They, by faith, accepted that down here they were only strangers and pilgrims and that in the future there was a brighter and perfect day.

How does the path get brighter? By living one day at a time, loving God and living for Him. By committing our ways and works to Him. By being confident "that He who has begun good work in you will complete it until the day of Jesus Christ" (Philippians 1:6). By daily reading and receiving His Word, because the entrance of His word gives light. By walking in obedience, that is walking in the light. How wonderful to walk in the path of the just: "the just shall live by faith" (Galatians 3:11).

It was said of Noah, who took a hundred years to build the ark, and was mocked and ridiculed for it, that he "was a *just* man, perfect in his generations [and] walked with God" (Genesis 6:9, emphasis added). He obeyed God – a brighter day was coming.

Joseph, the husband of Mary, the mother of Jesus, not understanding all that was happening was told by the angel, "do not be afraid to take to you Mary your wife" (Matthew 1:20). He obeyed the word and he is described as "a just man" (Matthew 1:19).

Yes, the pathway shines brighter and brighter unto the perfect day. Jesus has gone to prepare a place for us. One of these days,

> "... the Lord Himself will descend from heaven with a shout, with the voice of an archangel, and with the trumpet of God. And the dead in Christ will rise first. Then we who are alive and remain

shall be caught up together with them to meet the Lord in the air. And thus we shall always be with the Lord."

(1 Thessalonians 4:16–17)

. . . the perfect day has come.

"And God will wipe away every tear from their eyes; there shall be no more death, nor sorrow, nor crying. There shall be no more pain, for the former things have passed away." (Revelation 21:4)

. . . the perfect day has come.

With all the privileges and joys of walking with God here, and all the glorious prospects of the future, no wonder in this chapter Solomon exhorts and encourages his hearers and readers to live wisely and to live righteously. He not only taught the way, but he said, "I have taught you in the way of wisdom; I have led you in right paths" (v. 11). It is one thing to teach the truth and another to walk in the truth you teach. May our children and others follow what we are as well as what we say.

I remember reading of a man in the United States of America who become an alcoholic. Before going to work each day he called at a bar for a drink. One snowy winter morning when he was in the bar he felt a tug at his coat. With glass in hand he looked down and there was his little boy. "How did you get here?" he asked.

The little fellow said, "I just followed daddy's footsteps."

How are we leading?

The blessings of the just

The Word of God is such an encouragement. In several chapters in Proverbs Solomon reminds us of special blessings which accompany just and righteous living. Here are a few of them:

- God blesses the house of the just (3:33).
- The memory of the righteous is blessed (10:7).
- Blessings are on the head of the righteous (10:6).
- The tongue of the righteous is choice silver (10:20).
- The mouth of the righteous brings forth wisdom (10:31).

- Through knowledge the righteous will be delivered (11:9).
- The righteous will come through trouble (12:13).
- A righteous man may fall seven times but he will rise again (24:16). (So the saving is right, you cannot keep a good man down.)

Application

I am sure we all agree that for the Word of God to be beneficial it has to be applied. It is personal. God with His fatherly heart desires the very best for us and for His Kingdom. So in summary:

- Let us thank God for parents who brought us up in the right way. If that was not our experience, let us resolve to bring up our children with godly influence. Encourage children to honor their parents and thus fulfill God's commandment.
- Let us determine to be good listeners. In this chapter Solomon asked his children to hear, and also asked his son to hear.
- Let us guard our hearts. Solomon said, "Let your heart retain my words" (v. 4). We do not want merely to have a head knowledge of truth, but a heart knowledge.
- Let us pursue wisdom. Don't forget the promise: "If any of you lacks wisdom, let him ask of God, who gives to all liberally and without reproach, and it will be given to him" (James 1:5). Wisdom – don't leave home without it!
- Let us thank God for His so great salvation, and ask Him to help us, and enable us to live righteous lives, just lives.
- Let us praise God for every circumstance through which He has brought us, all evidence of His love, His care and the value He puts on us.
- Let us live in the present with eternity in the background. We are on a journey leading us to a glorious destination, and a glorious hope: we shall see the Lord . . . and we will be like Him.

Is there anything in my life that needs to be put right that has been brought to the light in this chapter? Anything relating to the way I have brought up my children? Have I been a good example? Am I living justly?

"If we confess our sins, He is faithful and just to forgive us our sins and to cleanse us from all unrighteousness." (1 John 1:9)

Thank God, if need be, we can start again, and our way can become brighter and brighter till we come to the perfect day.

*If any of you lacks wisdom, let him ask of God, who gives to all liberally and without reproach, and it **will** be given to him (James 1:5).*

Chapter 5

The peril of adultery

1. My son, pay attention to my wisdom; lend your ear to my understanding,
2. That you may preserve discretion, and your lips may keep knowledge.
3. For the lips of an immoral woman drip honey, and her mouth is smoother than oil;
4. But in the end she is bitter as wormwood, sharp as a two-edged sword.
5. Her feet go down to death, her steps lay hold of hell.
6. Lest you ponder her path of life – her ways are unstable; you do not know them.
7. Therefore hear me now, my children, and do not depart from the words of my mouth.
8. Remove your way far from her, and do not go near the door of her house,
9. Lest you give your honor to others, and your years to the cruel one;
10. Lest aliens be filled with your wealth, and your labors go to the house of a foreigner;
11. And you mourn at last, when your flesh and your body are consumed,
12. And say: "How I have hated instruction, and my heart despised correction!
13. I have not obeyed the voice of my teachers, nor inclined my ear to those who instructed me!
14. I was on the verge of total ruin, in the midst of the assembly and congregation."
15. Drink water from your own cistern, and running water from your own well.
16. Should your fountains be dispersed abroad, streams of water in the streets?
17. Let them be only your own, and not for strangers with you.
18. Let your fountain be blessed, and rejoice with the wife of your youth.
19. As a loving deer and a graceful doe, let her breasts satisfy you at all times; and always be enraptured with her love.

20. For why should you, my son, be enraptured by an immoral woman, and be embraced in the arms of a seductress?
21. For the ways of man are before the eyes of the LORD, and He ponders all his paths.
22. His own iniquities entrap the wicked man, and he is caught in the cords of his sin.
23. He shall die for lack of instruction, and in the greatness of his folly he shall go astray.

The warning and instruction in this chapter is so important, and Solomon implores to pay attention, to listen carefully. Obedience to the teaching will give discretion, understanding and wisdom. How this teaching is needed today. We live in a society where morality is scorned by so many, where standards have been ridiculed, where "sexual freedom" is the accepted thing, where "if it feels good, do it" is the advice. But what about the aftermath: the alarming statistics of increase in sexual disease; unwanted pregnancies; single mothers battling away on their own; the murder of innocents by abortion; broken marriages; broken families; broken hearts and broken bodies? Solomon's own parents had experienced the sorrow of immorality. David had committed adultery with Bathsheba, a married woman whose husband, Uriah, was a loyal soldier in David's army. What tragic consequences: the murder of Uriah; the death of the baby that was conceived in the adulterous affair; the terrible example. True, David really acknowledged and repented of his sin, and God in His great grace forgave him, but he could not escape some of the reaping process.

This chapter is an appeal for purity. It trumpets the seventh commandment, "You shall not commit adultery." God didn't give the Ten Commandments to harm people, but to protect them. They are a demonstration of His love for mankind. We break God's law at our peril. Immorality is firstly a sin against God; it is an act of rebellion and disobedience. In David's confession of his adultery he cried, "Against You, You only have I sinned, and done this evil in Your sight" (Psalm 51:4).

Portrait of a seductress

It is true that men seduce women, but women also seduce men. In this chapter the seductress is described as an immoral woman. The word "immoral" means "evil, decadent, impure, loose, promiscuous, sinful, unchaste, wanton, ungodly." In other chapters in Proverbs she is also described as: an immoral woman (2:16); a flatterer (2:16); a seductress (6:24); evil (6:24); a harlot (6:26); loud and rebellious (7:11); impudent (7:13); a foolish woman (9:13); clamorous (9:13); shameless. This is her true character. She can appear beautiful, alluring, attractive and appealing, but here is the X-ray of the real person:

> "... the lips of an immoral woman drip honey."　　　　(v. 3)

She speaks sweet attractive words, but like the bee that produces honey, it has honey in its month but a sting in its tail: "her mouth is smoother than oil" (v. 6) – slippery, deceiving, dulling the warning of man's conscience. Like the voice of Satan to our first parents, "You will not surely die ... you will be like God" (Genesis 3:4, 5). Every time you read an obituary or hear of a death you know the devil is a liar.

> "But in the end she is as bitter as wormwood,
> Sharp as a two-edged sword."　　　　(v. 4)

There is lust, but no love. There is no concern for the welfare of her victinm – just another conquest. Sweetness turns to bitterness – she has deeply wounded her consort.

> "Her feet go down to death,
> Her steps lay hold on hell."　　　　(v. 5)

Elsewhere in Scriptures we read:

> "The soul who sins shall die."　　　　(Ezekiel 18:4)

> "For the wages of sin is death."　　　　(Romans 6:23)

Beyond all the romance, the soft music, the perfume, the thrill, there is an end, there is reaping. "Her ways are unstable" (v. 6) – she cannot be trusted.

Hear me now

The warning cry goes out: hear ... listen ... pay attention ... don't go near her ... avoid her ... think of the consequences ... you have lost your honour, ruined your character. You will regret it and mourn at the results, and cry, "How I hated instruction and despised reproof. I have not obeyed the voice and advice of those who instructed me ... I face total ruin ... I will be exposed before many" (see vv. 12–14). Be sure your sin will find you out. Sin traps you, and to use Solomon's words, you will find yourself caught in the cords of your own sin (see v. 22).

Adultery may take place behind closed doors or places where no man can see, but verse 21 in this chapter says,

> "For the ways of man are before the eyes of the LORD,
> And He ponders all his paths."

No one can hide from God: "Thou God seest me" (Genesis 16:13 KJV). Billy Sunday, an American evangelist, used to preach a sermon he entitled "God's detective." Be sure your sin will find you out. Let us all take the advice given: pay attention ... listen ... remove your foot far from her, the adulteress ... don't go near the door of her house. Let's be morally pure.

Teaching in the New Testament

Because of the prevalence of the sins of immorality, it is taken up in the New Testament. There is the need today of having the knowledge of the cause, and results of the sins of fornication and adultery, fornication being consensual sexual intercourse between unmarried people, and adultery extramarital sexual intercourse by married people. This was counted a very serious sin in the Old Testament. According to the Levitical law, adulterers and fornicators were put to death. Paul, in writing to the church at Corinth, exhorted them to:

> "Flee sexual immorality. Every sin a man does is outside the body, but he who commits sexual immorality sins against his own body."
>
> (1 Corinthians 6:18)

He made it clear that:

> "... Neither fornicators, nor idolaters, nor adulterers, nor homosexuals, nor sodomites, nor thieves, nor covetous, nor drunkards, nor revilers, nor extortioners will inherit the kingdom of God."
>
> (1 Corinthians 6:9–10)

This is not man's assessment, but God's. Then he reminded them that some of them had participated in these sins, but when they came to Christ, repented of their sins and accepted Him as Savior, they "were washed ... sanctified ... justified in the name of the Lord Jesus" (1 Corinthians 6:11). Oh the grace of God.

Remember when the scribes and Pharisees brought a woman to Jesus who had been caught in the very act of adultery, they reminded Him of their law, which demanded the death penalty, and asked Him what His verdict was. He challenged them that if they were without sin they should cast the first stone. It is evident that they all had committed sin because they each, convicted by their own conscience, left one by one, till Jesus was left alone with the accused woman. "Where are those accusers of yours?" He asked her. "Has no one condemned you?"

She said, "No one, Lord."

That moment she confessed the Lordship of Jesus, He said, "Neither do I condemn you; go and sin no more" (see John 8:3–12).

Thank God there is forgiveness for adulterers and fornicators when they repent, confess and turn from their sin – go and sin no more.

Church discipline

It is an unfortunate fact that within the Church there is much immorality. The Bible gives clear instructions that when this is known by Church leaders it should be dealt with right away. The offender should be faced with the sin and, if true, should be encouraged to repent, confess, and turn from it. On the basis of God's Word, if that is done from the heart, the sin is forgiven. If the individual refuses to repent, it now becomes a church matter, and the person should be excommunicated or, to use Paul's instructions, "put away from yourselves the evil person" (1 Corinthians 5:13). Not only that, but Christians are instructed "not to keep company with anyone named a brother, who is sexually immoral . . . not even to eat with such a person" (1 Corinthians 5:11). The purpose of all discipline is to bring a person back to God. If sins are not dealt with they spread. How many of you have ever seen this discipline applied by Christian leadership?

Immorality is a heart problem

In the previous chapter Solomon encouraged his children to "keep your heart with all diligence, for out of it spring the issues of life" (4:23). Jesus taught that "out of the heart proceed . . . adulteries, fornications" (Matthew 15:19). Our actions and behavior are manifestations of what our hearts are like. Paul reminded the Galatians that adultery and fornication were "works of the flesh" (Galatians 5:19), works of the old sinful nature. How careful we should be in what we watch, what we read, what we listen to. We should not give room or place to what would stir up lust and wrongful desires. We have to guard our minds. Jesus spoke of whoever looks at a woman to lust after her, and said he "has already committed adultery with her in his heart" (Matthew 5:28). That is one reason why it so important to read, study, memorize and meditate on the Word of God. Every word of God is pure. Jesus said to His disciples, "You are already clean because of the word which I have spoken to you" (John 15:3). Jesus prayed for His own disciples, "Sanctify them by Your truth. Your word is truth" (John 17:17). Let us obey the Word and "flee, run away from sexual immorality."

We mentioned that there is forgiveness for the fornicator and adulterer. Forgiveness is also required by the party who has been also sinned against, the husband, or the wife, of the unfaithful spouse. I remember many years ago preaching in a church in the USA. At the end of the meeting many were getting right with God. I saw a lady weeping, and went up to see if I could help in any way.

She told me she was member of that church and that she had been committing adultery. She was truly repentant, and acknowledged and confessed her sin. I assured her of God's forgiveness, and asked her to go home and tell her husband and get right with him. She said. "I could never do that." I told her it was essential as she not only had sinned against God but against her husband. She said she would. Early next morning I had a phone call in the hotel where I was staying. It was this lady who was in great distress and told me she had told her husband and asked for his forgiveness, but things were terrible. I asked them both to come and see me right away. When they arrived the husband told me that their marriage had not been too easy, but he thought that realm was safe. He said, "I do forgive her but I have no affection for her any more." I asked him to get on his knees, and tell God that he had forgiven his wife. He did so and then I prayed for him. I asked God to do a miracle in this man's life and let the Holy Spirit shed abroad in his heart God's love for her, so that he would love her more than he ever had in his life. He got up and they left. That night I was preaching in that church again, and sitting on the platform could hardly believe my eyes. Here was this couple, who were in their forties, sitting together like a couple of teenagers deeply in love. After the meeting he came to me and said, "Campbell, God did it." I was back in that church a year later, met them again, and asked how they were. "Better than ever," they replied. There is an old chorus that says, "Jesus in me loves you." Thank God sins can be forgiven, marriages can be restored, and God can be glorified. Isn't He wonderful?

Maintaining a good marriage

One of the ways to protect against the sin of adultery is to guard, protect and maintain the marriage. Solomon encourages the married man to value his wife. He uses the terms "cistern," "running water," "fountain," "streams", all of which speak of refreshment, satisfaction, mutual joys. He wants his fountain, the source of his love, joy, companionship to be blessed. What a difference there would be in marriages if each desired the blessing of God on one another and desired to be an instrument of that blessing. Divorce is rampant these days and unfortunately and sadly there is much divorce among

Christians. Sometimes there is not divorce, but very unhappy marriages. This is a particular attack of the enemy. He knows that God will always bless true unity, and therefore he tries to bring disunity firstly in the home. If it is in the home, then it is in a church. No miracle happens when a married couple walk through the door of a church. They are still the same people they were half an hour previously at home. Sure, there are often many faults and complaints, such as taking one another for granted, poor communication, selfishness, criticisms, and failure to help one another.

In every aspect of life we need God, we need His help, we need His wisdom, and we need His love. It is interesting to note what Solomon advises; be a blessing to your wife and rejoice with her. Get the joy, the fun back into your relationship, restore romance. How about a lovely bunch of flowers, a box of favorite chocolates, breakfast in bed, a morning cup of tea before she rises. (Am I liable to get stoned for this?) Ask the question, "Is there anything I can do to help?"

What do your children see? Would you like your daughter to be a wife like you? Would you like your son to be a husband like you? A happy marriage is not merely an antidote to adultery, but it is meant to be a relationship which satisfies, fulfills and is enjoyable. My wife Shelagh and I were married for fifty-six years. We have five children and sixteen grandchildren. I do not for one minute set myself as a criterion as a husband, but I can testify to the goodness, grace, long-suffering, mercy and love of God. Like many marriages we knew such a variety of experiences, difficulties, illnesses, moving from one nation to another ... to Africa ... to New Zealand ... to the USA ... back to Britain, bereavements, times of separation due to our work, but our combined testimony is that God is wonderful. He is Jehovah Jireh, the God who meets our needs. If I was asked, and sometimes I am, for advice for a happy marriage, I answer in two words: pray together. I do not say, say prayers together, but really pray together. One cannot truly pray with anyone if there is anything between you. We can say words but not really pray. Sometimes, before I have prayed with my wife, I have had to apologise for wrong words, or attitudes, or actions and ask for forgiveness. The prayer the Lord Jesus taught His disciples is so wonderful and comprehensive, and includes "forgive me my sins as

I forgive..." Then, of course, marriage is enriched by reading God's Word together – we still do that.

Solomon is not shy or backward in his language. He encourages the pleasures of intimacy between husband and wife: "Let her breasts satisfy you at all times ... be enraptured [the word means "intoxicated"] with her love" (v. 19). It is a two-way thing, the man loving and wooing and the wife responding. The question is asked, "Why should you be enraptured, and embrace an immoral woman, when you can have so much better joy with your wife?"

Do any of us need to do some homework? How is your marriage? Does it need some repair? Are there apologies to be made? Is a humbling necessary? Perhaps you need to start and do what you may not have done for so long: pray together. Both put the Lord *first* in your lives and your marriage. The scripture is true:

> "Seek first the kingdom of God and His righteousness, and all these things shall be added to you."   (Matthew 6:33)

God is such a good God. Marriage was His idea – He wants you to be happy, to rejoice in Him and in one another.

Application

As we close, to get full benefit of this chapter let's firstly obey its instructions:

- Pay attention, listen, appreciate good judgment (vv. 1, 2).
- Hear and do not depart from the truth (v. 7).
- Avoid an adulteress; don't go near her house (v. 8).
- Find all your joys and satisfaction in your own marriage (vv. 15–20).

Promises

- If you pay attention to the Word you will be preserved and protected (vv. 1–2).

Conclusion

Lines from an old hymn come to mind:

> "Trust and obey,
> For there's no other way.
> To be happy in Jesus,
> But to trust and obey."   (John Henry Sammis)

If any of you lacks wisdom, let him ask of God, who gives to all liberally
*and without reproach, and it **will** be given to him* (James 1:5).

Chapter 6

Dangerous promises

1. My son, if you become surety for your friend, if you have shaken hands in pledge for a stranger,
2. You are snared by the words of your mouth; you are taken by the words of your mouth.
3. So do this, my son, and deliver yourself; for you have come into the hand of your friend: go and humble yourself; plead with your friend.
4. Give no sleep to your eyes, nor slumber to your eyelids.
5. Deliver yourself like a gazelle from the hand of the hunter, and like a bird from the hand of the fowler.

The folly of indolence

6. Go to the ant, you sluggard! Consider her ways and be wise,
7. Which, having no captain, overseer or ruler,
8. Provides her supplies in the summer, and gathers her food in the harvest.
9. How long will you slumber, O sluggard? When will you rise from your sleep?
10. A little sleep, a little slumber, a little folding of the hands to sleep –
11. So shall your poverty come on you like a prowler, and your need like an armed man.

The wicked man

12. A worthless person, a wicked man, walks with a perverse mouth;
13. He winks with his eyes, he shuffles his feet, he points with his fingers;
14. Perversity is in his heart, he devises evil continually, he sows discord.
15. Therefore his calamity shall come suddenly; suddenly he shall be broken without remedy.
16. These six things the LORD hates, yes, seven are an abomination to Him:
17. A proud look, a lying tongue, hands that shed innocent blood,
18. A heart that devises wicked plans, feet that are swift in running to evil,
19. A false witness who speaks lies, and one who sows discord among brethren.

Beware of adultery

20. My son, keep your father's command, and do not forsake the law of your mother.
21. Bind them continually upon your heart; tie them around your neck.
22. When you roam, they will lead you; when you sleep, they will keep you; and when you awake, they will speak with you.
23. For the commandment is a lamp, and the law a light; reproofs of instruction are the way of life,
24. To keep you from the evil woman, from the flattering tongue of a seductress.
25. Do not lust after her beauty in your heart, nor let her allure you with her eyelids.
26. For by means of a harlot a man is reduced to a crust of bread; and an adulteress will prey upon his precious life.
27. Can a man take fire to his bosom, and his clothes not be burned?
28. Can one walk on hot coals, and his feet not be seared?
29. So is he who goes in to his neighbor's wife; whoever touches her shall not be innocent.
30. People do not despise a thief if he steals to satisfy himself when he is starving.
31. Yet when he is found, he must restore sevenfold; he may have to give up all the substance of his house.
32. Whoever commits adultery with a woman lacks understanding; he who does so destroys his own soul.
33. Wounds and dishonor he will get, and his reproach will not be wiped away.
34. For jealousy is a husband's fury; therefore he will not spare in the day of vengeance.
35. He will accept no recompense, nor will he be appeased though you give many gifts.

Wisdom with our finances

We would all admit that we need wisdom in dealing with our financial affairs. The Bible gives sound instruction about money: not to love it.

> "The love of money is a root of all kinds of evil."
>
> (1 Timothy 6:10)

We are also encouraged to stay out of debt:

> "Owe no one anything except to love one another."
>
> (Romans 13:8)

We have already seen in a previous chapter that we should "honor the LORD with [our] possessions, and with the firstfruits of all [our] increase" (3:9). That is, we should honor God with our giving to Him. In the Old Testament God's people were obligated to give a tenth of their income to God.

Many years ago when I lived in South Africa I had a friend called David Naude, and I once heard him say, "for the Christian, tithing is the precipice line, that is we should never give less than that." His story was rather wonderful. His parents farmed in the Orange Free State. It was very difficult for them and they had a large family, mainly boys. They always honored God with what they received. The father became ill and one night had a dream. He dreamt that men came on his farm and started to drill. In the morning he asked his wife never to sell the farm, in spite of how difficult the circumstances might be, unless God clearly told her to. She promised and a little time later he died. Things did become very difficult, and although at times it would seem that the sensible thing to do would be to sell the farm, she kept her promise. One day a mining company came and asked permission to drill on her ground. It was there that they discovered gold, and she became rich overnight. However, they didn't change their standard of living but gave their proceeds to God and to His work. God always honors those who honor Him.

In this chapter Solomon warns his son about the danger of becoming "surety for your friend" (v. 1). That is, undertaking to pay another's debt should he become insolvent. He doesn't say he shouldn't help his friend, but that he should not make himself responsible by a contract to do so. In those days when you shook hands on an agreement it was sealed. He is advised that if he is in this position, to try and get out of it. In Proverbs 17:18 it says:

> "A man devoid of understanding shakes hands in a pledge,
> And becomes surety for his friend."

It is a snare to make such an agreement. It is like an animal being trapped or a bird being caught. He is advised to humble himself, and plead with his friend to release him from his commitment. Isn't it wonderful that God loves us so much, cares for us, and doesn't want us to he trapped in wrong financial dealings?

The lesson from these verses is that we should be wise with what we do with our money and be careful not to make commitments which embarrass and harm us, and put us into debt.

Warning against laziness

After dealing with the money situation, Solomon warns against the danger of laziness. True wisdom will cause a person to be diligent and hard working. He describes a lazy person as a sluggard, a lover of sleep. We have a word in the Oxford dictionary "slugabed", which means "a lazy person" – interesting that the word "bed" is included! The tendency in our society is get as much as we can with the minimum of effort. There is no substitute for hard work. This teaching is related to what we have just been considering about debt, and being surety for another's debt. Hard work will enable us to pay our accounts and keep out of debt. Laziness leads to poverty and robs us of what we need and could enjoy. As an illustration of hard work the reader is invited to look and learn from that tiny insect, the ant. I am sure we have all at some time watched ants scurrying continuously, carrying pieces of grass and other things into their nests. They are an object lesson. The lessons to be learned from them are:

- They are hardworking – diligent.
- They don't have overseers: they don't work because someone is watching them.
- They provide not only for the present but for the future: they take advantage of the now, the summer time, because winter is coming. They grasp the opportunity. Jesus said, "I must work the works of Him who sent Me while it is day; the night comes when no one can work" (John 9:4).
- They work in harmony: they are united, and have a common work and purpose. Each ant's contribution is so important. So is yours.

Have we learned the lesson from these little creatures? What are your thoughts on life? For it to be as easy as possible? Looking forward to a "doing nothing retirement"? What are you preparing for the future? One day we will all stand before the Lord to give account of the things we have done. Prepare for the future, lay up treasure in heaven.

Sometimes I am asked when I am going to retire. I am eighty-six years of age, but retirement isn't in my vocabulary. I have a contract to "serve the Lord all the days of nay life." Let us work while we have the opportunity, and let us work with joy. God's accusation against His people was "they served not the Lord their God with gladness." When everything we do is done unto the Lord and not unto men, we will have His blessing, His strength, His ability and, yes, His joy.

Are any changes needed in our attitude? In our program? What about the future? What about "the giving account day"?

Having shown the folly about laziness, Solomon proceeds to describe the behavior and character of those who chose to live contrary to God's ways. They are wicked, worthless, unstable. Often in Proverbs contrasts are made so that living the right way is the obvious thing to do. There is an instability and unreliability about a worthless person, a lazy person. You can know what he is like by the things that he says: he "walks with a perverse mouth" (v. 12).

The word "perverse" means "cantankerous, contrary, obstinate, self-willed." He is a trouble-maker. He winks with his eye, he shuffles his feet demonstrating his restlessness, his uneasiness. He points with his finger, the finger of accusation and criticism. This perversity is in his heart, it is part of his nature, he cannot hide it. He continually devises evil, trouble is his middle name, and wherever he goes he sows discord and disunity. Who wants to live like that? Again the Bible is true that "whatever a man sows, that he will also reap" (Galatians 6:7), and eventually calamity catches up with him, suddenly, without notice. He is broken.

We are told here that there are certain things which God hates. The word used is "abomination," which means "abhorrent, diabolical, evil, offensive, repugnant." He mentions seven of these things:

A proud look

The Amplified Bible defines that as "the spirit that makes one overestimate oneself and underestimate others." The look is the revelation of the heart. Later in Proverbs we read, "a haughty look, a proud heart, and the plowing of the wicked are sin" (21:4). God hates it.

A lying tongue

Solomon's father, David, prayed a good prayer: "Deliver my soul, O LORD, from lying lips and from a deceitful tongue" (Psalm 120:2).

Hands that shed innocent blood

Murder, abortion is shedding innocent blood. God hates it. The first murder in the Bible was Cain slaying his brother Abel. God said to Cain, "The voice of your brother's blood cries out to Me from the ground" (Genesis 4:10). God hates it.

A heart that devises wicked plans

Those who deliberately and maliciously plan to do all kinds of evil. God hates it.

Feet that are swift in running to evil

Those who are quick to put these wicked plans and schemes into action. God hates it.

A false witness who speaks lies

Those who deliberately give false evidence. How often does that happen in our courts today? God hates it.

One who sows discord among brethren

Those who are instruments of conflict, division, disunity. God hates it.

Obviously if we want to please God we should love what He loves and hate what He hates. Let us make sure we are not tainted by any of these things.

Let us humble ourselves under the mighty hand of God. We have nothing in ourselves to be proud about. The Lord taught us that even though we do everything we should do we should say, "we are unprofitable servants." Anything we can ever do to please God is done by His enabling, therefore God gets all the glory.

Let us ask God to deliver us and keep us from lying, from planning or doing evil or ever doing or saying anything that would cause discord or disunity among God's people.

After sharing these truths, Solomon pleads with his son to obey what he has been taught by his father and mother. Solomon exhorts him to bind them in his heart. Truth will always be protective; when you are traveling, even when you are sleeping, and when you wake up truth will be with you to lead you into another day. Truth, he tells him, will always be a lamp and a light, showing the way ahead and also showing the steps one should take. Another thing that truth will do is to preserve you and keep you from immorality.

Beware of adultery

Here we are again back to this subject. We saw it in the previous chapter, and now he brings it up again. Why? Because the danger presents itself, and we need to be continually reminded. When your children are young you don't tell them just once to look both ways before they cross the road! You tell them repeatedly till it becomes almost automatic in their lives. Repetition is so often used in Scripture. When we hear truth and receive it, it is planted in our hearts. When we hear again and agree with it, it is planted deeper in our hearts. The teaching of Jesus and the apostles contains much repetition. Obeying God's Word and obeying godly counsel will be a protection against adultery.

Here is more teaching: "Do not lust after her beauty in your heart" (v. 25). Don't be wrongly influenced by her flattering tongue, or her seductive beauty and seductive eyes. Adultery is dangerous. It is soul-destroying and brings trouble. You never ever escape its consequences; no more, says Solomon, than a man clutching fire and not expecting to be burned, or a man walking on hot coals and not expecting his feet to be burned and blistered. Just as surely as these things happen, so certain is it that any man who commits adultery will not be unharmed. He will not be innocent. You may say, this teaching is scary, frightening. Good, it is meant to be. Solomon talks about a starving man stealing food to keep alive, and says men will not despise him for that, but if he is caught he will be punished. But whoever commits adultery, steals another man's wife, will not get any sympathy. He is lacking in understanding. He hasn't counted the cost of his misdeeds. He will suffer from self-inflicted wounds. Whenever people think of him they will always remember what he did; he was an adulterer. That will stick with him for the rest of his life. Then he has a jealous husband to face. He is not only jealous, he is furious. You won't be able to pacify him with gifts. You cannot replace what you have stolen. He wants vengeance.

Conclusion and application

Again we underline the importance of not only listening to truth or reading about truth, but applying truth. We summarize the instructions given in this chapter:

- Do not become surety or guarantor for someone else's debts. If you have done so, try and be released from this commitment. This is going to involve humility, in acknowledging that although you did it with the best intentions, you realize it was a mistake. Don't procrastinate, do it as soon as possible.
- Learn the lessons from the ant, and resolve to be industrious. Don't just work well when someone is watching you. "Thou God seest me" (Genesis 16:13, KJV). Don't oversleep. Each day is a gift from God. Indolence leads to poverty; hard work leads to success.
- Avoid living a worthless life. Be reliable and trustworthy. Walk humbly, speak truth. Never be involved in plans or schemes that are not righteous. Don't ever be involved in the shedding of innocent blood, in abortion or anything that would destroy or curtail people's lives.
- Be truthful in every report and every witness.
- Avoid ever being a trouble-maker, a divider, a means of disunity.
- Obey God's commands and godly counsel. Remember your upbringing and follow the good advice your parents gave you. Also give good advice and counsel to your children so that they too will always respect and honor your teaching.

- Avoid immorality. Avoid adultery. Don't get in to compromising situations. Don't be trapped by flattery. Always remember the consequences of this sin, and how it not only harms and hurts others but also yourself. Remember, if you have been guilty of this sin, there is forgiveness from God when we acknowledge, repent, confess and forsake this sin. Seek the forgiveness of those involved. Show by your living that the repentance and sorrow was sincere.

Promises and assurances

- Obedience to truth will lead you wherever you go. It will keep you, and will speak to you. God's commandments and Word will always be a light and a lamp to you.
- Obedience to God's instructions will keep you from the wiles of the seductress.

Praying in truth

Having listened to God's instructions, and been encouraged by His promises, it is always wise to pray – sharing our desires, the intents of our hearts, the consciousness of our needs. Praying establishes these things with God. We may also be aware that there are others we know, perhaps some in our family or friends, who need to know and apply these truths. Why not pray for them too? Let's be still and quiet and do that now.

Add some of your own thoughts

---

*If any of you lacks wisdom, let him ask of God, who gives to all liberally
and without reproach, and it **will** be given to him* (James 1:5).

Chapter 7

1. My son, keep my words, and treasure my commands within you.
2. Keep my commands and live, and my law as the apple of your eye.
3. Bind them on your fingers; write them on the tablet of your heart.
4. Say to wisdom, "You are my sister," and call understanding your nearest kin,
5. That they may keep you from the immoral woman, from the seductress who flatters with her words.

The crafty harlot

6. For at the window of my house I looked through my lattice,
7. And saw among the simple, I perceived among the youths, a young man devoid of understanding,
8. Passing along the street near her corner; and he took the path to her house
9. In the twilight, in the evening, in the black and dark night.
10. And there a woman met him, with the attire of a harlot, and a crafty heart.
11. She was loud and rebellious, her feet would not stay at home.
12. At times she was outside, at times in the open square, lurking at every corner.
13. So she caught him and kissed him; with an impudent face she said to him:
14. "I have peace offerings with me; today I have paid my vows.
15. So I came out to meet you, diligently to seek your face, and I have found you.
16. I have spread my bed with tapestry, colored coverings of Egyptian linen.
17. I have perfumed my bed with myrrh, aloes, and cinnamon.
18. Come, let us take our fill of love until morning; let us delight ourselves with love.
19. For my husband is not at home; he has gone on a long journey;
20. He has taken a bag of money with him, and will come home on the appointed day."

21. With her enticing speech she caused him to yield, with her flattering lips she seduced him.

22. Immediately he went after her, as an ox goes to the slaughter, or as a fool to the correction of the stocks,

23. Till an arrow struck his liver. As a bird hastens to the snare, he did not know it would cost his life.

24. Now therefore, listen to me, my children; pay attention to the words of my mouth:

25. Do not let your heart turn aside to her ways, do not stray into her paths;

26. For she has cast down many wounded, and all who were slain by her were strong men.

27. Her house is the way to hell, descending to the chambers of death.

My son

What a privilege it is to explore the book of Proverbs, which is so full of good advice and encouragements for our day-by-day living. Once again this chapter opens with "My son". Isn't it a wonderful thing to be a Christian, a believer and follower of Jesus Christ? What a relationship we have. We are in His Kingdom, the Kingdom of God. We belong to God and are members of the family of God which consists of everyone who has come to God through the Lord Jesus Christ, believing that:

> "Christ died for our sins according to the Scriptures, and that He was buried, and rose again the third day according to the Scriptures."
>
> (1 Corinthians 15:3–4)

John reminds us that:

> "He who believes in the Son has everlasting life; and he who does not believe the Son shall not see life, but the wrath of God abides on Him." (John 3:36)

We are God's sons, and daughters, and as Jesus said to His disciples, "You are My friends if you do whatever I command you" (John

15:14). Let's start here by thanking God for making you His son, His daughter. Let us never lose the wonder of it. Because He is our Father in heaven, He loves to communicate with us. One of the main ways He does this is, of course, through His Word. What you have just read in this chapter is His Word: to teach, encourage and, yes, to warn.

Again, as always, we are totally reliant on the Holy Spirit to help us understand the Word of God and enable us to do it. The words that Mary, the mother of Jesus, gave to the servants at the wedding feast in Cana of Galilee, where Jesus did His first miracle by turning water into wine, are so relevant today:

> "Whatever He says to you, do it." (John 2:5)

The first thing we should always do is the last thing He told us to do. The more we obey truth, the more truth we will receive. How about starting with a prayer?

> "Father, help me to do whatever You tell me to do in this chapter. I choose to obey. Teach me today what I need to learn, and help me to receive it in my heart and apply it to my living. Amen."

We have already seen and will continue to see that the same truths are often repeated. We not only need to be taught but also reminded.

Again, the son is reminded to:

Keep my words (v. 1)
Guard them, don't let them slip. When Paul wrote to Timothy he gave him similar advice:

> To Timothy, a beloved son ... Hold fast the pattern of sound words which you have heard from me, in faith and love which are in Christ Jesus. That good thing which was committed to you, keep by the Holy Spirit who dwells in us." (2 Timothy 1:2, 13–14)

Keep my words: retain them; hold them fast; protect them. There is an enemy who would try to snatch away the word. The writer to the Hebrews warned of the danger of letting things slip:

"We must give the more earnest heed to the things we have heard, lest we drift away."   (Hebrews 2:1)

Sometimes things are lost, not by a deliberate decision to lose them but simply by neglect. You can lose a house, not by deliberately destroying it, but just neglecting it when it needs repair. You can lose your health by neglect and carelessness. You can lose truth by neglecting to apply it continually. Thank God when we seek to obey His Word and live for Him, we can trust God, as Jude reminds us:

"Now to Him who is able to keep you from stumbling,
And to present you faultless
Before the presence of His glory with exceeding joy.
To God our Savior,
Who alone is wise,
Be glory and majesty,
Dominion and power,
Both now and forever.
Amen."   (Jude 24–25)

Treasure my commands within you (v. 1)
Place great value on God's words and instructions. Treasure them within you. Make them part of your life. Our hearts are like banks, places of safety into which we deposit the valuables. The knowledge of God is priceless. Paul told the Corinthians:

"For it is the God who commanded the light to shine out of darkness, who has shone in our hearts to give the light of the knowledge of the glory of God in the face of Jesus Christ. But we have this treasure in earthen vessels, that the excellence of the power may be of God and not of us."   (2 Corinthians 4:6–7)

Keep my commands and live (v. 2)
God's words are life, as well as showing us how to live. Jesus said:

"The words that I speak to you are spirit, and they are life."
                                                             (John 6:63)

"Man shall not live by bread alone, but by every word of God."
(Luke 4:4)

Moses gave the children of Israel God's word, and said,

> "See, I have set before you today life and good, death and evil, in
> that I command you today to love the LORD your God, to walk
> in His ways, and to keep His commandments, His statutes, and His
> judgments, that you may *live* and multiply; and the LORD your God
> will bless you in the land which you go to possess."
> (Deuteronomy 30:15–16, emphasis added)

Guard them as the apple of your eye (v. 2)

How precious the eye is. Without our eyes we are blind, stumble
and live in darkness. Just as we protect and care for our eyes, so
precious is God's Word. It is light, it prevents us from falling, it
causes us to live and walk in light.

Bind them on your fingers, write them on the tablet of your heart (v. 3)

His Word will show us how to act, what to do with our hands.
When His Word is in our hearts it will rightly motivate all that we
do. Just as God wrote the Ten Commandments with His own hand
on the tablets of stone He gave to Moses, so the Holy Spirit can
imprint His precious Word in our hearts as we receive it.

Realize the value of wisdom (v. 4)

Treat wisdom as a close and needed friend, like a relative, part of
your family like a sister or nearest of kin, someone essential in your
life. In Proverbs 4 this was Solomon's plea:

> "Wisdom is the principal thing;
> Therefore get wisdom.
> And in all your getting, get understanding."   (4:7)

In previous chapters we have also been encouraged to:

- Incline your ear to wisdom (2:2).
- Know that the Lord gives wisdom (2:6).

- Know that happy is the man who finds wisdom (3:13).
- Keep sound wisdom (3:21).
- Pay attention to wisdom (5:1).

The summary of these opening verses is to exhort us to put great value on the teaching of God's Word. Be diligent to obey His commands. Don't neglect it. Don't be careless. Don't let things slip. Don't drop your standards.

What value do you put on God's Word? What place does it have in your life? Do you really treasure it? How much time do you give to it? What dependence do you put on it?

Obedience to God's Word will keep us from evil

When we keep and treasure God's commands they will keep us from evil. In this chapter Solomon says that when knowledge, wisdom and understanding are part of our lives they will keep us from the immoral woman. He is repeating what he taught in Proverbs 2. There, too, his son was exhorted to receive and treasure God's commands, apply his heart to wisdom, and they would "deliver [him] from the immoral woman" (2:16). Again in chapter 6 he is told that if he keeps the commands they will "keep [him] from the evil woman" (6:24). Now for the third time he brings the same teaching. If repetition of this teaching was relevant 3,000 years ago, how much more now? Fornication and adultery are glamorized. There seems to be no shame, but sometimes a boasting and glorying in immoral behavior. It is almost depicted as the norm. It is made to appear attractive, mysterious, pleasurable, but what about the consequences? What about the reaping? What about what God says, "You shall not commit adultery" (Exodus 20:14)? So to ease their conscience they say, "I don't believe there is a God." If you don't believe in God, then there is no need to believe His Word, His commands. If you don't believe in God, then you don't believe that judgment day is coming, and if you don't believe in God, the Bible says, "you are a fool."

> "The fool has said in his heart,
> 'There is no God.' "
>
> (Psalm 53:1)

However, not believing in God does not mean that He does not exist. Why, the very heavens declare the glory of God, and the earth shows forth His handiwork. One of the greatest evidences of the existence of God was through the coming to earth of the Lord Jesus: "God was manifested in the flesh" (1 Timothy 3:16) – God became man. His life clearly and wonderfully manifested the love of God, the holiness of God, the purity of God, the power of God, the compassion of God. His coming proved to the world that "God so loved the world that He gave His only begotten Son, that whoever believes in Him should not perish but have everlasting life" (John 3:16). That great love was manifested in the death of Jesus:

> "Greater love has no one than this, than to lay down one's life for his friends." (John 15:13)

Then, as now, men made their choice. Some followed Him, lived for Him, and some died for Him. Others cried out, "Crucify Him, crucify Him," and "We will not have this man to reign over us" (Luke 19:14). However, a day is coming when, whether men believe it or not, "every knee shall bow to Me, and every tongue shall confess to God" (Romans 14:11). The greatest question that still faces men today, which affects their whole lives and their eternity is, "What will *you* do with Jesus which is called the Christ"? For the followers of Jesus, knowing Him, following Him and obeying Him are the priorities of life. They wish to be kept from evil, and evil men and women. They will want to follow the teaching of this chapter.

To again underline the folly of immorality, Solomon tells a story of what he saw one evening, looking out of a window when it was getting dusk. He saw a young man walking down town who is approached by a woman. She is a married woman. Her husband is on a business trip, has just left and won't be back for a while. She is not a prostitute, but is behaving like one. She has dressed herself seductively, she wants action, she can't stand staying at home, she's restless. She is like a spider looking for a fly, and she finds one. She probably knows him and when they meet she takes the lead and kisses him. She professes to be good, even to be religious. She has made her offerings and paid her vows. She tells the young man how much she has been wanting to see him, actually looking for him and it has happened. Out comes more bait – the web is strong, and she describes what her bedroom is like: luxurious, beautiful, with perfumed cotton sheets. The whole scene is set and she says, "Come let us have a whole night of love. The coast is clear, my husband has gone ... no one will ever know." There is a battle of conscience in the young man's heart, but her enticing speech and flattering words trap him, and he yields and follows her like an ox going to the slaughter, or a fool going to be put in the stocks for punishment. A dart of passion strikes him, and he has become not a victor but a victim: a command remains unchangeable, "You shall not commit adultery."

After the story there comes the application: "Listen to me ... Pay attention to the words of my mouth ... Do not let your heart turn aside to her ways, do not stray into her paths" (vv. 24–25). He's not the first; many have been wounded, cast down, even slain. Sin is a killer. Her house is the way to death and hell.

Strong men have been slain and wounded

Samson was no weakling. He was reputed for his strength. Ropes could not bind him. He could snap them like threads, but what ropes could not do an evil woman did, and Delilah seduced him. He was wounded by blindness and died before his time.

David was a strong man – he once killed a giant and also killed a lion and a bear – but he was trapped by his own lust for a married woman.

And, yes, a very sad story – the very man who wrote this chapter was himself caught, and was influenced by evil women to sin:

> "King Solomon loved many foreign women ... when Solomon
> was old ... his wives turned his heart after other gods; and his heart
> was not loyal to the LORD his God."   (1 Kings 11:1, 4)

No wonder Paul wrote:

> "Let him who thinks he stands take heed lest he fall."
>   (1 Corinthians 10:12)

There is also his warning note to the Corinthians:

> "I discipline my body and bring it into subjection, lest, when I have
> preached to others, I myself should become disqualified."
>
> (1 Corinthians 9:27)

What warnings. Every single day we need God's help. We can
never take anything for granted. Again we are encouraged by Paul's
words:

> "No temptation has overtaken you except such as is common
> to man; but *God is faithful,* who will not allow you to be tempted
> beyond what you are able, but with the temptation will also make
> the way of escape, that you may be able to bear it."
>
> (1 Corinthians 10:13, emphasis added)

We never sin without first being tempted. When we are tempted
there is always a way of escape. James in his epistle talks about
temptation and says:

> "Let no one say when he is tempted, 'I am tempted by God'; for
> God cannot be tempted by evil, nor does He Himself tempt
> anyone. But each one is tempted when he is drawn away by his
> own desires and enticed. Then, when desire has conceived, it gives
> birth to sin; and sin, when it is full-grown, brings forth death."
>
> (James 1:13–15)

We cannot escape temptation, but we can avoid yielding to it.
Temptation is like a seed waiting to be planted in the heart, or to use
James' words, to be conceived. Conception cannot take place unless
the seed is received, but it need not be. There is always a way of
escape. We can always reject it, we can always say no. The
temptation itself is not sin. It may be a terrible thought or desire,
but need not be received. How do we deal with it? How did Jesus
deal with temptation? He responded by quoting God's Word. That
is the wonderful thing about God's Word. As we see in this chapter,
when the Word of God is kept, treasured and obeyed it keeps us
from sinning. David said:

> "Your word I have hidden in my heart,
> That I might not sin against You."   (Psalm 119:11)

And I like this verse:

> "For 'whoever calls upon the name of the LORD shall be saved.' "
>   (Romans 10:13)

That is, not only calling on the name of the Lord for salvation, conversion, but also when we are tempted we can say, "Lord Jesus help me." And He will. The young man we have just talked about in this chapter deliberately went into the realm of temptation rather than avoiding it. I once read of a vacancy for a job as a horse coach driver many years ago. The route the coach took daily was over a mountain pass. It was a very narrow road with a steep precipice on one side. After interviews there were two remaining applicants. One was asked, "How near could you steer the coach to the edge of the precipice?" "To within a few inches," he replied. The other was asked the same question, and replied, "I would keep as far away from the edge as possible." Who do you think got the job? Life is not free from temptation, but we can often avoid places and circumstances of temptation.

When we read or hear God's Word we are always faced with the question, "What are we going to do with it?" The answer is, obey it.

Application

Let us resolve to keep God's Word. Here is the summary of its instructions in this chapter:

- Keep my words (v. 1).
- Treasure my commands (v. 1)
- Keep my commands (v. 2).
- Bind them on your fingers (v. 3).
- Write them on the tablet of your heart (v. 3).
- Say to wisdom, "You are my sister" (v. 4).
- Call understanding your nearest kin (v. 4).
- Listen to me (v. 24).

- Pay attention to the words of my mouth (v. 24).
- Do not let your heart turn aside to her ways (v. 25).
- Do not stray into her paths (v. 25).

Promises

Here are the promises in this chapter:

- *Life*: "Keep my commands and live" (v. 2).
- *You will be kept*: God's Word will "keep you from the immoral woman" (v. 5).

Your own thoughts and prayers

*If any of you lacks wisdom, let him ask of God, who gives to all liberally and without reproach, and it **will** be given to him* (James 1:5).

Chapter 8

The excellence of wisdom

1. Does not wisdom cry out, and understanding lift up her voice?
2. She takes her stand on the top of the high hill, beside the way, where the paths meet.
3. She cries out by the gates, at the entry of the city, at the entrance of the doors:
4. "To you, O men, I call, and my voice is to the sons of men.
5. O you simple ones, understand prudence, and you fools, be of an understanding heart.
6. Listen, for I will speak of excellent things, and from the opening of my lips will come right things;
7. For my mouth will speak truth; wickedness is an abomination to my lips.
8. All the words of my mouth are with righteousness; nothing crooked or perverse is in them.
9. They are all plain to him who understands, and right to those who find knowledge.
10. Receive my instruction, and not silver, and knowledge rather than choice gold;
11. For wisdom is better than rubies, and all the things one may desire cannot be compared with her.
12. I, wisdom, dwell with prudence, and find out knowledge and discretion.
13. The fear of the LORD is to hate evil; pride and arrogance and the evil way and the perverse mouth I hate.
14. Counsel is mine, and sound wisdom; I am understanding, I have strength.
15. By me kings reign, and rulers decree justice.
16. By me princes rule, and nobles, all the judges of the earth.
17. I love those who love me, and those who seek me diligently will find me.
18. Riches and honor are with me, enduring riches and righteousness.

19. My fruit is better than gold, yes, than fine gold, and my revenue than choice silver.
20. I traverse the way of righteousness, in the midst of the paths of justice,
21. That I may cause those who love me to inherit wealth, that I may fill their treasuries.
22. The LORD possessed me at the beginning of His way, before His works of old.
23. I have been established from everlasting, from the beginning, before there was ever an earth.
24. When there were no depths I was brought forth, when there were no fountains abounding with water.
25. Before the mountains were settled, before the hills, I was brought forth;
26. While as yet He had not made the earth or the fields, or the primal dust of the world.
27. When He prepared the heavens, I was there, when He drew a circle on the face of the deep,
28. When He established the clouds above, when He strengthened the fountains of the deep,
29. When He assigned to the sea its limit, so that the waters would not transgress His command, when He marked out the foundations of the earth,
30. Then I was beside Him as a master craftsman; and I was daily His delight, rejoicing always before Him,
31. Rejoicing in His inhabited world, and my delight was with the sons of men.
32. Now therefore, listen to me, my children, for blessed are those who keep my ways.
33. Hear instruction and be wise, and do not disdain it.
34. Blessed is the man who listens to me, watching daily at my gates, waiting at the posts of my doors.
35. For whoever finds me finds life, and obtains favor from the LORD;
36. But he who sins against me wrongs his own soul; all those who hate me love death."

Introduction

In this chapter Solomon continues to extol the value, importance and blessing of wisdom. Remember right at the beginning of the book he said the purpose of the book was to know wisdom, and to receive the instruction of wisdom. God wants people to live happy, wise and useful lives. This wisdom is available to all. He illustrates this by depicting wisdom standing in a high place and crying out to all who will hear. The invitation is not restricted to people of good education or background. In God's great love He offers to all: everyone ... everywhere ... anywhere. Remember the promise which we continue to quote from the epistle of James 1:5:

> "If any of you lacks wisdom, let him ask of God, who gives to all liberally and without reproach, and it will be given to him."

God is the source of all true wisdom: not *a* source, but *the* source. That is why we are continually reminded that "the fear of the LORD is the beginning of wisdom," that is, we believe that God is God, and reverence Him, give Him first place in our lives. We can thank God again today that He has made a way to know Him, love Him, revere Him through the coming of the Lord Jesus to earth to live, to die for our sins, to rise from the dead so that we can have relationship and fellowship with the great eternal God. Jesus said, "No one comes to the Father except through Me" (John 14:6). When we repent of our sins, believe in the Lord Jesus Christ, confess with our mouths that He is Lord and choose to follow Him, then this great ocean of divine wisdom is open to us. Wisdom is not a mere philosophy or formula or prescription; wisdom comes from God. By His wisdom He created the heavens, earth, sun, moon, stars, oceans, rivers, mountains and hills. He spoke the word and it was done. By His wisdom He created man. Think of the wonders of the human body. Did we simply evolve? No, "God created man in His own image; in the image of God He created him; male and female He created them" (Genesis 1:27). We are described by David as being "fearfully and wonderfully made" (Psalm 139:14). No wonder Paul cries out:

> "Oh, the depth of the riches both of the wisdom and knowledge of God! How unsearchable are His judgments and His ways past finding out!"   (Romans 11:33)

Various types of wisdom

The Bible speaks of different kinds of wisdom:

Man's wisdom (1 Corinthians 2:13)

That is, man's human understanding. How limited that is, dependent on himself and the limitations of his own knowledge and understanding.

The wisdom of the world (1 Corinthians 3:19)

Paul says, "the wisdom of the world is foolishness with God." The world and its systems cannot meet man's greatest needs. Wisdom apart from that which comes from God is foolishness.

Earthly, sensual, devilish wisdom (James 3:15)

That is, so-called wisdom, which is self-centered and has no place for God. James writes:

> "If you have bitter envy and *self-seeking* in your hearts, do not boast and lie against the truth. This wisdom does not descend from above, but is earthly, sensual, demonic. For where envy and *self-seeking* exist, confusion and every evil thing are there."
>
> (James 3:14–16, emphasis added)

The wisdom of God

James asks the question: "Who is wise and understanding among you? and goes on to say, "Let him show by good conduct that his works are done in the *meekness of wisdom*" (James 3:13, emphasis added). The right kind of wisdom will cause people to live right ("good conduct"), will not make a person proud, or boastful, or flout their knowledge. Then he says:

> "The wisdom that is from above [God's wisdom] is first pure, then peaceable, gentle, willing to yield, full of mercy and good fruits, without partiality and without hypocrisy. Now the fruit of righteousness is sown in peace by those who make peace."
>
> (James 3:17–18)

Which wisdom would you choose? Man's? The world's? Earthly, sensual, demonic? *God's?* In Proverbs 8 wisdom is crying out for the right choice to be made. Remember in chapter 1 we saw that when wisdom was offered it was refused by some: "they . . . did not *choose* the fear of the LORD" (1:29, emphasis added), therefore, as this is the beginning of wisdom, they did not choose wisdom.

The blessings of God's wisdom

To encourage the right choice Solomon enumerates the blessings, advantages, values and consequences of choosing God's wisdom. They are:

- *Prudence* (v. 5) – that is, discretion, the ability to rightly assess situations and come to the right conclusions.
- *An understanding heart* (v. 5) – that is, God's wisdom enables us to use knowledge right. What's the use of knowledge if we do not know how to apply it?
- *Speak of excellent things* (v. 6) – not just good things, but the very best things. Receiving God's wisdom will cause us to excel in what we do. Paul encouraged the Corinthians that they should "seek to excel" (1 Corinthians 14:12). God's wisdom is excellent.
- *Always truthful* (v. 7) – there is nothing devious about God's wisdom. It is free of all deceit and wickedness. We read it is "with righteousness; nothing crooked or perverse" is in it (v. 8).
- *Of greater value than silver or the finest gold or of rubies* (vv. 10–11): "all the things one may desire cannot to be compared with her" (v. 11).
- *Always gives the right counsel* – "Counsel is mine" (v. 14). How important this is for us personally, and also when seeking to help others. It is vital not to depend on our own wisdom to counsel others but to look to God to give us His answers, His advice.
- *Brings honor, enduring riches, righteousness* (vv. 18, 21). Jesus said, "If anyone serves Me, him My Father will honor" (John 12:26). He gives us riches. The greatest wealth of all, as we have already seen, is "the riches both of the wisdom and knowledge of God" (Romans 11:33).

- *Life and favor* (v. 35). There is no greater favor than God's favor. It is His approval we should seek first and not man's. It is said of Jesus that He "increased in wisdom and stature, and in favor with God and men" (Luke 2:52). It was said of David that he "found favor before God" (Acts 7:46). God's wisdom will give us favor with God. What a thought! There is no approval like His approval. Jesus always had it: "This is My beloved Son, in whom I am well pleased" (Matthew 3:17).

God's wisdom is available for every circumstance

At the crossroads in our lives

Our lives are punctuated by circumstances and by choices. We read,

> "She [wisdom] takes her stand on the top of the high hill,
> Beside the way, where the paths meet." (v. 2)

What a great picture: wisdom on a high hill, able to see what is in the distance. She is standing there where the paths meet. *Quo vadis?* Which way should we go? What decisions should I make?. Think of all the crossroads in life: choosing a career, choosing jobs, choosing friends, choosing a wife or a husband, choosing where to stay, choosing how to handle our finances, choosing sometimes where we have to move and when. How terrible it is to make wrong choices: what regrets, what unhappiness and sorrows, what disappointments and frustrations. But here is the *good news*. There is wisdom available at the place where the paths meet. What should we do? What does wisdom say? What does God's Word say? Remember we saw the answer in chapter 3:

> "Trust in the LORD with all your heart,
> And lean not to your own understanding;
> In all your ways acknowledge Him,
> And He shall direct your paths.
> Do not be wise in your own eyes;
> Fear the LORD ... " (3:5–7)

God sees the future. God knows the very best way for us. He knows the end from the beginning. "The LORD is my shepherd; I shall not want ... He leads me..." (Psalm 23:1, 3). Solomon would have heard his father's counsel:

> "Trust in the LORD ...
> Delight yourself also in the LORD ...
> Commit your way to the LORD,
> Trust also in Him,
> And He shall bring it to pass ...
> Rest in the LORD, and wait patiently for Him." (Psalm 37:3–5, 7)

Are you facing an important decision? Are you at a crossroad? Be wise, acknowledge Him; commit it to Him, trust Him, and He will show you what to do. If God could lead, supply and guide over a million people in a wilderness, He certainly can guide you and supply your needs. Don't panic: rest, relax and wait patiently for Him. When we have handed it all over to Him, He has taken responsibility to bring the answer.

Isaiah wrote, "The LORD will guide you continually" (Isaiah 58:11). How many of you have already proved that? In the past fifty years the Lord has taken us from nation to nation: Britain to Africa; Africa to Britain; Britain to New Zealand; New Zealand to Britain; Britain to America; America to Britain. Not mere visits, but living and working in these countries, with all that in involved – family, homes, education of children, travel, never on anyone's payroll, and sometimes down to almost the last penny – but God is faithful and true: God leads, God supplies and God gets all the glory. Laban could say, "I have learned by experience" (Genesis 30:27) and I'm sure that many reading this can say that. I have learned by experience that God gives wisdom at the crossroads and shows the way. Blessed be the name of the Lord.

At the gates of the city

Wisdom is available at the gates of the city, with all its business, governments, commerce, legal institutions, universities and schools. Wherever you work or live, in a city or town, whatever work you do, whatever your profession, you can have God-given wisdom. Where there is God-given wisdom there will be righteousness, fairness and integrity. Later in Proverbs, Solomon writes:

"When it goes well with the righteous, the city rejoices . . .
By the blessing of the upright the city is exalted." (11:10–11)

History confirms that when nations and cities honored God there was blessing. Today you do not, or very rarely, hear of people in authority acknowledging their need of God and His wisdom. Rather, plans and promises are made which are dependent on man's wisdom and for man's acceptance, praise and glory. When the source of wisdom is not acknowledged, and rejected, no wonder so many mistakes are made and problems arise. Jesus wept over a city, a city that did not want God or His wisdom:

"O Jerusalem, Jerusalem, the one who kills the prophets and stones those who are sent to her! How often I wanted to gather your children together, as a hen gathers her chicks under her wings, but you were not willing!" (Matthew 23:37)

Thank God for every Christian in towns and cities who depends on God and His wisdom.

At the entrance of the doors
There is plenty of wisdom for every person, every place, every situation: the crossroads, the cities, and now the doors. The doors of opportunity. The doors of our homes. We need wisdom within our own doors. Wisdom in marriage, wisdom with our families, wisdom with our family decisions, wisdom in what we watch and what we read, wisdom with our health. Wisdom still cries out: "Ask, and you will receive," "Obey instructions and live." Keeping God's standards will always be blessed with God's wisdom.

Christ in all the Scriptures
In the latter part of this chapter there are some wonderful verses. It is like Jesus talking. It was said of Him when He was here on earth that He "was filled with wisdom" (Luke 2:40). People said, "Where did this Man get this wisdom . . . Is this not the carpenter's son?" (Matthew 13:54–55). We know the answer: His wisdom was God-given. He acknowledged, "I can do nothing of Myself; but as My Father taught Me, I speak these things" (John 8:28). God's wisdom

is eternal. John tells us, "He [Jesus] was in the beginning with God. All things were made through Him, and without Him nothing was made that was made" (John 1:2–3). Listen to these words as from Jesus:

> "When He [God] prepared the heavens, I was there.
> When He drew a circle on the face of the deep,
> When He established the clouds above . . .
> When He assigned to the sea its limit . . .
> When He marked out the foundations of the earth,
> *Then* I was beside Him as a master craftsman;
> And I was daily His delight,
> Rejoicing always before Him."   (vv. 27–30, emphasis added)

God's wisdom is eternal, creative, righteous, life-giving, protective and available.

Application

To receive the blessings of God's wisdom we should note His instructions. As we close let's look at them, and apply them:

- *Listen*, for I will speak. Hear and pay attention (vv. 6, 32).
- *Receive* my instructions. Say Amen to them (v. 10).
- *Fear God* – the fear of the LORD is to hate evil (v. 13).
- *Hear* instructions. Be wise . . . don't disdain . . . don't make light of the teaching (v. 33).
- *Watch* daily at my gates (v. 34).
- *Wait* at the posts of my doors. Daily come to Him with His Word. Wisdom increases with the knowledge of God. *Wait* on the Lord – give Him time to speak to you. Meditate on His Word. Value His Word.

His promises

- If you listen, God will speak (v. 6).
- If you listen God will bless (v. 34).
- I love those who love Me (v. 17).

- When you seek God He will give you riches, honor, enduring riches and righteousness (v. 18).
- God will bless those who keep His ways (v. 32).
- When you find wisdom you find life and obtain favor from the Lord (v. 35).

What has God said to you in this brief time? It is always good to pray in what we have heard, and express our desires, needs and thanksgiving to the Lord. Let's ask Him again to continually give us wisdom, to help us to listen and to hear. Help us to receive His Word, and to daily seek Him, to wait on Him, to learn of Him.

Let us be encouraged by His promises. The promise of God speaking to us, blessing us, loving us and showing us His favor.

---

*If any of you lacks wisdom, let him ask of God, who gives to all liberally and without reproach, and it **will** be given to him* (James 1:5).

Chapter 9

The way of wisdom

1. Wisdom has built her house, she has hewn out her seven pillars;
2. She has slaughtered her meat, she has mixed her wine, she has also furnished her table.
3. She has sent out her maidens, she cries out from the highest places of the city,
4. "Whoever is simple, let him turn in here!" As for him who lacks understanding, she says to him,
5. "Come, eat of my bread and drink of the wine I have mixed.
6. Forsake foolishness and live, and go in the way of understanding.
7. He who corrects a scoffer gets shame for himself, and he who rebukes a wicked man only harms himself.
8. Do not correct a scoffer, lest he hate you; rebuke a wise man, and he will love you.
9. Give instruction to a wise man, and he will be still wiser; teach a just man, and he will increase in learning.
10. The fear of the LORD is the beginning of wisdom, and the knowledge of the Holy One is understanding.
11. For by me your days will be multiplied, and years of life will be added to you.
12. If you are wise, you are wise for yourself, and if you scoff, you will bear it alone."

The way of folly

13. A foolish woman is clamorous; she is simple, and knows nothing.
14. For she sits at the door of her house, on a seat by the highest places of the city,
15. To call to those who pass by, who go straight on their way:
16. "Whoever is simple, let him turn in here"; and as for him who lacks understanding, she says to him,

17. "Stolen water is sweet, and bread eaten in secret is pleasant."
18. But he does not know that the dead are there, that her guests are in the depths of hell.

The house that wisdom built

In this chapter we are all given a great invitation by wisdom. She has built her house, prepared a great banquet, and sends out the invitation to all who will accept. It reminds us of the parable Jesus told of the man who prepared a great supper, sent out the invitation, "Come for all things are now ready," but some of those invited made their excuses, so the master told the servants to open the invitation to whoever would accept (see Matthew 22:1–14). As we have seen, wisdom's invitation is to all who lack wisdom and want to have it. True wisdom builds up, edifies. It is reliable, solid. Remember the story Jesus told about the wise and foolish men who built their houses, one on a rock the other on sand. God's wisdom is based on the Rock – Christ Jesus. As the old hymn says:

> On Christ the solid rock I stand
> All other ground is sinking sand.

Wisdom's house has seven pillars. Seven is the number of completeness, perfection. God's wisdom is perfect. James' description of wisdom has seven contents (see James 3:17). It is:

- Pure.
- Peaceable.
- Gentle.
- Willing to yield.
- Full of mercy.
- Full of good fruits.
- Without partiality and hypocrisy.

Remember too, the sevenfold description of Jesus in Isaiah 11:

- The Spirit of the Lord shall rest upon Him.
- The Spirit of wisdom.

- The Spirit of understanding.
- The Spirit of counsel.
- The Spirit of might.
- The Spirit of knowledge.
- The fear of the Lord.

> "But of Him you are in Christ Jesus, *who became for us wisdom from God.*" (1 Corinthians 1:30, emphasis added)

Anything we build requires God's wisdom; the building of:

- Our individual lives.
- Our homes and families.
- Our relationships.
- Our careers.
- Our churches.
- Our futures.

Everything is already prepared. All we will ever need is available, and wisdom sends her invitation, *"Come ..."*

- Eat of my bread (v. 5). Jesus said, "I am the bread of life" (John 6:48).
- Drink (v. 5). Jesus said, "If anyone thirsts, let him come to Me and drink" (John 7:37).
- Forsake foolishness (v. 6). To receive wisdom you have to forsake folly.
- Live, not merely exist (v. 6). Live life to the full with God's wisdom.
- Go in the way of understanding (v. 6), knowing what you are doing is according to truth and the right kind of knowledge.

"Wisdom has built her house" (v. 1). When you think of a house, you think of:

- Security, safety.
- Relationships, the home.
- Intimacy.

- Comfort.
- Supplies.

All these are found in the Lord. No wonder Paul talks about "the manifold wisdom of God" (Ephesians 3:10) and here we have the invitation, *"Come."* Do not lean to your own understanding. Divine wisdom is available.

> "Unless the LORD builds the house,
> They labor in vain who build it."   (Psalm 127:1)

Reaction to the invitation

How we react affects our lives. Solomon follows on the invitation by speaking about scoffers. The Greek work for scoffing means "holding up your nose in derision." It is mocking; making light of; not placing any value on it. It is pride, self-sufficiency. How many people today live or say, "I don't need God in my life"?

How we react to God's invitation affects our lives and our eternity. When He says to us, "believe on the Lord Jesus Christ and you will be saved," and we accept the invitation, we receive His salvation, everlasting life, His indwelling presence, and the promise of His presence and help.

When we accept wisdom's invitation we will live right.

Solomon says that if you reprove a scorner or rebuke a wicked man you will get shame and hatred. But if you rebuke a wise man he will love you. You have done him a favor:

> "Give instruction to a wise man, he will be still wiser;
> Teach a just man, and he will increase in learning."   (v. 9)

A person's character is revealed by the way he accepts correction and teaching.

How do you react to correction or rebuke? Your reaction will reveal whether you are wise or foolish. A proud heart will hate to be corrected and will probably scoff and shame the one who does it: "Who does he/she think they are?" Of course, anyone who seeks to correct should do it with an uncritical spirit, and sincere desire for the person's welfare. Paul gave some good advice about seeking to help a person with a fault:

> "Brethren, if a man is overtaken in any trespass, you who are spiritual restore such a one in the spirit of gentleness, considering yourself lest you also be tempted."   (Galatians 6:1)

How about the invitation? Sometimes when you receive an invitation, four letters are written: RSVP – *"respondez s'il vous plait."* Wisdom says: "Come . . . " RSVP.

The other voice

Wisdom has cried with her voice of invitation, but there is another voice. One is the voice of wisdom; the other is the voice of folly. This other voice is described as belonging to a clamorous woman. Clamorous means "noisy, boisterous, demanding." She sits at the open door of her house, which is by the highest place in the city. As people pass by who are going "straight on their way" (v. 15), she wants to stop them. She calls to them with tempting words:

> "Stolen water is sweet,
> And bread eaten in secret is pleasant."   (v. 17)

In other words, what is illegal or immoral is attractive. It is sweet and pleasant. She does not believe in the fear of the Lord, because the "fear of the LORD is to hate evil" (8:13). She is making sin attractive. It is the age-old temptation of the devil: if you obey God you are going to lose. It is the throw-back to the garden of Eden. It is still the same cunning voice, "Has God indeed said, 'You shall not eat of every tree of the garden?' " (Genesis 3:1). When Eve replied that they could eat of every tree in the garden except one, which they had not to touch, and if they did they would die, the devil told his lie, "You will not surely die" (Genesis 3:4). If you obey God you are going to lose? "[When] you eat of it your eyes will be opened, and you will be like God" (Genesis 3:5). She listens, she sees the tree is pleasant and desirable to make one wise ("stolen water is sweet", v. 17), and she took and ate the fruit.

> "Through one man sin entered into the world, and death through sin, and thus sin spread to all men, because all sinned."
>
> (Romans 5:12)

Every death is an evidence that the devil is a liar.

What stark differences there are in the invitations and offers of the two voices. Wisdom is open and honest. Wisdom underlines the importance of putting God first and obeying Him. Wisdom offers the right kind of knowledge and understanding. Wisdom is not deceitful, is not secret. Wisdom is obtained honestly. Wisdom prolongs life. Wisdom does you good. Folly is so different. It diverts one from a straight course. It leads astray. It is not open and honest, but secretive and tries to hide. It looks good from the outside; it is sin wrapped up in an attractive package. The one thing folly will not tell you, is the consequence. Those who accept the woman's attractive invitation and enter her house do not know that it leads to death, that "the soul who sins shall die" (Ezekiel 18:4), and that the destination is hell.

Then, too, one must consider those who issue the invitation, their character, their motives, their concern. Here God gives the invitation to the house of wisdom. He is perfect in character. He is love. He is the God who "so loved the world that He gave His only begotten Son," and wishes the best for those He invites. He is altogether righteous. The acceptance of His invitation brings freedom and joy and life. The voice of folly has no concern for the victim. She is loveless, impersonal, deceitful. Those who enter her doors become victims and not victors. You can write over the door, "Abandon hope, all you who enter here." The contrasts are meant to be so clear that the choice is obvious. Choose wisdom, choose God. Choose His Word, choose His will, choose His ways.

The fear of the Lord

It is not surprising that wisdom's invitation takes us back to the beginning:

"The fear of the LORD is the beginning of wisdom,
And the knowledge of the Holy One is understanding."   (v. 10)

There is no true wisdom without an acknowledgment and reverence for God. In the opening words of this book, Solomon said:

"The fear of the LORD is the beginning of knowledge,
But fools despise wisdom and instruction."   (1:7)

He described some who really got in to trouble because they "did
not choose the fear of the LORD" (1:29).

We cannot be wise without putting God first in our lives. If we
reject the source, we cannot have the product. Increase in wisdom is
determined by our increasing in the knowledge of God. That
increase will also give us an increase in understanding. What a
lovely phrase verse 10 is:

'The knowledge of the Holy One is understanding'

God is holy, sinless, righteous, perfect, pure, unchangeable, just and
blameless. Of all the sciences, philosophies, ideologies, there is none
greater than the knowledge of God, the Holy One. Oh, the glorious
wonder of God's salvation! We can know God. Oh, the greatness of
the Lord Jesus, who lived, died for our sins, rose again from the
dead, that we might know the Holy One! As He said:

'This is eternal life, that they may know You, the only true God,
and Jesus Christ whom You have sent."   (John 17:3)

Oh, the glory, that sinful, unholy man cannot only know the Holy
One, but be made holy! How powerful is the blood of Jesus that
cleanses us from all sin. How wonderful to be indwelt by the *Holy*
Spirit. His work within us is to make us holy too. Again, no wonder
that Paul cried out, "that I may know Him . . ." (Philippians 3:10).
The wisest men who have ever lived have been those who knew
and went on pursuing the knowledge of the Holy One. The more
we know Him, the more we will fear Him, reverence Him,
appreciate Him, obey Him, follow Him, live for Him and love

Him. The question is not just, "How well do you know the Bible?" but "How well do you know God?" Remember what Daniel said:

> "... the people who know their God shall be strong, and carry out great exploits. And those of the people who understand shall instruct many." (Daniel 11:32–33)

The proof of our desiring to be people of wisdom is evidenced by our hunger and thirst to know God. How is it with you? Is this the priority in your life? God is always a rewarder of those who diligently seek Him. Getting to know God is not meant to be boring, drudgery, or even just duty, but a delight. The "greats" in the Bible were those who knew the Holy One. Wise people will live longer than foolish people: "by me your days will be multiplied" (v. 11), and as we read in Proverbs 3:2: "Length of days and long life and peace they will add to you."

Application

God's Word and God's invitations, as we have already seen, require a response, or a confirmation of choices previously made. The wise and sensible thing to do, having read this chapter, is to fully accept God's invitation to partake of what His loving heart has provided. His grace and forgiveness are also available to those who have accepted the other invitation, and having recognized the foolishness of it, are deeply sorry, repent and confess, and return to the Lord, resolving as verse 6 says to "forsake foolishness and live, and go in the way of understanding."

The other encouragement we get from this chapter is to be continually getting to know God better; the knowledge of the Holy One. Are there any adjustments to be made in your life to do this? May I again encourage you to include reading one chapter in Proverbs every day as well any other reading plans you may have. This will be a continual reminder to seek wisdom, understanding and knowledge.

Let me encourage you to daily pray the prayer the Lord Jesus taught His disciples, praying it slowly and thoughtfully. There are varying voices of temptation which confront us every day. We need help, and it is good to ask of our Father, "Lead us not into temptation, but deliver us from evil." Why do we not do that right now?

> "Our Father in heaven,
> Hallowed be Your Name.
> Your kingdom come.
> Your will be done
> On earth as it is in heaven.
> Give us this day our daily bread.
> And forgive us our debts,
> As we forgive our debtors.
> And do not lead us into temptation,
> But deliver us from the evil one.
> For Yours is the kingdom and the power and
>   the glory forever. Amen."   (Matthew 6:9–13)

---

*If any of you lacks wisdom, let him ask of God, who gives to all liberally and without reproach, and it **will** be given to him (James 1:5).*

Chapter 10

Wise sayings of Solomon

1. The proverbs of Solomon: A wise son makes a glad father, but a foolish son is the grief of his mother.
2. Treasures of wickedness profit nothing, but righteousness delivers from death.
3. The LORD will not allow the righteous soul to famish, but He casts away the desire of the wicked.
4. He who has a slack hand becomes poor, but the hand of the diligent makes rich.
5. He who gathers in summer is a wise son; he who sleeps in harvest is a son who causes shame.
6. Blessings are on the head of the righteous, but violence covers the mouth of the wicked.
7. The memory of the righteous is blessed, but the name of the wicked will rot.
8. The wise in heart will receive commands, but a prating fool will fall.
9. He who walks with integrity walks securely, but he who perverts his ways will become known.
10. He who winks with the eye causes trouble, but a prating fool will fall.
11. The mouth of the righteous is a well of life, but violence covers the mouth of the wicked.
12. Hatred stirs up strife, but love covers all sins.
13. Wisdom is found on the lips of him who has understanding, but a rod is for the back of him who is devoid of understanding.
14. Wise people store up knowledge, but the mouth of the foolish is near destruction.
15. The rich man's wealth is his strong city; the destruction of the poor is their poverty.
16. The labor of the righteous leads to life, the wages of the wicked to sin.
17. He who keeps instruction is in the way of life, but he who refuses correction goes astray.

18. Whoever hides hatred has lying lips, and whoever spreads slander is a fool.
19. In the multitude of words sin is not lacking, but he who restrains his lips is wise.
20. The tongue of the righteous is choice silver; the heart of the wicked is worth little.
21. The lips of the righteous feed many, but fools die for lack of wisdom.
22. The blessing of the LORD makes one rich, and He adds no sorrow with it.
23. To do evil is like sport to a fool, but a man of understanding has wisdom.
24. The fear of the wicked will come upon him, and the desire of the righteous will be granted.
25. When the whirlwind passes by, the wicked is no more, but the righteous has an everlasting foundation.
26. As vinegar to the teeth and smoke to the eyes, so is the lazy man to those who send him.
27. The fear of the LORD prolongs days, but the years of the wicked will be shortened.
28. The hope of the righteous will be gladness, but the expectation of the wicked will perish.
29. The way of the LORD is strength for the upright, but destruction will come to the workers of iniquity.
30. The righteous will never be removed, but the wicked will not inhabit the earth.
31. The mouth of the righteous brings forth wisdom, but the perverse tongue will be cut out.
32. The lips of the righteous know what is acceptable, but the mouth of the wicked what is perverse.

Wisdom

The promised blessings given at the beginning of Proverbs, the book of wisdom, were to those who would hear the words, receive them, treasure them in their hearts, and apply them to their lives. One of the main purposes for the teaching is that we may be wise people. Solomon starts this chapter by saying that "a *wise* son makes a father glad" (v. 1, emphasis added), then contrasts that with "a foolish son is the grief of his mother" (v. 1). How true; children can bring their parents joy or sorrow. What joy Solomon must have been to David; Joseph to Jacob; Joshua to Nun, and what joy Jesus gave His Father, God. Then what grief and sorrow Cain gave to Adam and Eve when he murdered his brother Abel; what sorrow Absalom gave his parents.

How important it is that we bring up our children in the knowledge of God, encouraging them to put God first. Solomon says that "he who gathers in summer is a wise son" (v. 5), that is, he prepares for the future. He takes advantage of present-time opportunities, whereas "he who sleeps in harvest is a son who causes shame" (v. 5), that is, misses the opportunities. He also says in this chapter that a wise person will be someone who is obedient to God's instructions (v. 8); he/she will be a person of understanding who speaks the right thing (v. 13). A wise person will also "store up knowledge" (v. 14). What great and wonderful teaching in just a few words:

- A wise son gives joy to his parents (v. 1).
- A wise son gathers in summer (v. 5).
- A wise person obeys the commandments (v. 8).
- A wise person speaks with understanding (vv. 13, 23, 31).
- A wise person stores up knowledge (v. 14).

Contrasts

It may seem to the casual reader that this chapter is a list of disjointed statements. It may seem like that, but there is a definite theme throughout, and a clear purpose. There are continual contrasts, the little word "but" is mentioned twenty-six times. There are the contrasts between:

- Righteousness and wickedness.
- Diligence and laziness.
- Love and hatred.
- Unity and strife.
- Wisdom and folly.

It is a black and white presentation, facing us with the ability we have to choose.

The blessings of the righteous

We are presented with the benefits and blessings of living a righteous life, and also the sad and devastating result in living foolishly, wickedly. Let's look at righteousness.

Righteousness brings deliverance

Righteousness is simply doing what is right (it was formerly spelled "rightwiseness") and "righteousness delivers from death" (v. 2). To live right is self-preservation. Think of the multitudes who die because of doing the wrong thing.

Righteousness brings God's provision

"The LORD will not allow the righteous to famish" (v. 3). What a wonderful God. David said:

> "I have been young, and now am old;
> Yet I have not seen the righteous forsaken
> Nor his descendants begging bread."   (Psalm 37:25)

God fed Elijah at a brook in the time of famine. He fed over a million people daily in the wilderness. Paul said:

> "My God shall supply all your need according to His riches in glory
> by Christ Jesus."   (Philippians 4:19)

Righteousness brings God's blessing

"Blessings are on the head of the righteous" (v. 6). What an incentive to be righteous! There is no substitute for the blessing of the Lord. In verse 22 we read:

> "The blessing of the LORD makes one rich,
> And He adds no sorrow with it."

When Moses set before the people the instructions from the Lord, he promised "a blessing . . . if you obey the commandments of the LORD your God" (Deuteronomy 11:26–27)

Righteousness assures security

"He who walks with integrity walks securely" (v. 9). Righteousness brings security. There is no safer place on earth than in the will of God. When you are right, God is with you. David reminded us that:

> "Yea, though I walk through the valley of the shadow of death,
> I will fear no evil;
> For You are with me;
> Your rod and Your staff, they comfort me." (Psalm 23:4)

In the will of God, doing what is right assures us security and safety; confidence for the present and security for the future. Verse 28 speaks of the certain "hope of the righteous." In verse 25 we read: "the righteous has an everlasting foundation." They are built on the Rock. The righteous are strong: "the way of the LORD is strength for the upright" (v. 29); "the righteous will never be removed" (v. 30).

Righteousness blesses others

"The mouth of the righteous is a well of life" (v. 11). Righteous people will not only be blessed, but will be a blessing to others. They will minister life to people. Their conversation, their counsel, their advice will be a refreshment. They will encourage others in the paths of righteousness. Not only by what they say, but by what they do. We read in verse 16: "the labor of the righteous leads to life." Words will be matched with action. Both will be refreshing. In verse 20 we read: "the tongue of the righteous is choice silver." What they say is valuable and pure. Solomon also writes and says: "the lips of the righteous feed many" (v. 21). They will build people up and encourage them.

Righteousness is right, it:

- Delivers.
- Has God's provision.
- Has God's blessing.
- Makes one secure.
- Blesses others.

Let's choose righteousness.

Wickedness

Having described the blessing of righteousness, Solomon compares it with wickedness.

Wickedness causes grief to others

Not only does a wicked person hurt himself, but he grieves others. Solomon says, "a foolish son is the grief of his mother" (v. 1). How many parents are heart-broken because of the behavior of their unwise children?

- Adam and Eve were heart-broken when their son Cain murdered his brother Abel.
- Eli the priest was heart-broken over the wickedness of his sons Hophni and Phineas.
- David was heart-broken because of the rebellion of his son Absalom.

The character and assessment of the wicked

- "Violence covers the mouth of the wicked" (v. 6). He can speak pleasant words, but in his heart plans wickedness.
- "He who refuses correction goes astray" (v. 17). He hates to be corrected.
- "To do evil is like sport to a fool" (v. 23). He looks on evil as a sport. It is like a game and he hates to lose.

What the wicked sow they will reap

- "He [God] casts away the desire of the wicked" (v. 3). They will never, ever be truly satisfied.
- "The name of the wicked will rot" (v. 7). He will never leave behind any good memories.
- He will receive the wages for his misdeeds (v. 16).
- "The heart of the wicked is worth little" (v. 20). His life will be useless.
- "When the whirlwind passes by, the wicked is no more" (v. 25). The day will come when he is gone.

- "The years of the wicked will be shortened" (v. 27). Their lives are cut short.
- "The expectation of the wicked will perish" (v. 28). His expectations will never be realized.

Contrasts and differences between righteousness and wickedness

There are some contrasts, some differences, and again man faces the choice of what he wants to be and how he wants to live. We have the saying, "crime doesn't pay." Actually, it does: "the wages of sin is death" (Romans 6:23).

Righteousness has God's blessing; the righteous are safe and secure; the righteous bless others; the righteous have satisfaction; the righteous have hope; the righteous leave good memories; the righteous' lives are prolonged.

Wickedness is against the will of God; gives grief and hurts to the person and to others; the wicked are never satisfied; they are never secure; their lives are shortened; they face judgment. Again, what a choice: righteousness and blessing; or wickedness and a wasted life with no hope for the future. How the Lord desires the best for us.

In this chapter we read of:

- The *provision* of the Lord (v. 3).
- The *blessing* of the Lord (v. 22).
- The *fear* of the Lord (v. 27).
- The *way* of the Lord (v. 29).

If we walk in the way of the Lord, in the fear of the Lord, then we will know the blessing of the Lord and the provision of the Lord.

The contrast between diligence and laziness

Life is a one-way ticket. It is punctuated by opportunities. We are living in a day when many want to get as much as possible with as little effort as possible. However, in the Scriptures we are encouraged to work and to work well. In this chapter we read of dealing with a slack hand, or dealing with a diligent hand. If we are slack we will be poor; if we are diligent we will be rich (v. 4). We are also encouraged to make full use of opportunities to work, not only for the present but for the future:

> "He who gathers in summer is a wise son;
> He who sleeps in harvest is a son who causes shame."   (v. 5)

Christian employees should be the most reliable people. Their quality of work, dependability, honesty and integrity should be a testimony. They have available to them the wisdom of God to do their work. They are not merely serving an earthly employer, but a heavenly One. Paul exhorted employees:

> "Whatever you do, do it heartily, as to the Lord and not to men, knowing that from the Lord you will receive the reward of the inheritance; for you serve the Lord Christ." (Colossians 3:23–24)

Christian employees are not meant to steal their employer's time, telephone calls or stationery; they are primarily to be interested in pleasing the Lord. At the same time Christian employers are encouraged:

> "Masters, give your bondservants what is just and fair, knowing that you also have a Master in heaven."   (Colossians 4:1)

How the work place would be transformed by these principles. What kind of employee or employer are you? Does what you do please the Lord Jesus? Are there any adjustments that need to be made? In a later chapter Solomon says:

> "Do you see a man who excels in his work?
> He will stand before kings;
> He will not stand before unknown men."   (22:29)

Paul exhorted Timothy:

> "Be diligent to present yourself approved to God, a worker who does not need to be ashamed..."   (2 Timothy 2:15)

Other contrasts in this chapter are between *love and hatred* and *unity and strife.*

> "Hatred stirs up strife,
> But love covers all sins."   (v. 12)

Again we have a choice either to be peacemakers or trouble-makers. Jesus said:

> Blessed are the peacemakers,
> For they shall be called sons of God."   (Matthew 5:9)

What a terrible thing hatred is, with all its bitterness, contempt, spite, resentment and malignance. How it harms the person, and how it hurts others. It can be disguised. Verse 18 says:

> "Whoever hides hatred has lying lips,
> And whoever spreads slander is a fool."

As hatred is so evil, how wonderful true love is:

> "Love suffers long and is kind; love does not envy; love does not
> parade itself, is not puffed up; does not behave rudely, does not
> seek its own, is not provoked, thinks no evil; does not rejoice in
> iniquity, but rejoices in truth, bears all things, believes all things,
> hopes all things, endures all things. Love *never* fails."
>
> (1 Corinthians 13:4–8, emphasis added)

Again, what a comparison, what a choice: *love and hatred; unity and strife.* No wonder Paul calls *love* "a more excellent way" (1 Corinthians 12:31). Love brings unity; hatred brings strife. Jesus said to His disciples,

> "A new commandment I give to you, that you love one another; as
> I have loved you, that you also love one another. By this will all will
> know that you are My disciples, if you have love for one another."
>
> (John 13:34–35)

Let's go for the greatest:

> "And now abide faith, hope, love, these three; but the *greatest* of these is *love*."   (1 Corinthians 13:13, emphasis added)

Our mouths, tongues, lips

You will have noticed in this chapter how often what is said is mentioned; the *mouth*, the *tongue* and the *lips*. What we say reflects what we are: "out of the abundance of the heart the mouth speaks" (Matthew 12:23). Again, there is the comparison of speaking right, and speaking wrong. James described the tongue as "a fire, a world of iniquity" (James 3:6) and says,

> "If anyone does not stumble in word, he is a perfect man, able also to bridle the whole body."   (James 3:2)

What a contrast between the mouth of the righteous and the mouth of the wicked.

The mouth of the righteous

- The mouth of the righteous is a well of *life* (v. 11).
- *Wisdom* is found on the lips of him who has understanding (v. 13).
- He who *restrains* his lips is wise (v. 19).
- The tongue of the righteous is *choice silver* (v. 20).
- The lips of the righteous *feed* many (v. 21).
- The mouth of the righteous brings forth *wisdom* (v. 31).
- The lips of the righteous know what is *acceptable* (v. 32).

The mouth of the wicked

- Is *violent* (vv. 6, 11).
- Is *destructive* (v. 14).
- Speaks *lies* (v. 18).
- Spreads *slander* (v. 18).
- Is voluble, a multitude of words in which there is *evil* (v. 19).
- Is *perverse* (vv. 31, 32)

Application

- Let us choose to be righteous, doing what is right, with the aid of the Holy Spirit.
- Let us covet the continual blessing of the Lord.
- Let us desire to be a blessing to others; our own family and others, with knowledge, wisdom and love.

Again we are reminded in this chapter of the importance of the "fear of the LORD" and its rewards: "The fear of the LORD prolongs days" (v. 27). When we put God first, His blessings, provision, and presence are guaranteed.

Your own thoughts

*If any of you lacks wisdom, let him ask of God, who gives to all liberally and without reproach, and it **will** be given to him* (James 1:5).

Chapter 11

1. Dishonest scales are an abomination to the LORD, but a just weight is His delight.
2. When pride comes, then comes shame; but with the humble is wisdom.
3. The integrity of the upright will guide them, but the perversity of the unfaithful will destroy them.
4. Riches do not profit in the day of wrath, but righteousness delivers from death.
5. The righteousness of the blameless will direct his way aright, but the wicked will fall by his own wickedness.
6. The righteousness of the upright will deliver them, but the unfaithful will be caught by their lust.
7. When a wicked man dies, his expectation will perish, and the hope of the unjust perishes.
8. The righteous is delivered from trouble, and it comes to the wicked instead.
9. The hypocrite with his mouth destroys his neighbor, but through knowledge the righteous will be delivered.
10. When it goes well with the righteous, the city rejoices; and when the wicked perish, there is jubilation.
11. By the blessing of the upright the city is exalted, but it is overthrown by the mouth of the wicked.
12. He who is devoid of wisdom despises his neighbor, but a man of understanding holds his peace.
13. A talebearer reveals secrets, but he who is of a faithful spirit conceals a matter.
14. Where there is no counsel, the people fall; but in the multitude of counselors there is safety.
15. He who is surety for a stranger will suffer, but one who hates being surety is secure.

16. A gracious woman retains honor, but ruthless men retain riches.
17. The merciful man does good for his own soul, but he who is cruel troubles his own flesh.
18. The wicked man does deceptive work, but he who sows righteousness will have a sure reward.
19. As righteousness leads to life, so he who pursues evil pursues it to his own death.
20. Those who are of a perverse heart are an abomination to the Lord, but the blameless in their ways are His delight.
21. Though they join forces, the wicked will not go unpunished; but the posterity of the righteous will be delivered.
22. As a ring of gold in a swine's snout, so is a lovely woman who lacks discretion.
23. The desire of the righteous is only good, but the expectation of the wicked is wrath.
24. There is one who scatters, yet increases more; and there is one who withholds more than is right, but it leads to poverty.
25. The generous soul will be made rich, and he who waters will also be watered himself.
26. The people will curse him who withholds grain, but blessing will be on the head of him who sells it.
27. He who earnestly seeks good finds favor, but trouble will come to him who seeks evil.
28. He who trusts in his riches will fall, but the righteous will flourish like foliage.
29. He who troubles his own house will inherit the wind, and the fool will be servant to the wise of heart.
30. The fruit of the righteous is a tree of life, and he who wins souls is wise.
31. If the righteous will be recompensed on the earth, how much more the ungodly and the sinner.

As we have seen before there are continual comparisons between that which is right and that which is wrong. What a difference there would be in the world if everybody did that which was right. There would be no need of police forces, of armies or navies or air forces. There would be no criminal courts, no divorce court. Well, one day it is going to be like that when the Lord Jesus is reigning, when His Kingdom comes, and everything that is done will be right and righteous. However, as individuals we have the choice to be righteous or to be wicked. There is a standard laid down, which if people follow results in their welfare. That standard is God's standard. For example, think of something that affects all of us in our day-to-day living in the things we buy. We object to being cheated, short-changed, taken advantage of. What a need there is of the virtues, blessings and protection of righteousness, especially in our business dealings.

Righteousness in business

> "Dishonest scales are an abomination [God hates them] to the
> LORD,
> *But* a just weight is His delight."   (v. 1, emphasis added)

God loves integrity in business, and hates dishonesty. Men may cheat, and deceive, but what they forget is that God sees everything, and one day every individual is going to stand before the Judge of all the earth. I am sure we all have stories of people who have defrauded us. It is very unpleasant. However, the message to us personally is to be honest in all our dealings: paying our accounts, if business persons or traders; always seeking to have a righteous standard. It would be terrible to be doing anything that God hates. God loves righteousness, and loves the righteous.

You probably noticed reading this chapter, there was a recurrence of a certain word. Did you notice it? It is the word "righteous" or "righteousness"; mentioned at least twelve times. Also mentioned are the words "integrity," "just," "upright," "blameless." Let's look at the blessings of doing the right thing:

The virtues, blessings, and protection of righteousness

Righteousness delivers from death
"Righteousness delivers from death" (v. 4). How true and how obvious. How many lives have been cut short because of doing things that were not right. The premature death of drunkards, drug addicts, the immoral etc. Many of these lives would have been spared, if they had lived right and righteously.

Righteousness preserves

"The righteousness of the upright will deliver them" (v. 6). They will be saved from being trapped, deceived, making wrong decisions or forming wrong relationships.

Righteousness will deliver from trouble

"The righteous is delivered from trouble" (v. 8). The Bible doesn't say that Christians will not have trouble. Righteousness brings much trouble. Look at the troubles Joseph had and Moses, David, Paul, the disciples – most of whom were martyred. Look at the trouble Jesus had, even to death. The righteous are not delivered from not having trouble, but are delivered in it. There is a difference between self-inflicted trouble, and trouble that comes from others or from circumstances. When we are trusting God and seeking to do that which is right, God is with us.

David had his share of trouble but could say:

> "For in time of trouble
> He shall hide me in His pavilion;
> In the secret place of His tabernacle
> He shall hide me."   (Psalm 27:5)

Oh yes, when we seek to live righteously, He will provide for every need. We are not just living for time but for eternity. The righteous will come through trouble.

Righteousness brings blessings to our families

"The posterity of the righteous will be delivered" (v. 21). Righteousness not only blesses us, but our families and even our posterity. David said:

> "Blessed is the man who fears the LORD,
> Who delights greatly in His commandments.
> His descendants will be mighty on earth.
> The generation of the upright will be blessed."   (Psalm 112:1–2)

Many years ago someone traced the descendants of two men. The first was Jonathan Edwards, whom God greatly used in a great spiritual awakening in America. The other was a man called Jukes, who was a criminal. More than 400 of Jonathan Edwards' descendants were traced. They included:

- 14 college presidents.
- 100 professors.
- 100 ministers of the gospel, missionaries, Bible teachers.
- 100 lawyers and judges.
- 60 in the medical profession, authors, journalists.

1,200 descendants of Jukes were traced. They included:

- 400 who were physically self-wrecked.
- 310 who were paupers.
- 130 who were convicted criminals.
- 60 who were thieves or pickpockets.
- 7 who were murderers.
- 20 who had learned a trade – half of them owed it to prison discipline.

"The posterity of the righteous will be delivered." What foundations of influence are we laying for future generations?

Remember the Lord Jesus taught in His sermon on the Mount:

> "Seek first the kingdom of God and His righteousness, and all these things shall be added to you."   (Matthew 6:33)

Proverbs teaches us about righteous living and behavior, and we should seek to live to His standards by the help of His Holy Spirit. In this chapter we are given insight to the character of a righteous person. Let's look at them.

The character of righteous people

Remember we are not saved by our own righteousness for "there is none righteous, no, not one" (Romans 3:10), but when are saved we are enabled to live righteous lives. A righteous person will be:

A humble person

"With the humble is wisdom" (v. 2). Someone has said that "humility is the first letter in the Christian alphabet." The opposite to humility is pride. We are exhorted to "humble [ourselves] under the mighty hand of God" (1 Peter 5:6).

A person of integrity

"The integrity of the upright will guide them" (v. 3). The words of this phrase interpret what integrity is, being upright, that is, honest, incorrupt, virtuous, nothing crooked or devious.

A person who loves knowledge

"Through knowledge the righteous will be delivered" (v. 9). A righteous person will seek to increase in the knowledge of the righteous Holy God, His will and His ways, with the desire to obey them.

A person who is faithful

"He who is of a faithful spirit" (v. 13). A righteous person can be totally trusted. The verse says such a person "conceals a matter." He or she will be a person in whom you can have total confidence. You can share things with him or her, knowing that these matters will not be discussed or shared with anyone else.

A merciful person

"The merciful man . . ." (v. 17). A merciful person is not harsh, judgmental or critical, but gentle, tender, full of pity, forgiving, feeling for others, comforting and always truthful. He or she will "rejoice with those who rejoice, and weep with those who weep" (Romans 12:15).

A gracious person

"A gracious woman retains honor" (v. 16). How good that Solomon ascribes this virtue to a lady, but men too, should be gracious. One of the dictionary definitions of "graciousness" is "lady-likeness." Graciousness includes mercy, kindness, politeness, courtesy and gentleness.

A generous person

"The generous soul..." (v. 25). Generosity is giving liberally. Not merely money, but also time: a listening ear; sympathy; advice and counsel. The verse says that "the generous soul will be made rich." It is a biblical principle: "Give, and it will be given..." (Luke 6:38).

Righteousness always brings blessing

It brings blessing to the person:

- The merciful man does *good for his own soul* (v. 17).
- He who sows righteousness will have a *sure reward* (v. 18).
- He who earnestly seeks good finds *favor* (v. 27).
- The righteous will *flourish* like foliage (v. 28).
- The fruit of the righteous is a *tree of life* (v. 30).
- The righteous will be *recompensed* on the earth (v. 31).

It brings blessing to others:

- By the blessing of the upright the city is exalted (v. 11).
- When it goes well with the righteous, the city rejoices (v. 10).

When a city and a nation are governed by righteous, God-fearing people they prosper. When they are ruled by wicked, self-seeking, corrupt people the whole city or nation suffers. We have many illustrations of that in our present time,

> "Righteousness exalts a nation,
> But sin is a reproach to any people."   (14:34)

I am sure all of us are grateful to righteous people who have blessed our lives: generous people, merciful people, gracious people, faithful people. Their example should encourage us to be righteous too, and be a blessing to others.

Remember the story of David. One day he was wondering if there was any of Saul's family to whom he could show kindness. Saul had been his enemy and had sought to kill him on numerous occasions, but David never, ever sought revenge, and spared his life when he could have killed him. Here he is, being righteous, desiring to be gracious, generous and merciful. Do you want to show righteousness? Why not ask God to put into your heart someone to whom you can show kindness. Does someone come to mind? As Mary said at the wedding of Cana about Jesus, "Whatever He says to you, do it" (John 2:5). They will get blessed, and so will you. Isn't life exciting?

Having seen the blessings and rewards of righteousness, Solomon brings into stark contrast the character and results of wickedness. We have seen righteousness delivers from death; preserves lives; brings blessing to families; blesses cities, and now we see the effects and results of wickedness.

The effects and results of wickedness

Wickedness destroys
"The perversity [crookedness] of the unfaithful [treacherous] *will destroy* them" (v. 3, emphasis added). They not only destroy themselves but they destroy others:

- A city is overthrown by the mouth of the wicked (v. 11).
- The hypocrite with his mouth *destroys* his neighbor (v. 9).

Wickedness deceives
"A talebearer reveals secrets" (v. 13). The wicked cannot be trusted. Wickedness cheats:

- Dishonest scales . . . (v. 1).
- The wicked man does deceptive work (v. 18).

God hates wickedness
It is a frightful thing to have God's displeasure.

- Dishonest scales are an abomination to the the Lord (v. 1).
- Those who are of a perverse [contrary] heart are an abomination to the Lord (v. 20).

Wickedness and the wicked are doomed

Look at what God's Word says about their fate and future. Oh yes, they may prosper for a while. David once asked the question, "Why do the wicked prosper?" He was trying to do the right thing in pleasing God and being persecuted for it, while the wicked seemed to be getting away with it. When he thought about it all, he said:

> "It was too painful for me –
> *Until* I went into the sanctuary of God;
> Then I understood their end."   (Psalm 73:16–17)

In the presence of God he got the right perspective: they had an end. They would be cast down to destruction. See what this chapter says:

- Riches do *not profit* in the day of wrath (v. 4).
- The wicked will *fall* by his own wickedness (v. 5).
- The unfaithful will be *caught* by their lust (v. 6).
- When a wicked man dies his expectation will *perish* (v. 7).
- The hope of the unjust *perishes* (v. 7).
- When the wicked perish, there is *jubilation* (v. 10).
- He who pursues evil pursues it to his own *death* (v. 19).
- The wicked will *not go unpunished* (v. 21).
- The expectation of the wicked is *wrath* (v. 23).
- *Trouble* will come to him who seeks evil (v. 27).

These truths should be enough to scare anyone from wickedness to righteousness. There is an end. There is a judgment day. There is a verdict. There is a sentence.

The character of the wicked

Just as we saw a description in this chapter of the character of the righteous, so we also see a description of the character of the wicked. They may not seem like this outwardly, but God sees their hearts. They are:

- Proud (v. 2).
- Perverse (v. 3).

- Unfaithful (v. 3).
- Hypocritical (v. 9).
- Devoid of wisdom (do not fear God) (v. 12).
- Ruthless (v. 16).
- Cruel (v. 17).
- Deceptive (v. 18).
- Looking for trouble (v. 27).

Application

- The question comes, "What do I want to be: righteous, or wicked?" A wicked man by the name of Balaam once said, "Let me die the death of the righteous, and let my end be like his!" (Numbers 23:10). He wanted to live the life of the wicked, and die the death of the righteous!
- How wonderful is the grace and mercy of God. How glorious is the death and resurrection of the Lord Jesus who died "the just for the unjust, that He might bring us to God" (1 Peter 3:18). He makes sinners saints; He makes wicked righteous; He blots out all our sins and clothes us with a robe of righteousness. Hallelujah, what a Savior. Praise God now for His great salvation.
- Read again the attributes of the righteous and pray them in.
- *Pray* for people to be saved. Name some of them: family, friends, associates, your town and country. For all missionary outreaches. I love how this chapter ends: "He who wins souls is wise" (v. 30).

If any of you lacks wisdom, let him ask of God, who gives to all liberally and without reproach, and it **will** *be given to him* (James 1:5).

Chapter 12

1. Whoever loves instruction loves knowledge, but he who hates correction is stupid.
2. A good man obtains favor from the LORD, but a man of wicked intentions He will condemn.
3. A man is not established by wickedness, but the root of the righteous cannot be moved.
4. An excellent wife is the crown of her husband, but she who causes shame is like rottenness in his bones.
5. The thoughts of the righteous are right, but the counsels of the wicked are deceitful.
6. The words of the wicked are, "Lie in wait for blood," but the mouth of the upright will deliver them.
7. The wicked are overthrown and are no more, but the house of the righteous will stand.
8. A man will be commended according to his wisdom, but he who is of a perverse heart will be despised.
9. Better is the one who is slighted but has a servant, than he who honors himself but lacks bread.
10. A righteous man regards the life of his animal, but the tender mercies of the wicked are cruel.
11. He who tills his land will be satisfied with bread, but he who follows frivolity is devoid of understanding.
12. The wicked covet the catch of evil men, but the root of the righteous yields fruit.
13. The wicked is ensnared by the transgression of his lips, but the righteous will come through trouble.
14. A man will be satisfied with good by the fruit of his mouth, and the recompense of a man's hands will be rendered to him.
15. The way of a fool is right in his own eyes, but he who heeds counsel is wise.

16. A fool's wrath is known at once, but a prudent man covers shame.
17. He who speaks truth declares righteousness, but a false witness, deceit.
18. There is one who speaks like the piercings of a sword, but the tongue of the wise promotes health.
19. The truthful lip shall be established forever, but a lying tongue is but for a moment.
20. Deceit is in the heart of those who devise evil, but counselors of peace have joy.
21. No grave trouble will overtake the righteous, but the wicked shall be filled with evil.
22. Lying lips are an abomination to the LORD, but those who deal truthfully are His delight.
23. A prudent man conceals knowledge, but the heart of fools proclaims foolishness.
24. The hand of the diligent will rule, but the lazy man will be put to forced labor.
25. Anxiety in the heart of man causes depression, but a good word makes it glad.
26. The righteous should choose his friends carefully, for the way of the wicked leads them astray.
27. The lazy man does not roast what he took in hunting, but diligence is man's precious possession.
28. In the way of righteousness is life, and in its pathway there is no death.

The opening verse of this chapter reminds us of the importance of our attitude as we approach God's Word.

> "Whoever loves instruction loves knowledge;
> But he who hates correction is stupid."

Instruction is necessary for knowledge. As the verse implies, some people do not like knowledge because it sometimes includes correction, and many do not like to be corrected. Do you? However, the verse is very blunt, saying that those who hate correction are stupid. Humility will accept correction, but pride will resist it.

We are continually encouraged in Proverbs to be righteous and

this chapter is no exception. One of the rewards for doing good is
that we get the favor of God:

> "A good man obtains favor from the Lord."   (v. 2)

Having God's favor is the greatest blessing any one can know.
"Favor" means, "grace, peace, kindness, goodwill, delight." Jesus
always had God's favor: "This is My beloved Son, in whom I am
well pleased" (Matthew 3:17). It was written of Jesus when He was
growing up:

> "Jesus increased in wisdom and stature, and favor with God and
> men."   (Luke 2:52)

It is said of others who lived for God, that they had divine favor:
Moses, Samuel, David, Joseph, Esther, Mary etc. Thank God for all
His wonderful favor to His children.

> "Blessed be the God and Father of our Lord Jesus Christ, who has
> blessed us with every spiritual blessing in the heavenly places in
> Christ."   (Ephesians 1:3)

To enjoy and experience what has been provided for us in Christ,
we must live in obedience to His Word and His ways. David taught
us some of these ways:

- *Being right with God*
  > "He who has clean hands and a pure heart,
  > Who has not lifted up his soul to an idol
  > Nor sworn deceitfully.
  > He shall receive the blessing of the LORD,
  > And righteousness from the God of his salvation."
  >
  > (Psalm 24:4–5)

- *Trusting and believing God.*
  > "Blessed are all those who put their trust in Him."
  >
  > (Psalm 2:12)

- *Living in unity*

> "Behold, how good and how pleasant it is
> For brethren to dwell together in unity! . . .
> For there the LORD commanded the blessing –
> Life forevermore." (Psalm 133:1, 3)

- *Fearing God*

> "Blessed is the man who fears the LORD." (Psalm 112:1)

- *They are rooted*

> "The root of the righteous cannot be moved." (v. 3)

What an encouraging truth. Righteous people are secure, safe and confident. What is our root? Listen to Jesus:

> "I am the Root and Offspring of David, the Bright and Morning Star." (Revelation 22:16)

He, Jesus, is our root, our foundation, our salvation. Paul tells us:

> "As you have therefore have received Christ Jesus the Lord, so walk in Him, *rooted* and built up in Him and *established* in the faith." (Colossians 2:6–7, emphasis added)

Christians should be the most secure people on earth. Paul also reminded us that "we are rooted and grounded in love" (Ephesians 3:17). The root of the righteous cannot be moved. Hear David:

> "Those who trust in the LORD
> Are like Mount Zion,
> Which cannot be moved, but abides forever." (Psalm 125:1)

Enjoy your position in Christ: rooted, established; cannot be moved; abides forever.

- *They are fruitful*

> "The root of the righteous yields fruit." (v. 12)

Jesus is our root who bears fruit through us, as He told His disciples:

> "I am the vine, you are the branches. He who abides in Me, and I in him, bears much fruit; for without Me you can do nothing." (John 15:5)

What favor He has shown us, what blessings He gives us.

Praise God from Whom all blessings flow.
Praise Him all creatures here below.
Praise Him above ye heavenly hosts.
Praise Father, Son, and Holy Ghost.

Amen and Amen.

We continue with the blessings of the righteous.

They think right

Their thoughts are not warped:

"The thoughts of the righteous are right."   (v. 5)

Later on in Proverbs we read, "As [a man] thinks in his heart, so is he" (23:7). A man's thoughts reveal what the man is like. The blessing of being righteous is that our thoughts will be right. If our thoughts are right then our actions will be right. We are what we think. What do you think about most? If we think about ourselves we are selfish. If we are always thinking about things and possessions we are materialistic, and probably covetous. If we think about God we are godly.

They speak right

"He who speaks *truth* declares righteousness."
                                          (v. 17, emphasis added)

"The tongue of the wise promotes health."   (v. 18)

"The truthful lip shall be established forever."   (v. 19)

Jesus said, "Out of the abundance of the heart the mouth speaks. A good man out of the good treasure of his heart brings forth good things" (Matthew 12:34–35). A good man will bring forth treasures, good words, edifying words, encouraging words and sometimes, rebuking words. A righteous person will help those who are depressed:

> "Anxiety in the heart of man causes depression,
> But a good word makes it glad." (v. 25)

An encouraging word spoken at the right time can lift depression. How wonderful are the words of Paul to the Philippians:

> "Be anxious for nothing, but in everything by prayer and sup-
> plication, with thanksgiving, let your requests be made known to
> God; and the peace of God which surpasses all understanding, will
> guard your hearts and minds through Christ Jesus."
>
> (Philippians 4:6–7)

They act right

- They are kind to animals:

    "A righteous man regards the life of his animal." (v. 10)

- They are industrious, hard working:

    "He who tills his land will be satisfied with bread." (v. 11)

    "The hand of the diligent will rule." (v. 24)

    "Diligence is man's precious possession." (v. 27)

- They give good advice:

    "Counselors of peace have joy." (v. 20)

- They are honest in their business dealings:

    "Those who deal truthfully are His delight." (v. 22)

- They not only give man satisfaction, but also give God delight. How God loves righteousness.
- They choose their friends carefully:

    "The righteous should choose his friends carefully." (v. 26)

    There is the saying "a man is known by the company he keeps." Righteous people will want righteous friends. We are warned about being "unequally yoked together with unbelievers" (2 Corinthians 6:14). How much sadness there has been as a result of Christians marrying non-Christians. How many times have Christians been led astray because they chose the wrong friends,. A righteous man, one who wants to be right and do right will be very careful in his choice.

Their homes are blessed

"The house of the righteous will stand"   (v. 7).

Righteousness benefits marriages, children and those who enter the house. I am sure you have been to homes where there is an undescribable sense of peace, and in others there is a sense of tension and unease.

The blessings to the righteous

We are given a list of blessings that come to the righteous:

- They will come through trouble. They will not be trouble free but they will come through triumphantly:

  "The righteous will come through trouble."   (v. 13)

- They will be content:

  "A man will be satisfied with good by the fruit of his mouth."
                                                            (v. 14)

- They will be a delight to God:

  "Those who deal truthfully are His delight."   (v. 22)

  What a wonderful thing to be able to give God pleasure.

- They will be delivered from evil:

  "No grave trouble will will overtake the righteous."   (v. 21)

- They will walk in the way of life:

  "In the way of righteousness is life, and in its pathway there is no death."   (v. 28)

- Another wonderful blessing for a man is to have an excellent wife:

  "An excellent wife is the crown of her husband."   (v. 4)

The Amplified Bible puts it this way:

> "A virtuous and worthy wife – earnest and strong in character –
> is a crowning joy to her husband."   (v. 4)

What a blessing a righteous wife is to a righteous man. Later
on in Proverbs we read:

> He who finds a wife finds a good thing,
> And obtains favor from the LORD."   (18:22)

Surely these truths, and promises are a great encouragement to us
all to do what is right. How wonderful is Jesus, our Good Shepherd
who "leads me in the paths of righteousness for His name's sake"
(Psalm 23:3). If we follow Him we will be righteous.

As in previous chapters Solomon compares righteousness with
wickedness. In the Hebrew the word "proverb" means "comparison." Look at the comparisons in this chapter:

- Love and hate (v. 1).
- Favor and condemnation (v. 2).
- Insecure and established (v. 3).
- An excellent wife and one who causes shame (v. 4).
- Right thoughts and deceitful thoughts (v. 5).
- Entrapment and deliverance (v. 6).
- Overthrown and standing in safety (v. 7).
- Wisdom and folly (v. 8).
- Slighted and honored (v. 9).
- Kindness to animals and cruelty (v. 10).
- Seriousness and frivolity (v. 11).
- Covetousness and generosity (v. 12).
- Trouble and deliverance in trouble (v. 13).
- Self-righteousness and unselfishness (v. 15).
- Foolish anger and prudence (v. 16).
- Truth and lies (vv. 17, 22).
- Bitterness and health (v. 18).
- Devising evil and seeking peace (v. 20).
- Righteousness and evil (v. 21).
- Much speaking and silence (v. 23).
- Anxiety and gladness (v. 25).

- Good friends and bad companions (v. 26).
- Diligence and laziness (v. 27).

What a list!

As we have seen the virtues, and blessings of the righteous, here is a summary of wickedness and its results.

The way of the wicked

- They are under God's condemnation. What a dangerous place to be:

    "A man of wicked intentions He will condemn."   (v. 2)

- Man's approval without God's approval is useless and only temporary.
- They are insecure:

    "A man is not established by wickedness."   (v. 3).

    His life is built on wrong foundations: built on sand and all he seeks to build will fall.
- They are deceitful, cannot be trusted:

    "The counsels of the wicked are deceitful."   (v. 5)

    "Deceit is in the heart of those who devise evil."   (v. 20)

- They are doomed:

    "The wicked are overthrown and are no more."   (v. 7)

    "The way of the wicked leads them astray."   (v. 26)

- They are despised:

    "He who is of a perverse heart will be despised."   (v. 8)

    Men may flatter them and seek to have their approval, but in their hearts despise them.
- They are cruel:

    "The tender mercies of the wicked are cruel."   (v. 10)

- They are filled with evil:

    "The wicked shall be filled with evil."   (v. 21)

Conclusion and application

There are the comparisons between righteousness and wickedness. The wicked can camouflage their behavior and motives, but here is the divine description. So what should be the application to our own lives?

- We should always seek God's favor before man's.
- We should live within the boundaries of God's blessings. That is the way of righteousness.
- We should be grateful that there is a place of security, protection and joy in the ways of God. When we love righteousness, God is with us.
- Let us not only seek to be righteous but also seek to turn others to righteousness. I had a wonderful father. He was an evangelist and in his life led thousands to the Lord Jesus. When he died in New Zealand my old mother asked me what we should put on his grave stone. A scripture came to mind, which is inscribed:

> "Those who are wise shall shine
> Like the brightness of the firmament,
> And those who turn many to righteousness
> Like the stars forever and ever.' (Daniel 12:3)

What should we do?

- Deal with anything which is not righteous. When we confess and repent He forgives.
- Look to Jesus. He is our righteousness. Without Him we can do nothing. His indwelling life is a righteous life. When all is yielded to Him, He can fill us with His Holy Spirit, and the evidence of that fullness is holiness and righteousness.

Apply and pray in anything else God has said to you.

---

*If any of you lacks wisdom, let him ask of God, who gives to all liberally and without reproach, and it **will** be given to him* (James 1:5).

Chapter 13

1. A wise son heeds his father's instruction, but a scoffer does not listen to rebuke.
2. A man shall eat well by the fruit of his mouth, but the soul of the unfaithful feeds on violence.
3. He who guards his mouth preserves his life, but he who opens wide his lips shall have destruction.
4. The soul of a lazy man desires, and has nothing; but the soul of the diligent shall be made rich.
5. A righteous man hates lying, but a wicked man is loathsome and comes to shame.
6. Righteousness guards him whose way is blameless, but wickedness overthrows the sinner.
7. There is one who makes himself rich, yet has nothing; and one who makes himself poor, yet has great riches.
8. The ransom of a man's life is his riches, but the poor does not hear rebuke.
9. The light of the righteous rejoices, but the lamp of the wicked will be put out.
10. By pride comes nothing but strife, but with the well-advised is wisdom.
11. Wealth gained by dishonesty will be diminished, but he who gathers by labor will increase.
12. Hope deferred makes the heart sick, but when the desire comes, it is a tree of life.
13. He who despises the word will be destroyed, but he who fears the commandment will be rewarded.
14. The law of the wise is a fountain of life, to turn one away from the snares of death.
15. Good understanding gains favor, but the way of the unfaithful is hard.
16. Every prudent man acts with knowledge, but a fool lays open his folly.
17. A wicked messenger falls into trouble, but a faithful ambassador brings health.

18. Poverty and shame will come to him who disdains correction, but he who regards a rebuke will be honored.
19. A desire accomplished is sweet to the soul, but it is an abomination to fools to depart from evil.
20. He who walks with wise men will be wise, but the companion of fools will be destroyed.
21. Evil pursues sinners, but to the righteous, good shall be repaid.
22. A good man leaves an inheritance to his children's children, but the wealth of the sinner is stored up for the righteous.
23. Much food is in the fallow ground of the poor, and for lack of justice there is waste.
24. He who spares his rod hates his son, but he who loves him disciplines him promptly.
25. The righteous eats to the satisfying of his soul, but the stomach of the wicked shall be in want.

Introduction

There are many titles that could be given to this book: "the school of wisdom"; "the keys to successful living"; "a course for contentment" or perhaps "the paths of righteousness," reminding us of Solomon's father David's well-known twenty-third Psalm: "He leads me in the paths of righteousness for His name's sake" (Psalm 23:3). However, it is called "Proverbs," which we have seen in the Hebrew means "comparison." Throughout the book there are many comparisons. For example in this chapter there is:

A comparison of people

- The wise and the scoffer.
- The diligent and the lazy.
- The righteous and the wicked.
- The rich and the poor.
- The faithful messenger and the deceitful messenger.
- The prudent and the fool.
- The good man and the sinner.

A comparison of subjects

- Taking heed to advice or despising advice.
- Preservation and destruction.
- Riches and poverty.
- Righteousness and wickedness.
- Light and darkness.
- Health and trouble.
- Discipline and lack of discipline.
- Satisfaction and want.

It is amazing how much wisdom is condensed into the short space of twenty-five short verses. Such an economy of words, but such riches of counsel. Again we notice that in Proverbs there is a large amount of repetition. It is not repetition for the sake of repetition, but repetition with a purpose, because this is the inspired Word of God. Repetition deserves our full attention. Again we draw attention to the three essentials in dealing with truth:

- Knowledge;
- Understanding;
- Wisdom.

We also remind ourselves that truth is initially for ourselves. The teaching has to be personally applied to be profitable. We are continually faced with choices.

We can be

- Wise or foolish.
- Diligent or lazy.
- Righteous or wicked.
- Faithful or unfaithful.

We can choose

- Preservation or destruction.
- Righteousness or wickedness.
- Light or darkness.

- Honor or shame.
- Satisfaction or want.

Proverbs presents knowledge, the true facts. When we believe and receive that knowledge our lives are affected. Knowledge of facts faces us with decisions, choices. Again we remind ourselves that as we choose to obey, God gives us understanding of the facts, with His wisdom available to us to apply what we know and understand to our lives and living. With this in mind let's glean a few things from this chapter.

The right attitude to instruction

The opening verse tells us:

> "A wise son heeds his father's instruction,
> But a scoffer does not listen to rebuke."   (v. 1)

Yet again we are reminded of the great importance of bringing up our children, giving them the right instruction, and encouraging them to apply it. Sometimes instruction includes rebuke, and correction. Our reaction to correction manifests what kind of people we are. Remember the word given in the very first chapter of Proverbs, with its advice and encouragement:

> "Turn at my rebuke.
> Surely I will pour out my spirit on you;
> I will make my words known to you."   (1:23)

And then the warning of the danger of refusing correction:

> "Because I have called and you refused,
> I have stretched out my hand and no one regarded.
> Because you disdained all my counsel,
> And would have none of my rebuke,
> I will laugh at your calamity;
> I will mock when your terror comes."   (1:24–26)

An important question to ask ourselves is, "How do I respond to rebuke and correction?" This first verse says "a scoffer does not listen to rebuke." A wise person takes heed, a foolish person scoffs, scorns, mocks. In Proverbs this is how Solomon describes scoffers:

- "Scorners delight in their scorning" (1:22).
- "A scoffer seeks wisdom and does not find it" (14:6).
- "Poverty and shame will come to him who disdains correction" (14:18).
- "A scoffer does not love one who corrects him" (15:12).
- "Judgments are prepared for scoffers" (19:29).
- "A proud and haughty man – 'Scoffer' is his name" (21:24).
- "The scoffer is abomination to men" (24:9).

The right attitude to God's Word

> "He who despises the word will be destroyed,
> But he who fears the the commandment will be rewarded."
>
> (v. 13)

What a choice: destruction or reward! When Moses taught the children of Israel the ways of God he exhorted them: "I have set before you life and death ... choose life" (Deuteronomy 30:19).

Then again it is best to teach correction to children. Verse 24 is not very popular these days, but it is the Word of God:

> "He who spares his rod hates his son,
> But he who loves him disciplines him promptly."

New thoughts about this action have not produced improved youth, rather the opposite.

Let's have the right attitude towards correction, after all it is for our good and blessing. Have we had some rebuke or correction that we have refused? Let's apply whatever it was; it is foolish not to do so.

The blessings of wisdom

How God loves to encourage us. In this chapter we are encouraged to be wise. We have seen it is wise, for our good, to listen to a father's instruction.

Wisdom protects

- From death:

  "The law of the wise is a fountain of life,
  To turn one away from the the snares of death."　　　(v. 14)

- From saying the wrong thing:

  "He who guards his mouth preserves his life."　　　(v. 3)

Wisdom acts with knowledge

- Wisdom helps us to do the right thing:

  "Every prudent man acts with knowledge."　　　(v. 16)

Wisdom delights in wisdom

"He who walks with wise men will be wise."　　　(v. 20)

We have a saying, "a man is known by the company he keeps": how true. Again we are reminded, that "the fear of the LORD is the beginning of wisdom," therefore how good it is to have friends who fear God, and are wise. What company do you prefer? What are your friends like? Wise people will bless wise people. They will never boast about their wisdom, but will be people who agree with the question that the prophet Micah asked, "What does the LORD require of you?" And the answer was, "To do justly, to love mercy and to walk humbly with your God" (Micah 6:8). Or again the exhortation of the prophet Jeremiah:

" 'Let not the wise man glory in his wisdom . . .
But let him that glories glory in this,
That he understands and knows Me,

> That I am the LORD, exercising lovingkindness, judgment, and
>   righteousness in the earth,
> For in these I delight.' says the LORD."   (Jeremiah 9:23–24)

The blessings and rewards of righteousness

Wisdom and righteousness go together. See what we read in this
chapter about the blessings of being righteous, doing the right thing:

- Righteousness protects

  "Righteousness guards him whose way is blameless."   (v. 6)

- Righteousness rewards

  "To the righteous, good will be repaid."   (v. 21)

- Righteousness satisfies

  "The righteous eats to the satisfying of his soul."   (v. 25)

- Righteousness brings joy

  "The light of the righteous rejoices."   (v. 9)

- Righteousness blesses others

  "A good man leaves an inheritance to his children's children."

  (v. 22)

The folly and fruit of wickedness

Again here comes the contrast between. righteousness and wickedness, folly and wisdom:

- Wickedness ignores correction

  "A scoffer does not listen to rebuke."   (v. 1)

- Wickedness is violent

  "The soul of the unfaithful feeds on violence."   (v. 2)

- The wicked speak rashly

  "He who opens wide his lips shall have destruction."   (v. 3)

- The fool exposes his folly

  "A fool lays open his folly."   (v. 16)

- The fool hates to turn from evil

  "It is an abomination to fools to depart from evil." (v. 19)

- Fools destroy others

  "The companion of fools will be destroyed." (v. 20)

- The wicked will reap what they sow

  "Wickedness overthrows the sinner." (v. 6)

  "The lamp of the wicked will be put out." (v. 9)

  "A wicked messenger falls into trouble." (v. 17)

  "Evil pursues sinners." (v. 21)

All this reminds us of the consequences we can avoid so easily by choosing not to sin.

> "... whatsoever a man sows, that he will also reap. For he sows to the flesh will of the flesh reap corruption, but he who sows to the Spirit will of the Spirit reap everlasting life." (Galatians 6:7–8)

Riches and wealth

Several times in the book of Proverbs, Solomon teaches about riches and wealth, and its dangers. Most of us don't have that particular condition, but God's teaching brings everything, including money into right perspective. He writes:

> "There is one who makes himself rich, yet has nothing,
> And one who makes himself poor, yet has great riches." (v. 7)

Also:

> "Wealth gained by dishonesty will be diminished,
> But he who gathers by labor will increase." (v. 11)

Everything depends on what our value system is. Jesus taught us:

> "Do not lay up for yourselves treasures on earth, where moth and rust destroy and where thieves break in and steal; but lay up for

yourselves treasures in heaven, where neither moth nor rust destroys and where thieves do not break in and steal. For where your treasure is, there your heart will be also."

(Matthew 6:19–21)

A person can be rich and have nothing that will last. Riches cannot buy eternal life. Riches cannot give contentment. Riches do not guarantee happiness. So many rich people have been absolutely miserable. In a previous chapter Solomon says, "Riches do not profit in the day of wrath" (11:4). Verse 7 tells us that a man can be rich and have nothing of true value, but a man can make himself poor but have great riches, because he has given to God and His kingdom.

Jesus told the story of the rich fool who enlarged his barns, and boasted he had much laid up for many years. But that night he died. Jesus gave the point of the parable: "So is he who lays up treasure for himself, and is not rich toward God" (Luke 12:21). Let's resolve to lay up treasure in heaven – the finest investment we can ever make.

We have to admit that Proverbs deals with situations which face most of our lives. The teaching is so "down to earth," nitty-gritty. It does not use flowery or unnecessary language. We have seen that quite a number of subjects are dealt with in this chapter, and in concluding I wish to mention three others: hope, contention and discipline.

Hope

"Hope deferred makes the heart sick,
But when the desire comes, it is a tree of life."   (v. 12)

What a wonderful thing real hope is. Biblical hope is not a wishing for something, but an absolute guarantee. Sometimes there is a delay in what we are hoping for, and the verse says it makes the heart sick, but when fulfillment comes it is a "tree of life." One of the awful things of not being a Christian is being, as Paul says: "without Christ ... having no hope" (Ephesians 2:12). Life for so many is so hard, but how awful to live with no hope for the future, Hear what Solomon says in other chapters in Proverbs:

"The hope of the righteous will be gladness."   (10:28)

"The righteous hath hope in his death."   (14:32, KJV)

But:

"The hope of the unjust perishes."   (11:7)

"Do you see a man wise in his own eyes?
There is more hope for a fool than for him."   (26:12)

What wonderful hope the Christian has:

- The hope of Jesus coming again.
- The hope of one day being like Him.
- The hope that He will never leave us or forsake us.
- The hope that, "though I walk through the valley of the shadow of death, I will fear no evil; for You are with me" (Psalm 23:4).
- The hope of heaven where there is no sorrow or crying; no death; no parting; no sin. That is not wishful thinking but a divine guarantee. The best is yet to come.

Contention

I am sure none of us is a stranger to contention; that is, discord, disharmony; conflict; friction; rivalry; quarrelling. Solomon speaks several times about it:

"A fool's lips enter into contention."   (18:6)

"A brother offended is harder to win than a strong city,
And contentions are like the bars of a castle."   (18:19)

"As charcoal is to burning coals, and wood to fire,
So is a contentious man to kindle strife."   (26:21)

O the havoc wrought by contention, but in this chapter we are given not *a* cause of contention but *the* cause:

"Only by pride cometh contention."   (v. 10, KJV)

The pride that wants its own way; the pride that judges and criticizes; the pride that will not submit; the pride that refuses to acknowledge wrong and refuses to apologize; the pride that refuses to forgive; the pride which refuses to acknowledge fault. Pride is a killer. How wonderful if we all daily prayed the Lord's prayer and meant it: "Forgive us our trespasses as we forgive those who have trespassed against us." Are you out of relationship, fellowship with someone? Confess and repent of the root cause, pride. Go humble yourself, apologize, forgive:

"Humble yourself in the sight of the Lord, and He will lift you up."
(James 4:10)

Discipline

Proverbs reminds us of the importance of discipline in our lives. It requires both resolve and discipline to apply the truths we hear or read. There are three realms of discipline which are so important, but also so rewarding:

- Self-discipline.
- Home discipline.
- Church discipline.

in this chapter we are reminded that we need discipline, that after hearing instructions we obey them. When corrected we need discipline to accept it, and make what adjustments are necessary. We are also reminded of how much we need to discipline our tongues, or to use the expression in v. 3, "to guard our mouths."

When we are faced with contention we are faced with the discipline of humility, not allowing pride to continue it or feed it.

Then we need to rightfully discipline our children. According to verse 24, right discipline is an evidence of love. The children may not see it, but it's true. A friend of mine from America wrote a wonderful book entitled *The Christian Family*. He tells the story of a little girl who said to her Dad, "You don't love me as much as you love my brother." "Of course I do," remonstrated the father. "What gives you that idea?" he asked his daughter. She replied, "You don't smack me as much as you smack him!" Granted that is unusual, but it backs the scripture that right correction *is* an evidence of love.

Then we need the discipline of waiting on God and waiting for God to fulfill His promises, so that when there is a delay we don't get "sick," as verse 12 says: "Hope deferred makes the heart sick." We also need the discipline of diligence. There is no substitute for hard work:

> "The soul of a lazy man desires, and has nothing,
> But the soul of the diligent shall be made rich." (v. 4)

Application

Let us pray the truths of this chapter into our lives. Have we discovered some personal weakness?

- Our attitude to correction.
- Pride which causes contention.
- Lack of diligence.
- Lack of discipline.
- Lack of respect for the Word of God.
- Lack of being careful in what we speak.

Let us ask God to give us a love for righteousness, a hatred of evil, and also a love for true wisdom – and please don't forget to ask God for it.

---

*If any of you lacks wisdom, let him ask of God, who gives to all liberally and without reproach, and it **will** be given to him* (James 1:5).

Chapter 14

1. The wise woman builds her house, but the foolish pulls it down with her hands.
2. He who walks in his uprightness fears the LORD, but he who is perverse in his ways despises Him.
3. In the mouth of a fool is a rod of pride, but the lips of the wise will preserve them.
4. Where no oxen are, the trough is clean; but much increase comes by the strength of an ox.
5. A faithful witness does not lie, but a false witness will utter lies.
6. A scoffer seeks wisdom and does not find it, but knowledge is easy to him who understands.
7. Go from the presence of a foolish man, when you do not perceive in him the lips of knowledge.
8. The wisdom of the prudent is to understand his way, but the folly of fools is deceit.
9. Fools mock at sin, but among the upright there is favor.
10. The heart knows its own bitterness, and a stranger does not share its joy.
11. The house of the wicked will be overthrown, but the tent of the upright will flourish.
12. There is a way that seems right to a man, but its end is the way of death.
13. Even in laughter the heart may sorrow, and the end of mirth may be grief.
14. The backslider in heart will be filled with his own ways, but a good man will be satisfied from above.
15. The simple believes every word, but the prudent considers well his steps.
16. A wise man fears and departs from evil, but a fool rages and is self-confident.
17. A quick-tempered man acts foolishly, and a man of wicked intentions is hated.

18. The simple inherit folly, but the prudent are crowned with knowledge.
19. The evil will bow before the good, and the wicked at the gates of the righteous.
20. The poor man is hated even by his own neighbor, but the rich has many friends.
21. He who despises his neighbor sins; but he who has mercy on the poor, happy is he.
22. Do they not go astray who devise evil? But mercy and truth belong to those who devise good.
23. In all labor there is profit, but idle chatter leads only to poverty.
24. The crown of the wise is their riches, but the foolishness of fools is folly.
25. A true witness delivers souls, but a deceitful witness speaks lies.
26. In the fear of the LORD there is strong confidence, and His children will have a place of refuge.
27. The fear of the LORD is a fountain of life, to turn one away from the snares of death.
28. In a multitude of people is a king's honor, but in the lack of people is the downfall of a prince.
29. He who is slow to wrath has great understanding, but he who is impulsive exalts folly.
30. A sound heart is life to the body, but envy is rottenness to the bones.
31. He who oppresses the poor reproaches his Maker, but he who honors Him has mercy on the needy.
32. The wicked is banished in his wickedness, but the righteous has a refuge in his death.
33. Wisdom rests in the heart of him who has understanding, but what is in the heart of fools is made known.
34. Righteousness exalts a nation, but sin is a reproach to any people.
35. The king's favor is toward a wise servant, but his wrath is against him who causes shame.

One has to admire the scope of the book of Proverbs. In this chapter we find a list of descriptions of people:

- The wise and the foolish.
- The righteous and the wicked.
- The faithful and the false.

- The good and the evil.
- The quick-tempered and those slow to wrath.
- The rich and the poor.
- The hopeful and the hopeless.
- Those who pursue life, and those who pursue death.
- The upright and the crooked.
- The true and the deceiver.
- The merciful and the cruel.

These various categories are compared, with the purpose of convincing us that it is foolish to go the wrong way, and wise to go the right and righteous way. The readers of Proverbs can never say that they were never warned.

The fate of the foolish

The foolish are described as being perverse; that is crooked, distorted, twisted. They are scorners, scoffers, false, evil. Their behavior is described as those who "pull down and destroy."

Solomon speaks of a "foolish woman pulling down her house with her hands." She should be a home-maker, a home-builder but becomes a destroyer. Thank God for every wise woman; mothers who bless their family, bringing them up in the ways of God. Oh the sadness of those who fragmented or broke down families by their sinful behavior and selfish living.

- They become victims of their own mouth:

  "In the mouth of a fool is a rod of pride."   (v. 3)

  "A false witness will utter lies."   (v. 5)

  "A deceitful witness speaks lies."   (v. 25)

- They are deceitful:

  "The folly of fools is deceit."   (v. 8)

  They cannot be trusted. When Jesus was speaking about the last days He said: "Take heed that no one deceives you" (Matthew 24:4).

- They are mockers:

  "Fools mock at sin."   (v. 9)

  If it feels good do it. They call evil good, and good evil.

- They are angry people:

  "A fool rages and is self-confident."   (v. 16)

  "A quick-tempered man acts foolishly."   (v. 17)

  "He who is impulsive exalts folly."   (v. 29)

  Anger exposes a man's heart:

  "Out of the abundance of the heart the mouth speaks."

  (Matthew 12:34)

  "What is in the hearts of fools is made known."   (v. 33)

- They despise God:

  "He who is perverse in his ways despises Him."   (v. 2)

  What absolute folly to be against God!

  "The fool has said in his heart, 'There is no God.' "

  (Psalm 14:1)

- They are doomed to lose:

  "The house of the wicked will be overthrown."   (v. 11)

  "The wicked is banished in his wickedness."   (v. 32)

The way of the wise and righteous

What a comparison, surely the choice should not be difficult.

The wise

- Wisdom builds:

  "The wise woman builds her house."   (v. 1)

- Wisdom preserves:

  "The lips of the wise will preserve them."   (v. 3)

- Wisdom keeps from evil:

  "A wise man fears and departs from evil."   (v. 16)

- Wisdom protects:

 "The prudent considers well his steps."   (v. 15)

The righteous

- Flourish:

 "The tent of the upright will flourish."   (v. 11)

- Find favor:

 "Among the upright there is favor."   (v. 9)

- Are fulfilled:

 "A good man will be satisfied from above."   (v. 14)

 "He who has mercy on the poor, happy is he."   (v. 21)

 "Mercy and truth belong to those who devise good."

                (v. 22)

- Have a good future:

 "The righteous has a refuge in his death."   (v. 32)

- Righteousness is far reaching:

 "Righteousness exalts a nation,
 But sin is a reproach to any people."   (v. 34)

With these contrasts what would you choose?

The fear of the Lord

One is not surprised that one of the recurring themes in this book appears in this chapter too – the fear of the Lord. Remember:

 "The fear of the LORD is the beginning of knowledge." (1:7)

 "The fear of the LORD is the beginning of wisdom." (9:10)

Remember the fear of the Lord is reverence for God because of who He is, and also a love for God which does not in any way wish to hurt Him or grieve Him.

"He who walks in his uprightness fears the LORD" (v. 2)

The evidence of the fear of the Lord is right living:

> "He who walks in his uprightness fears the LORD" (v. 2)

It is not merely talk, but walk. Isn't "upright" a good word? It means "straight ... nothing crooked ... head lifted up looking straight ahead," and is a word that Solomon uses many times:

> "The way of the LORD is strength for the upright." (10:29)

> "The integrity of the upright will guide them." (11:3)

> "Righteousness keepeth him that is upright in the way."
>
> (13:6, KJV)

> "The prayer of the upright is His delight." (15:8)

> "The upright shall have good things in possession." (28:10, KJV)

"A wise man fears and departs from evil" (v. 16)

A wise man does not want to sin against God. He knows, "Thou God seest me"(Genesis 16:13, KJV). He has the consciousness that Elijah had of God "before whom I stand" (2 Kings 5:16). He knows that "whatever a man sows, that he will also reap" (Galatians 6:7). He realizes what David did when he cried, "Against You, You only, have I sinned" (Psalm 51:4) or the words of the prodigal to his father, "I have sinned against heaven and in your sight" (Luke 15:21). He knows, "Be sure your sin will find you out" (Numbers 32:23). A wise man fears and departs from evil.

"The fear of the LORD is a fountain of life, to turn one away from the snares of death" (v. 27)

The fear of the Lord is life-giving, and saves us from being trapped by sin:

> "For the wages of sin is death, but the gift of God is eternal life in Christ Jesus our Lord." (Romans 6:23)

Another thing the fear of the Lord will do will be to prevent us from *backsliding*.

Backsliding

"The backslider in heart will be filled with his own ways." (v. 14.)

This is such an important subject in these days in which we live. We are living in what the Bible calls "the last days." Paul mentions one of the signs of the last times:

"Now, brethren, concerning the coming of our Lord Jesus Christ and our gathering together to Him ... let no one deceive you by any means; for that Day will not come unless the falling away comes first..."
(2 Thessalonians 2:1, 3)

Again:

"Now the Spirit expressly says that in the latter times some will depart from the faith, giving heed to deceiving spirits, and doctrines of demons." (1 Timothy 4:1)

And Jesus talking about the signs of the last days:

"And then many will be offended, will betray one another, and will hate one another." (Matthew 24:10)

What is it to backslide?

- *It is not being what we used to be.* Something has happened, not perhaps a definite decision to turn from God, but more often "letting things slip." God remonstrated with His people Israel through Jeremiah:

  "I remember you,
  The kindness of your youth,
  The love of your betrothal...
  Israel *was* holiness to the LORD."

  (Jeremiah 2:2–3, emphasis added)

- *It is not loving Him as we used to.*

  "I have this against you, that you have left your first love. Remember therefore from where you have fallen."

  (Revelation 2:4)

- *It is not fearing God as we used to:*
  - Not reverencing Him.
  - Sins of the body are enjoyed without uproar of conscience.
  - We watch degrading films.
  - Our standards have dropped.

- *It is not having fellowship with God as we used to:*
  - Prayer has ceased to be essential.
  - The hunger for God and His Word has gone.
  - Eternal things have lost their value.
  - Husband and wife don't pray together or read the Word together.
  - Family devotions have gone.

- *It is a change in our priorities:*
  - We no longer "seek first the Kingdom of God and His righteousness."
  - Acquisition of money and things dominate our thinking.
  - Our giving to God has decreased or finished altogether.
  - The desire for Christ-likeness and holiness has gone.

- *It is a change of attitude to the world:*
  - We are more interested in the temporal than the spiritual.
  - Things which had lost their attraction have regained it. John said:

    > "Do not love the world or the things in the world. If anyone loves the world, the love of the Father is not in him. For all that is in the world – the lust of the flesh, the lust of the eyes, and the pride of life – is not of the Father, but is of the world."
    >
    > (1 John 2:15–16)

- *Our concern for the lost has gone.*

Are you a backslider? Backsliding brings God's chastening. He loves us so much, He will do what He wishes through circumstances, financial or otherwise, to try and get our attention. "As many as I love, I rebuke and chasten" (Revelation 3:19). To ignore it is dangerous.

Let's pause and question for a little. Have I backslidden? The first step back is honesty; to acknowledge it. Do you?

Thank God, there is a way back.

The way back

There is a way back for those who have ceased to follow Jesus as they should. Here are the steps involved:

1. Acknowledge it

God's instructions to backsliding Israel started here:

> "Only acknowledge your iniquity,
> That you have transgressed against the LORD your God,
> And have scattered your charms
> To alien deities under every green tree,
> And you have not obeyed My voice."   (Jeremiah 3:13)

It is easy to blame people, ministers, or circumstances, but these are only excuses. People may have acted wrongly, been unkind, been uncaring, but we did not choose to follow people but to follow Jesus. There is a cause for backsliding.

King Saul had known the power of God. He had been anointed by the prophet Samuel. "The Spirit of God came upon him, and he prophesied" (1 Samuel 10:10). He knew and witnessed the power of God, but he backslid through *disobedience* and *the fear of man*.

King Uzziah was another wonderful king who had been so zealous for God, but when he was strong he backslid because of *pride*, and was smitten with leprosy.

Demas was a close friend of the apostle Paul. He heard Paul's wonderful teaching and was his companion, but these sad words are recorded:

> "For Demas has forsaken me, having *loved this present world*, and
> has departed..."   (2 Timothy 4:10, emphasis added)

How very sad.

Ananias and Saphira knew the blessing of the day of Pentecost, yet backslid by coveting man's approval and lied to the Holy Spirit, pretending to give all the proceeds of a sale to God, but *kept back* some of it for themselves.

It is good therefore to acknowledge the cause with frank honesty, and confess the sin of it with the assurance that:

"If we confess our sins, He is faithful and just to forgive us our sins and to cleanse us from all unrighteousness."　　　(1 John 1:9)

2. Turn

This was God's second instruction – *turn*; that is, stop going in the wrong direction. Turn back to God. He also said *return*, with the promise, "I will heal your backslidings" (Jeremiah 3:22). The words of an old hymn take words of regret and repentance:

I've wandered far away from God,
Now I'm coming home.
The paths of sin too long I've trod,
Now I'm coming home.

Coming home, coming home,
Never more to roam,
Open wide Thine arms of love;
Lord I'm coming home.　　　(William J. Kirkpatrick, 1892)

3. Start afresh

Get back to the Word of God and prayer; back to church, back to loving and following Jesus. Stop being filled with our own ways; instead want His ways and His will. Now it is:

- Walking in righteousness and not in foolishness.
- Being faithful instead of false.
- Following good instead of evil.
- Being hopeful instead of hopeless.
- Being upright instead of being deceitful.
- Building up instead of pulling down.
- Being devoted to God instead of despising Him.
- Fearing God instead of fearing man.
- Being a winner instead of being a loser.
- It is life instead of death:

    "There is a way that seems right to a man,
    But its end is the way of death."　　　(v. 12)

- It is satisfaction instead of disappointment:

> "The backslider in heart will be filled with his own ways,
> But a good man will be satisfied from above." (v. 14)

What a wonderful time for some. What joy in heaven over a prodigal coming home.

You may not be a backslider but you know someone who is; perhaps in your own family. Why not pray for them that they will return to the Lord. Seek God's wisdom as to what you can do to influence them to return to the Lord. In verse 25 of this chapter we read, "a true witness delivers souls." What a privilege.

As we come to the close of our chapter the important question is, "What has God said to me?"

- Let us choose to fear the Lord.
- Let us choose to walk in His ways.
- Let us daily ask Him for His wisdom, knowledge and understanding.
- Let us praise and worship Him for His greatness; His compassion; His pardon; His enabling power.
- Let us thank Him for ever sending Jesus to be our sin bearer.
- Let us thank Him for the preciousness of His blood which cleanses from all sin.
- Let us thank Him for His Holy Spirit who can empower us to live for Him, walk with Him, be His witnesses. What a privilege to know *Him*. What sheer joy to *serve Him*.
- Let us pray.

Application

- What has God said to me?
- What is my response to God?
- Pray *now*.

---

*If any of you lacks wisdom, let him ask of God, who gives to all liberally and without reproach, and it **will** be given to him* (James 1:5).

Chapter 15

1. A soft answer turns away wrath, but a harsh word stirs up anger.
2. The tongue of the wise uses knowledge rightly, but the mouth of fools pours forth foolishness.
3. The eyes of the LORD are in every place, keeping watch on the evil and the good.
4. A wholesome tongue is a tree of life, but perverseness in it breaks the spirit.
5. A fool despises his father's instruction, but he who receives correction is prudent.
6. In the house of the righteous there is much treasure, but in the revenue of the wicked is trouble.
7. The lips of the wise disperse knowledge, but the heart of the fool does not do so.
8. The sacrifice of the wicked is an abomination to the LORD, but the prayer of the upright is His delight.
9. The way of the wicked is an abomination to the LORD, but He loves him who follows righteousness.
10. Harsh discipline is for him who forsakes the way, and he who hates correction will die.
11. Hell and Destruction are before the LORD; so how much more the hearts of the sons of men.
12. A scoffer does not love one who corrects him, nor will he go to the wise.
13. A merry heart makes a cheerful countenance, but by sorrow of the heart the spirit is broken.
14. The heart of him who has understanding seeks knowledge, but the mouth of fools feeds on foolishness.
15. All the days of the afflicted are evil, but he who is of a merry heart has a continual feast.

16. Better is a little with the fear of the LORD, than great treasure with trouble.
17. Better is a dinner of herbs where love is, than a fatted calf with hatred.
18. A wrathful man stirs up strife, but he who is slow to anger allays contention.
19. The way of the lazy man is like a hedge of thorns, but the way of the upright is a highway.
20. A wise son makes a father glad, but a foolish man despises his mother.
21. Folly is joy to him who is destitute of discernment, but a man of understanding walks uprightly.
22. Without counsel, plans go awry, but in the multitude of counselors they are established.
23. A man has joy by the answer of his mouth, and a word spoken in due season, how good it is!
24. The way of life winds upward for the wise, that he may turn away from hell below.
25. The LORD will destroy the house of the proud, but He will establish the boundary of the widow.
26. The thoughts of the wicked are an abomination to the LORD, but the words of the pure are pleasant.
27. He who is greedy for gain troubles his own house, but he who hates bribes will live.
28. The heart of the righteous studies how to answer, but the mouth of the wicked pours forth evil.
29. The LORD is far from the wicked, but He hears the prayer of the righteous.
30. The light of the eyes rejoices the heart, and a good report makes the bones healthy.
31. The ear that hears the rebukes of life will abide among the wise.
32. He who disdains instruction despises his own soul, but he who heeds rebuke gets understanding.
33. The fear of the LORD is the instruction of wisdom, and before honor is humility.

I don't suppose there is another Old Testament book that deals so much with practical Christian living than the book of Proverbs. If we follow its precepts we will know the blessing of God on our lives. We will be led in the paths of righteousness, and know His direction for our lives. Centuries pass, customs change, nations rise and fall, generation follows generation, but basically man's heart is the same, and the answer to man's needs remains constant – God Himself. This chapter teaches us about:

- The Lord.
- The heart.
- The mouth.
- The righteous.
- The wicked.
- Attitudes towards correction.
- Laziness and diligence.
- Greed and contentment.

Solomon rightly keeps the focus on God Himself. If we walk in the "fear of the Lord" we will know the blessing of the Lord. In this chapter he speaks of:

The eyes of the Lord

> "The eyes of the LORD are in every place,
> Keeping watch on the evil and the good."   (v. 3)

What a truth. God sees everything. Remember the story of Hagar, Sarah's maid, who ran away because of her harsh treatment, and an Angel of the Lord appeared to her and asked her the question, "Where have you come from, and where are you going?" (Genesis 16:8). She replied that she was fleeing from Sarai. The Angel told her to return and submit herself to her mistress, and gave her the promise that her seed would be multiplied. So awesome was this experience that she called the name of the Lord, "You are the God Who sees" (Genesis 16:13) and called the place "the Well of the One Who Lives and Sees Me" (Genesis 16:14). No one can hide from God. A prophet called Hanani said to King Asa:

> "The eyes of the LORD run to and fro throughout the whole earth,
> to show Himself strong on behalf of those whose heart is loyal to
> Him."   (2 Chronicles 16:9)

In a previous chapter Solomon wrote:

> "The ways of man are before the eyes of the LORD,
> And He ponders all his paths."   (5:21)

O yes, we may hide from people, but cannot hide from God. "Thou God seest me." He knows everything about you and me.

The ears of the Lord

> "He hears the prayers of the righteous."   (v. 29)

How wonderful that our God not only sees but hears. David, Solomon's father, was so conscious of this and one day expressed:

> "O You who hear prayer,
> To You all flesh will come."   (Psalm 65:2)

Think of, and thank God for, all the prayers in your life He has answered. God hears. He hears our worship; He hears our cries for help; He hears our intercession for others; He hears our heartbreak; He hears our confessions; He hears our questions. Thank God ... God hears.

The delights of the Lord

> "The prayer of the upright is His delight."   (v. 8)

Isn't it wonderful that we can give pleasure to God? Not only does He hear prayer, but He delights to hear the prayer of the upright. The next verse says:

> "He loves him who follows righteousness."   (v. 9)

The Lord abominates

There are things that God loves, and things that God hates. In this chapter he mentions certain things that God hates:

> "The sacrifice of the wicked is an abomination to the LORD."
>   (v. 8)

The Lord does not look initially at what we offer to him, but to the heart that brings it.

> "The way of the wicked is an abomination to the LORD."
> (v. 9)

> "The thoughts of the wicked are an abomination to the
> LORD." (v. 26)

The judgments of the Lord

"The LORD will destroy the house of the proud." (v. 25)

"The LORD is far from the wicked." (v. 29)

"Harsh discipline is for him who forsakes the way,
And he who hates correction will die." (v. 10)

Some people do not like God's judgments to be mentioned but if He was not the God of judgment, He could not be the God of righteousness. People would agree today that offenders, thieves, rapists, murderers and fraudsters should be caught and punished. A government would not be righteous or fair if they did not judge and punish the criminal. Judgment is an essential part of righteousness. One day every person who has ever been born will stand before God and hear the verdict on their lives. Paul preached God is going to judge the world:

> "He [God] has appointed a day on which he will judge the world in righteousness by the Man whom He has ordained." (Acts 17:31)

It is all very personal. One day you and I will stand before God. The greatest thing in that day will be our relationship and fellowship with God and His Son Jesus Christ.

The fear of the Lord

"Better is a little with the fear of the LORD,
Than great treasure with trouble." (v. 16)

"The fear of the LORD is the instruction of wisdom." (v. 33)

Holiness is loving what God loves and hating what God hates. God is perfect in all His ways. There is a perfect balance in His character – as for God His way is perfect. He is the God who:

- Sees.
- Hears.
- Delights.
- Loves.
- Hates.
- Judges.

Blessed be the Name of the Lord.

The mouth, tongue, lips

Again in this chapter Solomon speaks about the tongue. God not only hears what we say to Him, but He also hears what we say to others. What a blessing or a curse the tongue can be. James refers to it as a little member that boasts great things, a fire, a world of iniquity. It can defile the whole body and set on fire the course of nature and is set on fire by hell (James 3:5–6). What we say reflects what we are. Jesus said, "Out of the abundance of the heart the mouth speaks" (Matthew 12:34). What we say is what we are. What tragedies, unhappiness, conflict, contentions and hatred have resulted in words that have been said. Again quoting James:

> "If anyone does not stumble in word, he is a perfect man, able also to bridle the whole body."
> (James 3:2)

How wonderful the Lord Jesus was here on earth. He never said a wrong word. People "marveled at the gracious words which proceeded out of His mouth" (Luke 4:22).

Listen to what Solomon said in this chapter about the tongue:

> "A soft answer turns away wrath."   (v. 1)

> "The tongue of the wise uses knowledge rightly."   (v. 2)

> "A wholesome tongue is a tree of life."   (v. 4)

> "The lips of the wise disperse knowledge."   (v. 7)

"A word spoken in due season [at the right time], how good it is." (v. 23)

"The words of the pure are pleasant." (v. 26)

"The heart of the righteous studies how to answer." (v. 28)

"A good report makes the bones healthy." (v. 30)

What a list to covet. Speaking right:

- Turns away wrath.
- Uses knowledge right.
- Disperses knowledge.
- Brings goodness.
- Is a tree of life.
- Is pleasant.
- Promotes health.

David's prayer is a good one to borrow:

"Let the words of my mouth and the meditation of my heart
Be acceptable in Your sight,
O LORD, my strength and my Redeemer." (Psalm 19:14)

Again there is a contrast between right words and wrong words, remembering that the mouth reveals the heart:

"A harsh word stirs up anger." (v. 1)

"The mouth of fools pours forth foolishness." (v. 2)

"Perverseness in it [the tongue] breaks the spirit." (v. 4)

"The heart of the fool does not do so [disperse knowledge]." (v. 7)

"The mouth of fools feeds on foolishness." (v. 14)

"The mouth of the wicked pours forth evil." (v. 28)

What a contrast between good words and wrong words.

Righteousness of heart will bring forth righteousness in talk

Again in this chapter we are encouraged to be righteous. It always brings its rewards. It will also bring opposition from others, but we are here to please God, not to please men. The most perfect words spoken on earth were spoken by Jesus, and He was always being opposed, ridiculed, accused, mocked and eventually crucified. But righteousness always brings its rewards.

The house of the righteous

> "In the house of the righteous there is much treasure."   (v. 6)

This is not referring to the building but to those who live in it – the household. What a privilege for children to be brought up in a righteous home with righteous parents, righteous husband, righteous wife, righteous standards. What is your home like? The greatest treasure is the knowledge of God, as Paul reminded us:

> "For it is God who commanded the light to shine out of darkness, who has shone in our hearts to give the light of the knowledge of the glory of God in the face of Jesus Christ. But we have this treasure in earthen vessels, that the excellence of the power may be of God and not of us."   (2 Corinthians 4:6–7)

The treasure, Paul says, is the knowledge of God as we see it in Jesus Christ. Isaiah tells us that, "the fear of the LORD is His treasure" (Isaiah 33:6). Reverence and love for God is treasure greater than all the riches of the world. It is greater because it is God-given. It is greater because it is eternal. It is greater because it is not dependent on circumstances. It is this treasure which enabled the martyrs to face death. It is this treasure which has enabled the saints to endure in dire circumstances.

The way of the righteous

Righteous people walk on a righteous road. It is called a "highway." It is a narrow way and leads to life.

> "The way of the upright is a highway."   (v. 19)

Isaiah describes this way:

> "A highway shall be there and a road,
> And it shall be called the Highway of Holiness.
> The unclean shall not pass over it,
> But is shall be for others.
> Whoever walks the road, although a fool,
> Shall not go astray."   (Isaiah 35:8)

What is the way of the righteous? It is the way of holiness. What is holiness?

- It is a right relationship with God.
- It is being separated to God.
- It is righteousness.
- It is purity.
- It is a God-pleasing, God-fearing life.

The prayer of the righteous

> "The LORD ... hears the prayer of the righteous."   (v. 29)

Why are some prayers not answered? David said,

> "If I regard iniquity in my heart,
> The LORD will not hear."   (Psalm 66:18)

But the Lord hears the prayer of the righteous. Thank God He does hear the prayer of the unrighteous who want to be righteous and cry, "God, have mercy on me, a sinner." Thank God, too, that He hears the prayers of sinners who want to repent of their sin.

> "If we confess our sins, He is faithful and just to forgive us our sins
> and to cleanse us from all unrighteousness."   (1 John 1:9)

But if one has known sin in his life and is unwilling to turn from it, don't expect God to answer prayer.

Love for the righteous

> "He loves him who follows righteousness."   (v. 9)

What an encouraging word. What would life be like without the love of God. Let's follow after righteousness and give Him pleasure. Amen?

Correction

Solomon once more reminds us in this chapter of the importance of a right attitude to being instructed and corrected. Correction is not our favorite experience! People may correct us with the wrong attitude, being critical, or judgmental, or wanting their own way. However, when God corrects us, it is because He has our well-being at heart: "As many as I love, I rebuke and chasten" (Revelation 3:19). Note what Solomon says in this chapter:

> "A fool despises his father's instructions,
> But he who receives correction is prudent."   (v. 5)

> "Harsh discipline is for him who forsakes the way,
> And he who hates correction will die."   (v. 10)

> "A scoffer does not love one who corrects him,
> Nor will he go to the wise."   (v. 12)

> "The ear that hears the rebukes of life
> Will abide among the wise."   (v. 31)

> "He who disdains instruction despises his own soul,
> But he who heeds rebuke gets understanding."   (v. 32)

God uses a variety of means both to instruct and correct:

The Word

> "All Scripture is given by inspiration of God, and is profitable for doctrine, for reproof, for correction, for instruction in righteousness."   (2 Timothy 3:16)

When a person is living in disobedience, and is backsliding, they cease, or minimise the reading of the Bible. Why? Because the Bible is going to reprove and seek to correct what they are doing. How foolish, because the Word of God shows the way of forgiveness and restoration, if they will acknowledge, confess and repent.

Our conscience
When we do wrong our conscience tells us so, and will continue to do so until we wilfully refuse to respond. Then our conscience becomes, what the Bible calls, "seared" (cauterised) (1 Timothy 4:2).

People
Sometimes friends or relatives who love us will point out the error of our ways. Abraham was told by God to listen to his wife. Pilate's wife pleaded with him, saying, "Have nothing to do with that just Man [Jesus]" (Matthew 27:19). In a later chapter in Proverbs we read: "Faithful are the wounds of a friend" (27:6).

Spiritual leadership
Thank God for pastors and leaders who care enough for us to counsel us when they see faults.

Circumstances
At times God allows or ordains circumstances as a means of His reproof and correction.

Judgment
Isaiah the prophet wrote:

> "... when Your judgments are in the earth,
> The inhabitants of the world will learn righteousness."
>
> (Isaiah 26:9)

Lack of peace and joy
When we are outside the will of God we lose our peace and joy. When David had sinned, part of his prayer was, "Restore to me the joy of Your salvation" (Psalm 51:12). And talking about joy, we are encouraged to have:

A merry heart

"A merry heart makes a cheerful countenance,
But by sorrow of the heart the spirit is broken."   (v. 13)

"He who is of merry heart has a continual feast."   (v. 15)

In a later chapter we read:

"A merry heart does good, like a medicine."   (17:22)

Nehemiah said:

"The joy of the LORD is your strength."   (Nehemiah 8:10)

Paul several times encouraged the saints to "rejoice in the Lord." This joy is not something which is worked up, or dependent on circumstances, but is the evidence of the fruit of the Holy Spirit.

"The fruit of the Spirit is ... joy ..."   (Galatians 5:22)

Are we good advertisements for God's salvation?

Application

Remember the words of Mary, at the wedding in Cana: "Whatever He says to you, do it" (John 2:5). What has God said to you in this chapter? Do it.

---

*If any of you lacks wisdom, let him ask of God, who gives to all liberally and without reproach, and it **will** be given to him (James 1:5).*

Chapter 16

1. The preparations of the heart belong to man, but the answer of the tongue is from the LORD.
2. All the ways of a man are pure in his own eyes, but the LORD weighs the spirits.
3. Commit your works to the LORD, and your thoughts will be established.
4. The LORD has made all for Himself, yes, even the wicked for the day of doom.
5. Everyone proud in heart is an abomination to the LORD; though they join forces, none will go unpunished.
6. In mercy and truth atonement is provided for iniquity; and by the fear of the LORD one departs from evil.
7. When a man's ways please the LORD, He makes even his enemies to be at peace with him.
8. Better is a little with righteousness, than vast revenues without justice.
9. A man's heart plans his way, but the LORD directs his steps.
10. Divination is on the lips of the king; his mouth must not transgress in judgment.
11. Honest weights and scales are the LORD's; all the weights in the bag are His work.
12. It is an abomination for kings to commit wickedness, for a throne is established by righteousness.
13. Righteous lips are the delight of kings, and they love him who speaks what is right.
14. As messengers of death is the king's wrath, but a wise man will appease it.
15. In the light of the king's face is life, and his favor is like a cloud of the latter rain.
16. How much better to get wisdom than gold! And to get understanding is to be chosen rather than silver.
17. The highway of the upright is to depart from evil; he who keeps his way preserves his soul.
18. Pride goes before destruction, and a haughty spirit before a fall.

19. Better to be of a humble spirit with the lowly, than to divide the spoil with the proud.
20. He who heeds the word wisely will find good, and whoever trusts in the LORD, happy is he.
21. The wise in heart will be called prudent, and sweetness of the lips increases learning.
22. Understanding is a wellspring of life to him who has it. But the correction of fools is folly.
23. The heart of the wise teaches his mouth, and adds learning to his lips.
24. Pleasant words are like a honeycomb, sweetness to the soul and health to the bones.
25. There is a way that seems right to a man, but its end is the way of death.
26. The person who labors, labors for himself, for his hungry mouth drives him on.
27. An ungodly man digs up evil, and it is on his lips like a burning fire.
28. A perverse man sows strife, and a whisperer separates the best of friends.
29. A violent man entices his neighbor, and leads him in a way that is not good.
30. He winks his eye to devise perverse things; he purses his lips and brings about evil.
31. The silver-haired head is a crown of glory, if it is found in the way of righteousness.
32. He who is slow to anger is better than the mighty, and he who rules his spirit than he who takes a city.
33. The lot is cast into the lap, but its every decision is from the LORD.

One of the purposes of this wonderful book of Proverbs is to give us a true value system for living. Its instructions, inspired by God, portray His love for mankind, and His desire for people to live a full and effective lives. It is the heart of the Good Shepherd seeking to lead us in the "paths of righteousness for His name's sake." His instructions and advice leave us with choices. There are ways we can travel: our own way, or God's way. In life we have only a one-way ticket. We cannot retrace our steps, or turn the clock back. This chapter underlines the importance of making the right plans, living with right attitudes, and right motives. Planning our ways affects our own life and the life of many others too. This chapter speaks of man's way and God's way.

Man's way

The chapter opens with the statement:

> "The preparations of the heart belong to man,
> But the answer of the tongue is from the LORD." (v. 1)

That is, we can make our own plans, but it is foolish to make these plans without committing them to the Lord. James in his epistle advised that whatever plans we make we ought to say, "If the Lord wills, we shall live and do this or that" (James 4:15). The next verse says:

> "All the ways of a man are pure in his own eyes,
> But the LORD weighs the spirits." (v. 2)

We all want our own way, but without God it is the wrong way. Isaiah wrote:

> "All we like sheep have gone astray;
> We have turned, every one, to his own way." (Isaiah 53:6)

Verse 25 in this chapter says:

> "There is a way that seems right to a man,
> But its end is the way of death."

Making our plans without God is evidence of pride, of independence – an "I am the master of my own fate" attitude. Verse 18 reminds us that:

> "Pride goes before destruction,
> And a haughty spirit before a fall."

Thank God for His grace and mercy. When we have made our own plans, and left God out of them, there is a way of forgiveness when we acknowledge, confess and repent. This requires honesty. Facing up to mistakes, and facing up to truth. We are reminded of God's grace in verse 6:

> "In mercy and truth
> Atonement is provided for iniquity."

Thank God for the glorious atoning work of the Lord Jesus. He is our way, our truth, our life. He has provided His forgiveness through His precious blood. He is our guide and our provider.

God's ways

The way of His Word
This is the wonderful thing about the Word of God: in it we discover His will, His plans, His ways His standards.

The way of the right motive
The important thing is not merely what we do, but why we do it. Verse 2 tells us: "the LORD weighs the spirits." That is, He tests the motives. The motive in Christian living should be the same motive that Jesus had, which was to do everything for the glory of God. Just before going to the cross He told His Father:

> "I have glorified You on the earth. I have finished the work which You have given me to do."   (John 17:4)

The way of the fear of the Lord
How often "the fear of the LORD" is mentioned in Proverbs. The starting point; the beginning of wisdom; the beginning of knowledge; holy reverence and love for God; that which causes us to hate evil as verse 6 tells us:

> "By the fear of the LORD one departs from evil."

The way of commitment
How can I make the right plans and go the right way? Verse 3 tells us:

> "Commit your works to the LORD,
> And your thoughts will be established."

What a wonderful promise. When we commit to Him all we are going to do, He will cause us to think right. When we commit what we do to the Lord, that indicates our desire to do His will. Solomon's father David gave this great advice in Psalm 37:

> "Commit your way to the LORD,
> Trust also in Him,
> And He shall bring it to pass . . .
> Rest in the LORD, and wait patiently for Him."   (Psalm 37:5, 7)

Job with the many troubles said:

> "But as for me, I would seek God,
> And to God I would commit my cause."   (Job 5:8)

The word "commit" means "to throw, to let go, to give it entirely to Him." Have you a situation just now which is causing trouble, worry, distress? Why not throw it to the Lord? Then trust Him, and then wait patiently for Him. He never misses a catch!

The way of trust
When we have committed then we must trust:

> "Without faith it is impossible to please Him, for he who comes to God must believe that He is, and that He is a rewarder of those who diligently seek Him."   (Hebrews 11:6)

I am sure most of us can praise God for so much of His faithfulness in the past, for circumstances which we committed to Him, and in which we trusted Him. We can praise Him for all that is past, and trust Him for all that's to come, or as the old hymn puts it:

> "Count your many blessings, name them one by one,
> And it will surprise you what the Lord hath done."
>   (Johnson Oatman, 1897)

The way of contentment
The result of committing and trusting is resting, relaxing, and being satisfied with our circumstances. Verse 8 says:

"Better is a little with righteousness,
Than vast revenues without justice."

The writer to the Hebrews exhorts us to:

" . . . be content with such things as you have. For He Himself has said, 'I will never leave you nor forsake you.' So we can boldly say:

'The LORD is my helper;
I will not fear.
What can man can do to me?' "   (Hebrews 13:5–6)

What a wonderful thing contentment is. Paul could say:

"I have learned in whatever state I am, to be content."
(Philippians 4:11)

And again when writing to Timothy:

"Godliness with contentment is great gain."   (1 Timothy 6:6)

Aren't these great ways? God's ways:

- The way of His Word.
- The way of the right motive.
- The way of the fear of the Lord.
- The way of commitment.
- The way of trust.
- The way of contentment.

Isn't it right to choose God's way? Let's do it.

Pleasing God

One of the great things about walking in God's way is that we give pleasure to God. Verse 7 tells us:

"When a man's ways please the LORD
He makes even his enemies to be at peace with him."

Don't you think that it is a glorious thing, to be able to give pleasure to Almighty God and His beloved Son Jesus? When we live to please God, God is pleased. Jesus said while here on earth, "I always do those things that please Him" (John 8:29). The result was, God spoke from heaven and said:

> "This is My beloved Son, in whom I am well pleased."
>
> (Matthew 3:17; 17:5; see also 12:18)

Remember what was said of Enoch: "he walked with God" (Genesis 5:22, 24); that is, he walked in the ways of God and the writer to the Hebrews says: "he had this testimony, that he pleased God" (Hebrews 11:5).

Now that is a good commendation to desire, a good testimony to have; not living initially to please men but to please God. Paul said, "If I still pleased men, I would not be a bondservant of Christ" (Galatians 1:10). That is, if his initial motive was to get man's commendation, he could not please God. Sometimes we are all faced with the choice, whether to please men or please God. Pleasing God often brings opposition, but pleasing God will always have God's approval. Paul exhorted the Colossians:

> "that you may walk worthy of the Lord, fully pleasing Him, being fruitful in every good work and increasing in the knowledge of God."
>
> (Colossians 1:10)

When you love someone you find out the things that give him or her pleasure. So it is with God, we should find out the things that please Him.

Things that please God

We find in this chapter some of the things that please God:

- When we commit what we do to the Lord:

  > "Commit your works to the LORD." (v. 3)

- When we live righteously:

  "Better is a little with righteousness,
  Than vast revenues without justice."   (v. 8)

- When there is integrity in our business dealings:

  "Honest weights and scales are the LORD's."   (v. 11)

- When we speak right:

  "Righteous lips are the delight of kings,
  And they love him who speaks what is right."   (v. 13)

- Being upright:

  "The highway of the upright is to depart from evil."   (v. 17)

- Being humble:

  "Better to be of a humble spirit."   (v. 19)

- Being obedient to God's Word:

  "He who heeds the word wisely will find good."   (v. 20)

- When we trust the Lord:

  "Whoever trusts in the LORD, happy is he."   (v. 20)

- When we speak pleasant words:

  "Pleasant words are like a honeycomb,
  Sweetness to the soul and health to the bones."   (v. 24)

- When older people live right:

  "The silver-haired head is a crown of glory,
  If it is found in the way of righteousness."   (v. 31)

- When we are not quick-tempered and irritable:

  "He who is slow to anger is better than the mighty,
  And he who rules his spirit than he who takes a city."   (v. 32)

It is good to ask ourselves the question, "Am I pleasing God in these things?" Shall we check?

- Have I committed everything I do to the Lord?
- Am I living righteously?
- Am I completely righteous in my business dealings, and personal affairs?

- Are my lips righteous? Do I speak truth?
- Am I living uprightly?
- Am I humble or proud?
- Am I being obedient to the Word of God?
- Am I trusting God for everything?
- Are there areas of unbelief?
- Are my words pleasant words; sweet and health-giving?
- As an older person am I walking in the way of righteousness?

The Word of God is so practical, but useless to us if we don't apply and obey its truths. Again let me say, God, our loving heavenly Father wants the very best for us: the best quality of life; the ability to please Him; the privilege of our lives influencing others for good, being examples in integrity and right living; our words blessing and encouraging people.

A great encouragement to please God is given to us by John in his first epistle:

> "Whatever we ask we receive from Him, because we keep His commandments and do those things that *are pleasing in His sight.*"
> (1 John 3:22, emphasis added)

And a further encouragement from the writer to the Hebrews who talks not just about pleasing, but "well pleasing":

> "Now may the God of peace who brought up our Lord Jesus from the dead, that great Shepherd of the sheep, through the blood of the everlasting covenant, make you complete in every good work to do His will, working in you what is well pleasing in His sight, through Jesus Christ, to whom be glory forever and ever. Amen."
> (Hebrews 13:20–21)

What a truth. What a comfort. He, Jesus, in us gives us the ability to live to please Him and to give Him pleasure. God can look on you and say, "This is my beloved son ... beloved daughter ... in whom I am well pleased." Isn't God wonderful? Isn't His Word precious? Aren't His promises exceedingly great and precious? And all the people said. Amen.

Further observations

In this chapter of Proverbs the comparisons continue. He contrasts:

- The wicked and upright.
- The proud and humble.
- The wise and foolish.
- The perverse and righteous.
- The violent and he who rules his own spirit.
- Enemies and friends.
- Kings and laborers.

We also see the variety of subjects mentioned:

- The ways of man and the ways of God.
- What appears to be right, and what is right.
- Mercy and truth.
- The fear of the Lord.
- Wisdom and understanding.
- Great riches and possessing a little.
- Life and death.
- Man's thoughts and God's answers.
- Integrity in business.
- Prudence.
- Value of speaking right.

It is also rewarding to see what a chapter says about the Lord. In this one:

- The answer comes from the Lord (v. 1).
- The Lord weighs the spirit (v. 2).
- We should commit to the Lord (v. 3).
- The Lord has made all things for Himself (v. 4).
- The proud are an abomination to the Lord (v. 5).
- The fear of the Lord (v. 6).
- Pleasing the Lord (v. 7).
- The Lord directs our steps (v. 9).
- A just balance is the Lord's (v. 11).
- Trust in the Lord (v. 20).
- Every decision is from the Lord (v. 33).

Instructions to be obeyed

It is always profitable when reading the Bible to ask the question: "Are there any clear instructions from the Lord, that I should obey?" For example, in this chapter many subjects are dealt with, advice given, and warnings too. We should seek to apply the truth we hear or read but again discover any clear instruction. There is one in this chapter:

> "Commit your works to the LORD,
> And your thoughts will be established."
> (v. 3)

Many times you will find that with the instruction there is a promise, as in this verse. One of the important keys in Christian living is to obey the last thing the Lord told us to do. We should not expect to hear from the Lord if we do not obey what He previously said. Sometimes Christians can stay in the same place or condition for years, with little or no progress, because a previous instruction has not been obeyed. Let us be practical and obey this one: "Commit your works to the LORD."

What is your circumstance? Perhaps a difficulty, a problem, a need, a relationship? With the situation there come so many thoughts, sometimes questions, sometimes doubts. Then let us all obey this clear but simple instruction – "Commit it to the Lord." Obviously committing it to the Lord indicates that we want the will of God to be done. We haven't the answer but He has. We don't know what to think, but if we commit it to Him our thoughts will be established: firm and reliable. There is no safer place to put it that in His wonderful hands. If we place it in His hands we have to trust Him with it, and you know He is completely trustworthy. Why not do it now? Ready?

- *What is the circumstance . . . the problem . . . the worry?* Imagine it is something you can put in your hand and close your hand over it. Now tell the Lord what it is: "Lord, here's my financial need . . . my physical need . . . my husband . . . my wife . . . my child . . . my business . . . my home . . . my church . . . my future . . . my job . . . my addiction-habit . . ."

- *Now commit it.* Remember the word *commit* means "throw." Now open your hand and throw it to Him, with the assurance that you will do whatever He tells you. Now leave it there – don't take it back. Remember the words of David:

  > "*Commit* your way to the LORD,
  > *Trust* also in Him,
  > And He shall bring it to pass . . .
  > *Rest* in the LORD, and *wait* patiently for Him."
  >
  > (Psalm 37:5, 7, emphasis added)

What is the main purpose of all this? It is that we *might please the Lord.* It pleases Him when we obey Him. It pleases Him when we trust Him.

Let's pray:

> Our loving gracious heavenly Father. We come to You in the name of your beloved Son the Lord Jesus. We praise You for Your great love and faithfulness to us. We thank You You are the God who hears and answers prayer. We do, Father, commit our ways and our works to You. We desire to love for Your glory, and for Your pleasure. All that we have committed to You we leave in Your hands, and thank You in anticipation for the answers You are going to bring, the needs You are going to meet, the people You are going to bless. In Jesus' name. Amen.

> "Be anxious for nothing, but in everything by prayer and supplication, with thanksgiving, let your requests be made known to God, and the peace of God, which surpasses all understanding, will guard your hearts and minds through Christ Jesus."
>
> (Philippians 4:6–7)

---

*If any of you lacks wisdom, let him ask of God, who gives to all liberally and without reproach, and it **will** be given to him* (James 1:5).

Chapter 17

1. Better is a dry morsel with quietness, than a house full of feasting with strife.
2. A wise servant will rule over a son who causes shame, and will share an inheritance among the brothers.
3. The refining pot is for silver and the furnace for gold, but the LORD tests the hearts.
4. An evildoer gives heed to false lips; a liar listens eagerly to a spiteful tongue.
5. He who mocks the poor reproaches his Maker; he who is glad at calamity will not go unpunished.
6. Children's children are the crown of old men, and the glory of children is their father.
7. Excellent speech is not becoming to a fool, much less lying lips to a prince.
8. A present is a precious stone in the eyes of its possessor; wherever he turns, he prospers.
9. He who covers a transgression seeks love, but he who repeats a matter separates friends.
10. Rebuke is more effective for a wise man than a hundred blows on a fool.
11. An evil man seeks only rebellion; therefore a cruel messenger will be sent against him.
12. Let a man meet a bear robbed of her cubs, rather than a fool in his folly.
13. Whoever rewards evil for good, evil will not depart from his house.
14. The beginning of strife is like releasing water; therefore stop contention before a quarrel starts.
15. He who justifies the wicked, and he who condemns the just, both of them alike are an abomination to the LORD.
16. Why is there in the hand of a fool the purchase price of wisdom, since he has no heart for it?
17. A friend loves at all times, and a brother is born for adversity.

18. A man devoid of understanding shakes hands in a pledge, and becomes surety for his friend.
19. He who loves transgression loves strife, and he who exalts his gate seeks destruction.
20. He who has a deceitful heart finds no good, and he who has a perverse tongue falls into evil.
21. He who begets a scoffer does so to his sorrow, and the father of a fool has no joy.
22. A merry heart does good, like medicine, but a broken spirit dries the bones.
23. A wicked man accepts a bribe behind the back to pervert the ways of justice.
24. Wisdom is in the sight of him who has understanding, but the eyes of a fool are on the ends of the earth.
25. A foolish son is a grief to his father, and bitterness to her who bore him.
26. Also, to punish the righteous is not good, nor to strike princes for their uprightness.
27. He who has knowledge spares his words, and a man of understanding is of a calm spirit.
28. Even a fool is counted wise when he holds his peace; when he shuts his lips, he is considered perceptive.

In this chapter there is the following list of people who cause contentions and strife:

- The evildoer who has a spiteful tongue and is a liar (v. 4).
- The talebearer, the gossip who repeats a matter and separates the best of friends (v. 9).
- An evil man who seeks only rebellion (v. 11).
- Those who reward evil for good (v. 13).
- Those who justify the wicked (v. 15).
- Those who love strife and sin and exalt themselves (v. 19).
- Those with a deceitful heart and perverse tongue (v. 20).
- Those who are wicked and accept bribes (v. 23).

What a rogues gallery! Trouble makers. But there are others who abhor their behavior and have a desire to please God. They are described in this chapter as:

- Wise (v. 2).
- Those of excellent speech (v. 7).
- Those who cover transgression and seek love (v. 9).
- A friend who loves at all times, and a brother in adversity (v. 17).
- The righteous (v. 26).
- The man who is sparing in his words (v. 27).
- The person with understanding and a calm spirit (v. 27).

There are the contrasts. The choice is: What kind of people do we want to be?

The cure of contention

Let's consider what the answer is to contention, and what we should do to prevent it, and to stop it.

Love

Love seeks to help people with their faults and not to expose these faults to others:

> "He who covers a transgression seeks love."   (v. 9)

In a previous chapter Solomon says:

> "Hatred stirs up strife,
> But love covers all sins."   (10:12)

Think of the love of God which forgives and covers all our sins and says, "their sins and their lawless deeds I will remember no more" (Hebrews 8:12; 10:17; cf. Jeremiah 31:34).

Avoid strife

Verse 14 tells us:

> "The beginning of strife is like releasing water;
> Therefore stop contention before a quarrel starts."

Once trouble starts it is difficult to stop it, and prevent it from spreading. A woman who was a great gossip went to a minister and confessed her fault. He told her to go back home get a pillow, and walk from her home to the church, and as she walked to throw out the feathers. She got to the church, told the minister she had done what he told her do. Then he told her to do the next part: go back down the street and collect the feathers. When she got back there were few feathers that she had collected. She got the lesson. When you spread gossip it is difficult and sometimes impossible to take back the damage caused.

Paul said:

> "Let nothing be done through selfish ambition or conceit, but in lowliness of mind let each esteem others better than himself."
>
> (Philippians 2:3)

Strife hurts people: love heals them.

The cause of contention

Let's also consider the causes of contention.

Loving sin

> "He who loves transgression loves strife." (v. 19)

Hatred

> "Hatred stirs up strife,
> But love covers all sins." (10:12)

Talebearing

> "He who repeats a matter separates friends." (v. 9)

> "Where there is no wood, the fire goes out;
> And where there is no talebearer, strife ceases." (26:20)

Isn't it good to find the cause so that we can find a cure? How strife, contention and quarreling spoil life. What an unpleasant, tense atmosphere it creates. It forces people to take sides and therefore causes divisions.

Remember the story about Abraham and his nephew Lot? God had prospered them and they had an abundance of flocks and herds. Then there came trouble between Abraham's herdsmen and Lot's. Abraham didn't claim seniority in the situation, but he said, "Let there be no strife ... for we are brethren" (Genesis 13:8). Then Abraham did a wonderful thing. Although it was his right to choose, he told Lot he could choose whatever part of the land he wanted. Lot chose what seemed to be the best, the well-watered plain of Jordan. Abraham's answer to the crisis was humility.

Then remember too when the disciples of Jesus had strife between themselves because they were arguing as to which of them was considered the greatest. Jesus intervened and said:

> "He who is greatest among you, let him be as the younger, and he who governs as he who serves."   (Luke 22:26)

Again the answer was humility.

Are you having problems in this area, or do you know of some who are? The best thing to do is to deal with the causes. Some of these, as we have seen, are pride, carnality, anger, envy, loving sin, hatred, talebearing, gossiping and whispering. Another cause is that we are liable to blame others, or our circumstances, when the problem lies with ourselves. Let's be honest about it, then we can go on to consider the cure.

Here again in this chapter of Proverbs, a variety of subjects are mentioned: strife, reproof, deceitful heart, perverse tongue, friendship, a broken spirit, justifying the wicked, good speech, covering faults, a merry heart, wisdom, being sparing with words. Different kinds of people are also mentioned: the wicked, liars, mockers, fools, those who cause shame, the wise, children, grandchildren, the righteous.

Contention, strife and quietness

I am sure that all of us desire as peaceful a life as possible. Life is certainly not trouble free, but there are troubles that can be avoided.

The most common causes of trouble and problems are contention and strife. What personal unhappiness, what vast numbers of broken marriages and relationships have been adversely affected by strife. This chapter opens with the statement:

> "Better is a dry morsel with quietness,
> Than a house full of feasting with strife."   (v. 1)

How true. It's better to eat bread and cheese in a peaceful atmosphere than have a great feast with disagreements and unpleasantness. How is it with you, your home, your marriage, your relationships, your church? The Bible is very blunt and very plain about the reasons and causes of strife. The initial cause of strife is pride, though, as we shall see, there are others.

Pride

Paul writing to Timothy spoke of those who were "obsessed with disputes and arguments over words, from which come envy, strife, reviling, evil suspicions" (1 Timothy 6:4), and puts his finger on the root cause of those in this category – *pride*.

Solomon says a similar thing in a later chapter:

> "He who is of a proud heart stirs up strife."   (28:25)

And remember in a previous chapter he said:

> "By pride comes nothing but strife."   (13:10)

So we do not need to search too long for the cause of most quarrels and strife. It is pride. Pride that wants its own way. Pride that wants to impose its will on others. Pride that refuses to admit we may be wrong.

Carnality

The other cause of strife is carnality; that is, the work of the flesh, of the old nature, that which is not submitted to the will of God. Paul makes that clear:

"For you are still carnal. For where there are envy, strife and divisions among you, are you not carnal and behaving like mere men?"   (1 Corinthians 3:3)

Examples of carnality are:

- *Anger.* In other chapters Solomon says:

  "A wrathful man stirs up strife,
  But he who is slow to anger allays contention."   (15:18)

  "An angry man stirs up strife."   (29:22)

- *Envy.* James says:

  "For where envy and self-seeking exist, confusion and every evil thing are there."   (James 3:16)

Avoiding strife and contention

Don't be a talebearer

How we need to control our tongues, and our ears. When people come and say, "Have you heard about . . . ?" the best answer would be, "No, but I don't want to hear unless the person is present." How that would shorten conversations! The Levitical law stated:

"You shall not go about as a talebearer among your people; nor shall you take a stand against the life your neighbor: I am the Lord."   (Leviticus 19:16)

Solomon also mentions talebearing in other chapters:

"A talebearer reveals secrets,
But he who is of a faithful spirit conceals a matter."   (11:13)

"The words of a talebearer are like tasty trifles,
And they go down into the inmost body."   (18:8)

"He who goes about as a talebearer reveals secrets;
Therefore do not associate with one who flatters with his lips."
(20:19)

"Where there is no talebearer, strife ceases."   (26:20)

Have you been a talebearer? Let's resolve to stop as from *now*, and seek to make restitution where it is needed.

Fear God

"The fear of the LORD is to hate evil" (8:13) and that includes causing strife, or talebearing. Fearing God is also a place of safety for us. Listen to a great promise given through David in Psalm 31:19–20:

> "Oh, how great is Your goodness,
> Which You have laid up for those who *fear You*,
> Which You have prepared for those who *trust* in You
> In the presence of the sons of men!
> You shall hide them in the secret place of Your presence
> From the plots of man;
> You shall keep them secretly in a pavilion
> From the the *strife of tongues*."   (emphasis added)

Avoid the company of those who cause strife

The work of the enemy is to bring divisions among God's people. He will fight against unity and promote strife. Those who cause divisions in the church are meant to be disciplined. If the problem is not dealt with, it will spread. Paul laid down this disciplinary action:

> "Reject a divisive man after the first and second admonition."
> (Titus 3:10)

That is, after two warnings, if there is no change, reject him; excommunicate him, until he repents. Also in a later chapter Solomon says:

> "Cast out the scoffer, and contention will leave;
> Yes, strife and reproach will cease."   (22:10)

Let us all strive to be peacemakers.

> "Blessed are the peacemakers,
> For they shall be called sons of God."   (Matthew 5:9)

Let us love, avoid strife and never be talebearers. Fear God, and avoid those who would be initiators of strife. With God's help we can be unifiers and not dividers.

> "Behold, how good and how pleasant it is
> For brethren to dwell together in unity! . . .
> For there the LORD commanded the blessing –
> Life forevermore."   (Psalm 133:1, 3)

God's purpose – to make us like Jesus

God works in us to refine us, purify us, to make us Christ-like. How perfect He was here in earth. How perfect He is. Pilate could say, "I find no fault in this Man." He uses different means by which to purify us. In verse 3 we read:

> "The refining pot is for silver and the furnace for gold,
> But the LORD tests the heart."

Just as there are means for purifying precious metals, so the Lord Himself tests our hearts. Strife and contention are evidences of heart problems. Jesus said:

> "For from within, out of the heart of men, proceed evil thoughts, adulteries, fornications, murders, thefts, covetousness, wickedness, deceit, lewdness, an evil eye, blasphemy, pride, foolishness. All these evil things come from within and defile a man."
>
> (Mark 7:21–23)

Jeremiah said:

> "The heart is deceitful above all things,
> And desperately wicked;
> Who can know it?
> I, the LORD, search the heart,
> I test the mind,
> Even to give to every man according to his ways,
> According to the fruit of his doings."   (Jeremiah 17:9–10)

Malachi reminds us that:

> "He [God] is like a refiner's fire
> And like launderers' soap.
> He will sit as a refiner and a purifier of silver;
> He will purify the sons of Levi,
> And purge them as gold and silver,
> That they may offer to the LORD
> An offering in righteousness."   (Malachi 3:2–3)

The Word – the means of purifying

One of the main ways of His testing and purifying is through the Word of God. Jesus said, "You are already clean because of the word which I have spoken to you" (John 15:3). We find this true in our study of Proverbs. His Word tests us, and His Word when obeyed purifies us. Some of us may have discovered, or been reminded, that we cause strife and contentions, or that we are guilty of talebearing, or that we are proud and hate correction. This is the purifying process, and, thank God, the Word that reveals the faults is the same Word that reveals the cures. Thank God for whatever means He uses to purify us. He is not bent on hurting us but blessing us. Are we open to Him to test our hearts? Not just what we do, but why we do it. Not merely our actions, but our motives. We can learn from David's attitude to testing. He prayed to God:

> "Search me, O God, and know my heart,
> Try me, and know my anxieties;
> And see if there is any wicked way in me,
> And lead me in the way everlasting."   (Psalm 139:23–24)

He could also say to God:

> "You have tested my heart;
> You have visited me in the night;
> You have tried me and have found nothing;
> I have purposed that my mouth shall not transgress."
>
>   (Psalm 17:3)

This chapter has revealed the wicked heart, the false lips, the spiteful tongue, talebearing, deceit and rebellion.

Other means of testing

- Our conscience.
- Conviction by the Holy Spirit.
- Through God-allowed or God-ordained circumstances, revealing our reactions and attitudes.
- By our reaction to the criticism of others.
- By our reaction to the praise of others: whether we accept the glory, or give all the glory to God.
- By delayed answers to prayer.
- Through testing in the home, business, church.

In times of scarcity, and times of plenty. Paul could say:

> "I have learned in whatever state I am, to be content: I know how to be abased, and I know how to abound. Everywhere and in all things I have learned both to be full and to be hungry, both to abound and suffer need. I can do all things through Christ who strengthens me." (Philippians 4:11–13)

What an example! He passed the test!

God is not a schoolmaster but a Father. He not only wants us to have a pure life but a happy one. There is no joy like God's joy. "The joy of the LORD is your strength" (Nehemiah 8:10), and we are told in this chapter of Proverbs that:

> "A merry heart does good, like a medicine,
> But a broken spirit dries the bones." (v. 22)

In a previous chapter Solomon also says:

> "A merry heart makes a cheerful countenance." (15:13)

God's joy doesn't only make you feel better, but also look better! It is not dependent on pleasant circumstances but on a right relationship with God. Paul and Silas could rejoice in a prison cell.

Conclusion and application

Let God's Word do its work in our hearts. What has the Lord said to you through this chapter? Is there anything to be put right? Then let's do it. Does it remind us of some who need prayer? Then let's pray for them. Does it give us a sense of need? Then let's commit that need to the Lord. He will supply. May His peace, His purity, His presence be your experience and the Lord bless you abundantly.

*If any of you lacks wisdom, let him ask of God, who gives to all liberally and without reproach, and it **will** be given to him* (James 1:5).

Chapter 18

1. A man who isolates himself seeks his own desire; he rages against all wise judgment.
2. A fool has no delight in understanding, but in expressing his own heart.
3. When the wicked comes, contempt comes also; and with dishonor comes reproach.
4. The words of a man's mouth are deep waters; the wellspring of wisdom is a flowing brook.
5. It is not good to show partiality to the wicked, or to overthrow the righteous in judgment.
6. A fool's lips enter into contention, and his mouth calls for blows.
7. A fool's mouth is his destruction, and his lips are the snare of his soul.
8. The words of a talebearer are like tasty trifles, and they go down into the inmost body.
9. He who is slothful in his work is a brother to him who is a great destroyer.
10. The name of the LORD is a strong tower; the righteous run to it and are safe.
11. The rich man's wealth is his strong city, and like a high wall in his own esteem.
12. Before destruction the heart of a man is haughty, and before honor is humility.
13. He who answers a matter before he hears it, it is folly and shame to him.
14. The spirit of a man will sustain him in sickness, but who can bear a broken spirit?
15. The heart of the prudent acquires knowledge, and the ear of the wise seeks knowledge.
16. A man's gift makes room for him, and brings him before great men.

17. The first one to plead his cause seems right, until his neighbor comes and examines him.
18. Casting lots causes contentions to cease, and keeps the mighty apart.
19. A brother offended is harder to win than a strong city, and contentions are like the bars of a castle.
20. A man's stomach shall be satisfied from the fruit of his mouth; from the produce of his lips he shall be filled.
21. Death and life are in the power of the tongue, and those who love it will eat its fruit.
22. He who finds a wife finds a good thing, and obtains favor from the LORD.
23. The poor man uses entreaties, but the rich answers roughly.
24. A man who has friends must himself be friendly, but there is a friend who sticks closer than a brother.

This chapter deals with certain dangers in life, and also the greatest protection we can have. Here are some of the dangers:

The danger of isolation

> "A man who isolates himself seeks his own desire;
> He rages against all wise judgment." (v. 1)

The word "isolates" infers "being unfriendly, estranging himself from God and man; a spirit of independence." He wants to do his own thing without interference from anyone. If anyone gives him advice or counsel he gets angry. There is no one living who does not need God and his fellow man. Isolation can be an escape route from the responsibilities of life. People can isolate themselves by choice, preferring their own company. Sometimes because of disagreement or quarrel people say, "I will never speak to him/her again," thinking they can solve the problem by trying to escape from it. It doesn't work, does it? A person needs friends. The last verse of this chapter says:

> "A man who has friends must himself be friendly,
> But there is a friend who sticketh closer than a brother." (v. 24)

This reminds us of that lovely old hymn:

> "What a Friend we have in Jesus,
> All our sins and griefs to bear!
> What a privilege to carry
> Everything to Him in prayer!
> O what peace we often forfeit!
> O what needless pain we bear!
> All because we do not carry
> Everything to God in prayer."
>
> (Charles C. Converse, 1832–1918)

Who would want to isolate himself from such a wonderful Friend?

The danger of ignorance

> "A fool has no delight in understanding,
> But in expressing his own heart."   (v. 2)

This is an "I know it all person" – unteachable. But the Bible calls such a person "a fool." This word "fool" is not used lightly in the Scriptures. It is used to describe an evil person; a boaster; self-confident; empty; unwise; thoughtless. There are further descriptions of a fool in this chapter:

> "A fool's lips enter into contention."   (v. 6)

> "A fool's mouth is his destruction,
> And his lips are the snare of his soul."   (v. 7)

> "He who answers a matter before he hears it,
> It is folly and shame to him."   (v. 13)

Let's avoid being willingly ignorant. Several times in Paul's epistles he says, "I would not have you ignorant." There is such a vast undiscovered knowledge of God for all of us. Let us go on to know Him.

Remember earlier in Proverbs we were told that "the fear of the LORD is the beginning of knowledge . . . the beginning of wisdom"

(1:7; 9:10). It is foolish not to have reverence and love for God. "The fool has said in his heart, 'There is no God' " (Psalm 14:1). A fool is also a person who does not prepare for the future. Remember the parable Jesus told about the rich man who had an abundance, and was about to pull down his barns and build bigger ones and said to himself, "You have many goods laid up for many years; take your ease; eat, drink and be merry." But God said to him, "Fool! This night your soul will be required of you" (Luke 12:19–20). Let's not be foolish through ignorance; through causing contention by what we say; by not preparing for eternity.

The danger of partiality

"It is not good to show partiality to the wicked."   (v. 5)

God is no respecter of persons. He is completely just and fair. James tells us that God's wisdom is the wisdom which is from above, without partiality. Partiality leads to injustice, to favoritism. Paul felt very strongly about this when he wrote to Timothy and said:

"I charge you before God and the Lord Jesus Christ and the elect angels that you observe these things without prejudice, doing nothing with partiality."   (1 Timothy 5:21)

The danger of gossip

"The words of a talebearer are like tasty trifles,
And they go down into the inmost body."   (v. 8)

We saw in the previous chapter the havoc that is wrought in talebearing, gossip and all the dangers that brings.

The danger of laziness

"He who is slothful in his work
Is a brother to him who is a great destroyer."   (v. 9)

Laziness is not only non-productive but destructive. It not only fails to build up but breaks down. One of the evidences in Christian living should be diligence in all we do, remembering we are encouraged to do everything as unto the Lord and not unto men. Jesus said:

> "I must work the works of Him who sent Me while it is day; the night is coming when no one can work." (John 9:4)

He could also say just before going to the cross:

> "I have finished the work which You have given me to do."
> (John 17:4)

One day we are all going to stand before Him to account of the things we have done in the body. May we receive the "well done good and faithful servant."

The danger of being offended

> "A brother offended is harder to win that a strong city,
> And contentions are like the bars of a castle." (v. 19)

There are two dangers: one of giving offence and the other of taking offence. How very many people are offended with some who harmed them, or hurt them, or spoken against them. We are called upon to forgive men their trespasses, and if we don't, neither will our heavenly Father forgive us. What a horrendous thought. Are you offended with anyone? Put it right, forgive. Have you offended anyone? Apologize, get reconciled.

The danger of pride

> "Before destruction the heart of man is haughty,
> And before honor is humility." (v. 12)

We saw laziness was destructive, and so is pride. God hates it. Let us obey Scripture and "humble [ourselves] under the mighty hand of God" (1 Peter 5:6).

The dangers expressed are for our good, our benefit. Let's heed the warnings and teachings and we will be blessed and bless others.

The danger of what we say

In almost every chapter in Proverbs, including this one, mention is made of the importance of what we say. Solomon speaks about words, the mouth, the lips:

- Flattering words.
- Words of the wicked.
- Grievous words.
- Words of a talebearer.

In contrast he writes about:

- Pure words.
- Pleasant words.
- Wise words.
- Sweet words.

Then he writes about the mouth:

- The deceitful mouth.
- The violent mouth.
- The hypocritical mouth.
- The mouth of fools.
- The mouth of a strange woman.

Again in contrast he mentions:

- A righteous mouth.
- The mouth of the upright.
- A mouth of wisdom.

In speaking about lips he says:

- Perverse lips.
- Lying lips.
- False lips.
- Deceitful lips.

Then he also commends:

- Lips of righteousness.
- Lips of truth.
- Lips of knowledge.

We all, without exception have been guilty of saying wrong things: words that hurt and wound, judgmental words, critical words, spiteful words, lying words, hypocritical words, deceitful words. How many times have we regretted what we said, and had to repent, confess and apologise? What we say reveals what we are. Jesus said, "out of the mouth the heart speaks" (Matthew 12:34). James called the tongue:

- A fire.
- A world of iniquity.
- A defiler of the whole body.
- An unruly evil.
- Full of deadly poison.
- With it we bless God and curse man.

No wonder he said, "My brethren, these things ought not to be so" (James 3:10).

In this chapter we read about a fool's mouth and lips:

> "A fool's lips enter into contention,
> And his mouth calls for blows." (v. 6)

> "A fool's mouth is his destruction,
> And his lips are the snare of his soul." (v. 7)

He not only destroys others, but destroys himself.

> "The words of a talebearer are like tasty trifles,
> And they go down into the inmost body." (v. 8)

Then there are those who speak without thinking; judge without knowing the facts.

"He who answers a matter before he hears it,
It is a folly and a shame to him."   (v. 13)

And we are reminded of the awesome power of words:

"Death and life are in the power of the tongue,
And those who love it will eat its fruit."   (v. 21)

What a challenge! We can destroy with our mouths, or build up and
bless. Jesus could say, "The words that I speak to you are spirit, and
they are life" (John 6:63). People wondered at "the gracious words
that proceeded from His mouth." With our mouths we can
encourage or discourage, give hope or sow hopelessness. We can
bring joy or sorrow.

Let us covet the mouth mentioned in verse 4:

"The words of a man's mouth are deep waters;
The wellspring of wisdom is a flowing brook."

When a person has a right heart and God-given wisdom, he or she
will bring refreshment, encouragement, hope and life. Wholesome
words will sustain and not break. It is so good to know that we can
be instruments of good by what we say today, but let me repeat it is
not initially the mouth but the heart. When our hearts are right
with God and one another then our words will be right.

We not only need wisdom in what we say, but also when we
should say nothing or little. In a previous chapter we read:

"He who has knowledge spares his words . . .
Even a fool is counted wise when he holds his peace." (17:27, 28)

How important timing is. In chapter 15 Solomon speaks about "a
word in season" that is the right word at the right time. I am sure
that in considering these truths about the tongue, we would again
like to borrow David's prayer:

"Let the words of my mouth and the meditation of my heart,
Be acceptable in Your sight,
O LORD, my strength and my Redeemer."   (Psalm 19:14)

The place of safety

We have been reminded in Proverbs 18 of some dangers, but there is a glorious encouragement in this chapter of a place of safety for His people:

> "The name of the LORD is a strong tower;
> The righteous run to it and are safe." (v. 10)

By the "name of the LORD" is meant all that God is. We understand what He is like by the many glorious names He has, and which describe Him: He is our strong tower, our refuge from the storm, our fortress, our Deliverer, our strength, our salvation, He is our Righteousness, our peace, our banner.

Our God is:

- The God of hosts.
- The most High God.
- Our provider.
- Our healer and sanctifier.
- The Creator of the heavens and the earth.
- The God who always was, is, and always will be; the eternal God.
- He is the Mighty God – the Champion.

When David went against the giant Goliath with a few small stones, He was safe, protected because he said:

> "I come to you in the name of the LORD of hosts, the God of the armies of Israel, whom you have defied. This day the LORD will deliver you into my hand . . . that all the earth may know there is a God in Israel." (1 Samuel 17:45, 46)

How wonderful that God has revealed Himself as who He is, and what He can do. He revealed what He was to Moses on Mount Sinai: God stood with him there and "proclaimed the name of the LORD" (Exodus 34:5), proclaimed what He was like:

"The LORD, the LORD God, merciful and gracious, longsuffering, and abounding in goodness and truth, keeping mercy for thousands, forgiving iniquity and transgression and sin."

(Exodus 34:6–7)

Oh how great is our God! What safety in Him. What glorious revelations of what He is like through the Lord Jesus: "He who has seen Me has seen the Father" (John 14:9). He revealed the wonders of God through His name. He is the beginning and the end, He is the Good Shepherd, He is the way, the truth and the life, He is the Blessed and only Potentate, He is faithful and true, He is the friend of sinners, He is the Holy One of God, He is the Righteous Judge, He is the Lamb of God who takes away the sins of the world, He is the King of saints, the King of glory, the King of kings, He is the Light of the world, He is the Morning Star, and the Dayspring from on high, He is the power and wisdom of God, He is our Redeemer, He is the resurrection and the Life ... Oh, *Yes*, in Him is perfect safety. He is prophet, priest and King, He is the Judge of the quick and the dead.

> "The name of the Lord *is* a strong tower;
> The righteous run to it and are safe."   (v. 10, emphasis added)

We can join wholeheartedly with the psalmist and say:

> "Blessed be the name of the LORD
> From this time forth and forevermore!
> From the rising of the sun to its going down
> The LORD's name is to be praised."   (Psalm 113:2–3)

Whatever the circumstance of life, whatever the problem, whatever the questions, whatever the dangers, when we run to Him, we run to the place of absolute safety and security. When the prodigal wandered from home, he remembered there was a place of safety, and returned home to the Father.

When Peter preached on the Day of Pentecost he said:

> "... whoever calls on the name of the LORD
> Shall be saved."   (Acts 2:21)

Three thousand ran into that name and were saved.

One day everyone who has ever been born is going to acknowledge that Wonderful Name.

> "God also has highly exalted Him and given Him the name which is above every name, that at the name of Jesus every knee should bow, of those in heaven, and of those on earth, and of those under the earth, and that every tongue should confess that Jesus Christ is Lord, to the glory of God the Father." (Philippians 2:9–11)

Yes, there is safety for the righteous, those who are right with God. We were all at one time unrighteous, "there is none righteous, no, not one" (Romans 3:10), but we became righteous when we ran in to that name for salvation:

> " . . . not having my own righteousness, which is from the law, but that which is through faith in Christ, the righteousness which is from God by faith." (Philippians 3:9)

If you do not have that righteousness, "whoever calls on the name of the LORD shall be saved" (Romans 10:13). We must acknowledge our unrighteousness, our sinfulness, be ready to repent and turn from sin, believe that the Lord Jesus died for our sins and rose again from the dead, yield the totality of our lives to His Lordship, and be *saved*. He is now our/*my* strong tower, knowing from the assurance of God's Word:

> "that if you confess with your mouth the Lord Jesus and believe in your heart that God has raised Him from the dead, you will be saved." (Romans 10:9)

Those who are saved have that assurance of glorious salvation, so let us by His grace live righteously. Let nothing mar fellowship and relationship with God. When we have failed we can still run into that name for forgiveness. When we are weak we can run into that strong name, for He is our strength. When we do not know what to do, He is our wisdom. When we do not know which way to go, He is our guide. Whatever the circumstance, "God is . . . a very present help in trouble" (Psalm 46:1) "Whoever calls on the name of the LORD shall be saved." What a glorious God; what a Wonderful Savior.

Apply all He has said to you in this chapter, and do not forget to praise Him.

---

*If any of you lacks wisdom, let him ask of God, who gives to all liberally and without reproach, and it **will** be given to him* (James 1:5).

Chapter 19

1. Better is the poor who walks in his integrity than one who is perverse in his lips, and is a fool.
2. Also it is not good for a soul to be without knowledge, and he sins who hastens with his feet.
3. The foolishness of a man twists his way, and his heart frets against the LORD.
4. Wealth makes many friends, but the poor is separated from his friend.
5. A false witness will not go unpunished, and he who speaks lies will not escape.
6. Many entreat the favor of the nobility, and every man is a friend to one who gives gifts.
7. All the brothers of the poor hate him; how much more do his friends go far from him! He may pursue them with words, yet they abandon him.
8. He who gets wisdom loves his own soul; he who keeps understanding will find good.
9. A false witness will not go unpunished, and he who speaks lies shall perish.
10. Luxury is not fitting for a fool, much less for a servant to rule over princes.
11. The discretion of a man makes him slow to anger, and his glory is to overlook a transgression.
12. The king's wrath is like the roaring of a lion, but his favor is like dew on the grass.
13. A foolish son is the ruin of his father, and the contentions of a wife are a continual dripping.
14. Houses and riches are an inheritance from fathers, but a prudent wife is from the LORD.

15. Laziness casts one into a deep sleep, and an idle person will suffer hunger.
16. He who keeps the commandment keeps his soul, but he who is careless of his ways will die.
17. He who has pity on the poor lends to the LORD, and He will pay back what he has given.
18. Chasten your son while there is hope, and do not set your heart on his destruction.
19. A man of great wrath will suffer punishment; for if you rescue him, you will have to do it again.
20. Listen to counsel and receive instruction, that you may be wise in your latter days.
21. There are many plans in a man's heart, nevertheless the LORD's counsel – that will stand.
22. What is desired in a man is kindness, and a poor man is better than a liar.
23. The fear of the LORD leads to life, and he who has it will abide in satisfaction; he will not be visited with evil.
24. A lazy man buries his hand in the bowl, and will not so much as bring it to his mouth again.
25. Strike a scoffer, and the simple will become wary; rebuke one who has understanding, and he will discern knowledge.
26. He who mistreats his father and chases away his mother is a son who causes shame and brings reproach.
27. Cease listening to instruction, my son, and you will stray from the words of knowledge.
28. A disreputable witness scorns justice, and the mouth of the wicked devours iniquity.
29. Judgments are prepared for scoffers, and beatings for the backs of fools.

Introduction

Once more as we go into this chapter we are impressed at the variety of people who are mentioned, and also the variety of subjects. The people mentioned are:

- The king.
- A wife.

- Nobility.
- The poor.
- The fool.
- The false witness.
- The careless.
- The lazy.
- The scoffer.
- The disreputable witness.
- The son who causes shame.

The subjects mentioned are:

- Integrity.
- Wisdom, understanding, discretion.
- Obedience.
- The Lord's counsel.
- The fear of the Lord.
- Chastening.
- Poverty.
- Ignorance.
- Wealth.
- Lying.
- Laziness.
- Contention.
- Disrespect to parents.

All these people and subjects are mentioned in twenty-nine short verses. Let us remind ourselves of the purposes that Solomon had in mind when he wrote these sayings and which he gave us in the first chapter (1:2–4):

- To know wisdom and instruction.
- To perceive words of understanding.
- To receive instruction on wisdom, justice, judgment, equity.
- To give prudence.
- To give young men knowledge and discretion.

Every chapter we read has these purposes in view.

The fear of the Lord

In this book we are never allowed to forget the importance of the fear of the Lord. This is the starting point, "the beginning of wisdom" and "the beginning of knowledge." That means in everything we should put God first, reverence Him, obey Him, love Him. The Scottish catechism states, "man's chief end is to glorify God and to enjoy Him for ever." Putting God first in our lives is an evidence that we fear Him. We saw in the first chapter that fearing God is a choice. He said of some, that they "did not choose the fear of the LORD" (1:29). A wonderful promise is given in verse 23 in this chapter:

> "The fear of the LORD leads to life,
> And he who has it will abide in satisfaction;
> He will not be visited with evil."

We may live in an evil environment, many suffering at the hands of wicked men, but evil will not invade our soul. In this verse are three wonderful promises to those who fear God:

- *Life* – real life; fulfilling life; purposeful life.
- *Satisfaction* – abiding in it; not craving for what we do not have, but being content.
- *Protection from evil.*

These blessings should encourage us all to choose the fear of the Lord.

The poor

Much prominence is given to the poor in the Bible, because they represent the majority of mankind. When Jesus was on earth, it was the poor who heard Him gladly. It was to the poor He preached the gospel. He did not live on earth as a wealthy man, but a poor man. He had nowhere to lay His head. He did not have a permanent home. He knew what it was to be hungry and thirsty. Paul told the Corinthians:

"Though He was rich, yet for your sakes He became poor, that you through His poverty might become rich." (2 Corinthians 8:9)

Look at what this chapter says about the poor:

"The poor is separated from his friend." (v. 4)

Poor people don't have too many friends. The same verse says, "wealth makes many friends." How many poor friends do you have? Even relatives avoid their poor relations. Verse 7 says:

"All the brothers of the poor hate him;
How much more do his friends go far from him!
He may pursue them with words, yet they abandon him."

But the Word makes it clear that it is better to be poor and live with integrity, than to be rich but unrighteous. Verse 22 says:

"A poor man is better than a liar."

In verse 17 God gives a wonderful promise to those who consider the poor:

"He who has pity on the poor lends to the LORD,
And He will pay back what he has given."

James tells us:

"Has God not chosen the poor of this world to be rich in faith and heirs of the kingdom which He promised to those who love Him?" (James 2:5)

Poor but rich . . . heirs of a kingdom. Now, there is true riches.
Do you know of any who are poor, and you would like to lend to the Lord? He will repay – what a joy to give to Him.

The fool

Quite often in Proverbs Solomon speaks about the fool. Obviously foolishness is the opposite to wisdom, and the contrasts are meant to encourage us not to be fools, but wise. In this chapter he mentions some of the characteristics and behavior of fools:

> "One who is perverse in his lips, and is a fool."   (v. 1)

"Perverse" means "self-willed; cantankerous; obstinate; crooked." He is a trouble-maker, contentious, and a fool.

A fool's thinking is warped. Verse 3 says:

> "The foolishness of a man twists his way;
> And his heart frets against the LORD."

He doesn't think straight, and he is resentful towards God, because his ways and his thinking are contrary, opposed to God's ways.

A fool does not only hurt himself but hurts and grieves others:

> "A foolish son is the ruin of his father."   (v. 13)

How many parents grieve because of the foolish actions of their children. Fools will not escape punishment. Verse 29 says:

> "Judgments are prepared for scoffers,
> And beatings for the backs of fools."

How foolish to be foolish.

The lazy and careless

Proverbs continually encourages diligence. Today many want as much as they can for as little they can do. There is no substitute for hard work. God's perfect plan for mankind was, "six days you shall labor and do all your work" (Exodus 20:9). In six days God created the heavens and the earth, the sea and all that is in them, then He rested the seventh day. No one can ever better God's standard of living. In this chapter Solomon points out the dangers of laziness:

> "Laziness casts one into a deep sleep,
> And an idle person will suffer hunger." (v. 15)

How lazy can one be? Listen to verse 24:

> "A lazy man buries his hand in the bowl,
> And will not so much as bring it to his mouth again."

The false witness

A false witness is simply someone who does not tell the truth. He does not accurately tell what he has seen, heard or knows. How many times do people take a vow on the Bible in court to tell the truth, the whole truth, and nothing but the truth, and then lie? One day they have to stand before the Judge of all the earth, and give account. Verse 5 says:

> "A false witness will not go unpunished,
> And he who speaks lies will not escape."

So important is this warning that it is repeated almost verbatim in verse 9:

> "A false witness will not go unpunished,
> And he who speaks lies shall perish."

It is the ninth commandment:

> "You shall not bear false witness against your neighbor."
> (Exodus 20:16)

When Jesus faced the Sanhedrin, the chief priests and elders and council sought false witness against Him. No one could ever accuse Him of sin. Pilate had to admit, "I find no fault in this Man" (Luke 23:4). False witness is something that God "hates." It is included in a list of seven things that are an abomination to Him, that we read about in chapter 6. The seven things are:

1. A proud look.
2. A lying tongue.
3. Hands that shed innocent blood.
4. A heart that devises wicked plans.
5. Feet that are swift in running to evil.
6. A false witness who speaks lies.
7. One who sows discord among brethren.

How dangerous to be doing anything that God hates.

May God give us a love for truth, and a hatred of lying. We can give facts, but exaggerate. We can make statements, but omit certain facts. We can say things, and add to them. All these can distort the truth.

Verse 12 tells us:

"The king's wrath is like the roaring of a lion,
But his favor is like dew on the grass."

Truth and speaking truth always brings God's favor. False witness and lying bring His judgments.

The scoffer

"Judgments are prepared for scoffers."   (v. 29)

To scoff is to mock, to belittle, to jeer, to make fun of, to scorn. They scorned and scoffed Jesus. They jeered at Him on the cross. They crowned Him with thorns, bowed the knee and mocked, saying, "Hail King of the Jews." Peter said in the last days scoffers would come, "saying, 'Where is the promise of His coming?'" (2 Peter 3:4). Christians are many times scoffed at, and scorned because of their faith and trust in Jesus. Just before going to the cross Jesus told His disciples what some people's reactions would be to them, because they followed Him:

"You will be betrayed even by parents and brothers, relatives and friends; and they will put some of you to your death. And you will be hated by all for My name's sake."   (Luke 21:16–17)

The servant is not greater than the Master. They mocked, scorned, scoffed at Him, so we must not be surprised when that sometimes happens to us. Foolishness brings self-inflicted wounds but wisdom brings blessing. Verse 8 tells us:

> "He who gets wisdom loves his own soul,
> He who keeps understanding will find good."

So let's be wise and avoid foolishness.

It is always profitable in reading Scriptures to note, amidst all the teaching, what is said about the Lord. In this chapter we read about:

Being resentful against the Lord

> "The foolishness of a man twists his way,
> And his heart frets against the LORD." (v. 3)

How foolish to be against the Lord. There is one thing for sure, you will never win. How often people blame God for circumstances with questions like: "If God is a God of love, why...?" There is one thing to be clearly understood about God: it is totally impossible for God to do one thing which is unrighteous or unfair – He is the Holy God. For the Christian, no circumstance will ever come without a divine purpose. That purpose can be to strengthen our faith; to prove the absolute reliability of the promises of God; to teach and to train us; and, yes, sometimes to chastise and correct us. In all things God never changes. God is love. When He corrects us, it is because He loves us: "As many as I love, I rebuke and chasten" (Revelation 3:19). Never ever blame God: He is blameless.

"A prudent wife is from the LORD" (v. 14)

In the previous chapter we were told that:

> "He who finds a wife finds a good thing,
> And obtains favor from the LORD." (18:22)

"Prudent" means "wise, discreet, sensible, thoughtful." What an encouragement for wives to be prudent. Husbands should realize their wives are gifts from God to be valued and appreciated.

Lending to the Lord

"He who has pity on the poor lends to the LORD."   (v. 17)

Sometimes we may have lent money and never been repaid, and never will be. But God not only pays back but pays back with interest.

"The fear of the LORD leads to life" (v. 23)

We have already seen that living for and loving God results in a life of satisfaction.

The Lord's counsel

"There are many plans in a man's heart,
Nevertheless the LORD's counsel – that will stand."   (v. 21)

What a thought! Man can plan his way but it is God who will direct our steps if we will let Him. One of the reasons why we are going through Proverbs is to obtain counsel, advice and instruction from the Lord. These are not merely the proverbs of Solomon, but the inspired Word of God. There is nothing in this book with which God does not agree. As we have been continually reminded:

"All Scripture is given by inspiration of God, and is profitable for doctrine, for reproof, for correction, for instruction in righteousness."   (2 Timothy 3:16)

There was a human instrument but a divine author. Think about it. The finest, best, most reliable counsel is available to us, the main means of that being through the Word of God.

He is the God of *all* knowledge, *all* wisdom, *all* understanding. He knows the past, the present and the future. He knows the way we should live, where we should live and how we should live. Here are some scriptures describing God's counsel:

"Wonderful Counselor." (Isaiah 9:6, NIV)

"...the LORD of hosts,
Who is wonderful in counsel, and excellent in guidance."
(Isaiah 28:29)

"With Him are wisdom and strength.
He has counsel and understanding." (Job 12:13)

His counsel, as we have said, is totally reliable:

"The counsel of the LORD stands forever,
The plans of His heart to all generations." (Psalm 33:11)

How unwise not to seek His counsel, or to ignore it, or go against it:

"Those who sat in darkness and in the shadow of death,
Bound in affliction and irons –
Because they rebelled against the words of God,
And *despised the counsel of the Most High.*"
(Psalm 107:10–11, emphasis added)

Ignoring or refusing God's counsel leads to trouble: darkness; death and danger; affliction.

We read in the first chapter of Proverbs a warning to those who would not accept God's counsel:

"Because I have called and you *refused*,
I have stretched out my hand and no one regarded,
Because you *disdained all my counsel*,
And would have none of my rebuke." (1:24–25, emphasis added)

The choice is ours: yours and mine. We can accept and obey God's counsel, or we can despise it, rebel against it, refuse it, and disdain it. David's attitude to God's counsel was:

"I will bless the LORD who has given me counsel." (Psalm 16:7)

What counsel have we received from this chapter?

- To walk in integrity (v. 1).
- To pursue knowledge (v. 2).
- To speak truth at all times (v. 5)
- To acquire wisdom (v. 8).
- To be slow to anger (v. 11).
- To be diligent and not lazy (v. 15).
- To keep God's commandments (v. 16).
- To pity the poor (v. 17).
- To chasten our children when needed (v. 18).
- To listen to counsel (v. 20).
- To show kindness (v. 22).
- To fear the Lord (v. 23).
- To treat parents well (v. 26).

This is not merely good counsel: it is, but it is the *best* counsel because it is the counsel of the Lord. With God's counsel there is always God's provision to enable us not merely to obey it, but to enjoy it. Let's affirm or reaffirm our choice to walk in the counsel of the Lord. Let us ask for His help.

Prayerfully apply these truths.

*If any of you lacks wisdom, let him ask of God, who gives to all liberally and without reproach, and it **will** be given to him* (James 1:5).

Chapter 20

1. Wine is a mocker, strong drink is a brawler, and whoever is led astray by it is not wise.
2. The wrath of a king is like the roaring of a lion; whoever provokes him to anger sins against his own life.
3. It is honorable for a man to stop striving, since any fool can start a quarrel.
4. The lazy man will not plow because of winter; he will beg during harvest and have nothing.
5. Counsel in the heart of man is like deep water, but a man of understanding will draw it out.
6. Most men will proclaim each his own goodness, but who can find a faithful man?
7. The righteous man walks in his integrity; his children are blessed after him.
8. A king who sits on the throne of judgment scatters all evil with his eyes.
9. Who can say, "I have made my heart clean, I am pure from my sin"?
10. Diverse weights and diverse measures, they are both alike, an abomination to the LORD.
11. Even a child is known by his deeds, whether what he does is pure and right.
12. The hearing ear and the seeing eye, the LORD has made them both.
13. Do not love sleep, lest you come to poverty; open your eyes, and you will be satisfied with bread.
14. "It is good for nothing," cries the buyer; but when he has gone his way, then he boasts.
15. There is gold and a multitude of rubies, but the lips of knowledge are a precious jewel.
16. Take the garment of one who is surety for a stranger, and hold it as a pledge when it is for a seductress.
17. Bread gained by deceit is sweet to a man, but afterward his mouth will be filled with gravel.

18. Plans are established by counsel; by wise counsel wage war.
19. He who goes about as a talebearer reveals secrets; therefore do not associate with one who flatters with his lips.
20. Whoever curses his father or his mother, his lamp will be put out in deep darkness.
21. An inheritance gained hastily at the beginning will not be blessed at the end.
22. Do not say, "I will recompense evil"; wait for the LORD, and He will save you.
23. Diverse weights are an abomination to the LORD, and dishonest scales are not good.
24. A man's steps are of the LORD; how then can a man understand his own way?
25. It is a snare for a man to devote rashly something as holy, and afterward to reconsider his vows.
26. A wise king sifts out the wicked, and brings the threshing wheel over them.
27. The spirit of a man is the lamp of the LORD, searching all the inner depths of his heart.
28. Mercy and truth preserve the king, and by lovingkindness he upholds his throne.
29. The glory of young men is their strength, and the splendor of old men is their gray head.
30. Blows that hurt cleanse away evil, as do stripes the inner depths of the heart.

✢ ✢ ✢

As we continue in this wonderful book, let me remind you of its purposes:

- To know wisdom.
- To perceive the words of understanding.
- To receive instruction.
- To give prudence.
- To give knowledge and discretion.

It also tells us how we should respond to what we read or hear:

- To receive the words.
- To treasure them – value, and respect them.
- To apply the word to our hearts.

God in His love for us wants us to live wisely. We have often been reminded that the beginning of wisdom, and the beginning of understanding, is to fear the Lord. That is, we give God His rightful place in our lives in reverence and in love.

We find in this chapter advice and counsel, warnings and instructions, all with the purpose that we should live lives which are righteous and fulfilling. We are told of things that will help us, and warned about things that will hurt us. Proverbs teaches us how God views things. His teachings are an evidence of His love. He is the God who "so loved the world that He gave His only begotten Son" (John 3:16). In this chapter Solomon speaks about the Lord.

The Lord

The Lord abominates, hates unfair, unrighteous trading. How disappointing it is for any of us to be cheated, short-changed, let down or deceived. What does God think about it?

> "Diverse weights and diverse measures,
> They are both alike, an abomination to the LORD." (v. 10)

And this is repeated in verse 23:

> Diverse weights are an abomination to the LORD,
> And dishonest scales are not good."

Some traders had two different scales. One for selling and another for buying. How difficult it seems these days to find honest tradesmen. Men may think they are smart but eventually they have to stand before God and give account.

An illustration is also given in this chapter of a buyer who comes to buy some object, and declares, "It is good for nothing," then goes and boasts about the good deal he has just made (v. 14). Let us resolve always to be just in our business affairs, to be honest, to be truthful.

We are also reminded that it is the Lord who has given us ears to hear and eyes to see:

"The hearing ear and the seeing eye.
The LORD has made them both."   (v. 12)

He is Creator God. What precious gifts to hear and see. May we
always have ears to hear what He is saying to us, and eyes to look at
what is pleasing to Him.
    The third mention about the Lord is in verse 22:

"Do not say, 'I will recompense evil';
Wait for the LORD, and He will save you."   (v. 22)

Although we may be unfairly treated we should not take vengeance:

" 'Vengeance is Mine, I will repay,' says the LORD."
                            (Romans 12:19; cf. Deuteronomy 32:35)

We should commit our causes, our ways to the Lord, and wait on
Him, and wait for Him. Again this reminds us of what David wrote
in Psalm 37:

"Do not fret about evildoers . . .
Commit your way to the LORD,
Trust also in Him . . .
. . . and wait patiently for Him."   (vv. 1, 5, 7)

The fourth mention of the Lord in this chapter is in verse 24:

"A man's steps are of the LORD;
How then can a man understand his own way?"

We are so completely dependent on Him. He knows the way we
should take. He knows the past, present and future. He not only
knows the way, but also the path, and also the very steps we should
take. We read in Job:

"Does He not see my ways,
And count all my steps?"   (Job 31:4)

Can you remember times in childhood when walking in the dark with a parent, who would say, "It is only four more steps"? David said:

> "The steps of a good man are ordered by the LORD,
> And He delights in his way." (Psalm 37:23)

In Proverbs 16:9 we read:

> "A man's heart plans his way,
> But the LORD directs his steps."

When we commit everything to the Lord, He will lead us in the right way. He leads us in the paths of righteousness for His own name's sake.

How wonderful the Lord is:

- He is righteous, hating unrighteous trade.
- He is the great Creator, giving us ears to hear, eyes to see.
- He is the God who takes our causes: we do not need to recompense evil. Commit it to Him.
- He is the One who guides and orders our very steps.

Yes, let us "Commit our way to the LORD and He will direct our paths."

> "The LORD is my shepherd;
> I shall not want." (Psalm 23:1)

Let's thank Him; commit to Him; trust Him; wait for Him; love Him; get to know Him.

As we proceed in this chapter we are taught the right way to go. We are also warned of things that could harm us.

The dangers of intoxicating drink

How true are the words:

> "Wine is a mocker,
> Strong drink is a brawler,
> And whoever is led astray by it is not wise." (v. 1)

What havoc is wrought in people's bodies, marriages, homes, through strong drink. It is a deceiver. It promises what it cannot give. People may say, "Let's drink and forget our circumstances and sorrows," but when the drinking is finished, the situations haven't changed. It is a mocker. What fools it makes of people in their behavior when inebriated. It causes discord, brawling, fights, broken relationships, broken homes, and broken bodies. People become enslaved, bound, victims. Jesus can break every bondage when our lives are submitted to Him. Every person who has ever become a drunkard started with one drink. Solomon tells us that to be a slave to drink is not wise.

The danger of laziness

Diligence is a virtue. Hard work is good for us.

> "Do you see a man who excels in his work?
> He will stand before kings;
> He will not stand before unknown men."   (22:29)

If you want a harvest you must plow: that's hard work.

> "The lazy man will not plow because of winter,
> Therefore he will beg during the harvest and have nothing."
>   (v. 4)

And later in verse 13:

> "Do not love sleep, lest you come to poverty;
> Open your eyes, and you will be satisfied with bread."   (v. 13)

When Paul wrote to the church at Colosse he encouraged masters and servants:

> "Whatever you do, do it heartily, as to the Lord and not to men."
>   (Colossians 3:23)

Christians should be the best employers and the best employees, not initially seeking man's approval, but God's.

The danger of talebearing

What unnecessary trouble and problems are caused by gossip and talebearing – breaking confidences.

> "He who goes about as a talebearer reveals secrets;
> Therefore do not associate with one who flatters with his lips."
>
> (v. 19)

We have a saying that, "a man is known by the company he keeps." Talebearers attract talebearers, but we are counseled to avoid them, to refuse to listen to them, to refuse to pass on what they would say.

The danger of strife

God wants us to be peacemakers, not trouble-makers. We read in verse 3:

> "It is honorable for a man to stop striving,
> Since any fool can start a quarrel."

What wise and good advice to do the honorable thing. Let's avoid strife. Let's seek peace and pursue it.

The danger of disrespect to parents

We are living in a day when so much of family life has broken, or is breaking, down. Standards have been lowered. God's commandment to "Honor your father and your mother" (Exodus 20:12) is much disregarded. Parental love and discipline is often missing. Frequently this has been caused by divorce and wrong marital relationships. Later on in Proverbs we read:

> "There is a generation that curses its father,
> And does not bless its mother."
>
> (30:11)

It seems we are in that generation now. True, many times parents do not live in a way that earns respect, the main cause being that children are not brought up for God. But God's standards do not change, even though man's behavior does. In verse 20 we read:

"Whoever curses his father or his mother,
His lamp shall be put out in deep darkness."

Let's commit ourselves to be good parents, and good children. Let us obey God's Word and honor our fathers and mothers. For many of us, our parents have already gone, but I, with you and so many others, honor the memory of good and godly parents.

Two questions

Two questions are asked in this chapter. The first is: "Who can find a faithful man?" (v. 6).

"Most men will proclaim each his own goodness,
But who can find a faithful man?"

How true. Paul's words come to mind:

"God forbid that I should boast except in the cross of our Lord Jesus Christ."   (Galatians 6:14)

We have nothing of ourselves in which to boast. Remember Jesus taught His disciples that even though they did everything they should do, they should say, "We are unprofitable servants" (Luke 17:10). God help us to be faithful. When Jesus was here on earth, He declared that He could do nothing of Himself, but gave His Father God all the glory. God help us to be faithful, trustworthy, honest, not seeking our own glory. Abraham is described as "faithful Abraham." Timothy was described by Paul as "faithful in the Lord." Epaphras as a "faithful minister"; Sylvanus as a "faithful brother." But greatest of all Jesus: "Christ, the faithful witness" (Revelation 1:5). May the question encourage us to be faithful.

The second question asked is: "Who can say, 'I have made my heart clean, I am pure from my sin'?" (v. 9). Good works cannot cleanse our hearts. Penance cannot cleanse our hearts. Good intentions cannot cleanse our hearts. How then can our hearts be cleansed? The answer is in the old hymn.

> "What can wash away my sin?
> Nothing but the blood of Jesus.
> What can make me whole again?
> Nothing but the blood of Jesus.
>
> O precious is the flow
> That makes me white as snow;
> No other fount I know,
> Nothing but the blood of Jesus."   (Robert Lowry)

Who can say, "I have made my heart clean"?

> "If we confess our sins, He is faithful and just to forgive us our sins
> and to cleanse us from all unrighteousness."   (1 John 1:9)

Hallelujah! What a Savior.

Righteousness

Proverbs continually teaches us and encourages to do that which is right, to live righteously. Righteousness always brings its reward. It often brings trouble, criticism and even opposition but in the end righteousness will prevail. We read in verse 7:

> "The righteous man walks in his integrity;
> His children are blessed after him."

Integrity is the standard of living of a righteous man or woman. "Integrity" means "character, honesty, principle, morality, rectitude." As we have just seen, he will not take credit for what he is, will not proclaim his own goodness, but give glory to God. Not only is his own life blessed but blessing is promised to his children. Malachi tells us that God "seeks godly offspring" (Malachi 2:15). John could say, "I have no greater joy than to hear that my children walk in truth" (3 John 4). Righteous lives and living will affect others and influence their lives for God and for good. Even little children can be rightly affected. Verse 11 tells us:

> "Even a child is known by his deeds,
> Whether what he does is pure and right."

How true. Again we are reminded of the exhortation and promise:

> "Train up a child in the way he should go,
> And when he is old he will not depart from it."   (22:6)

Children should be taught righteousness, both by the Word and by example. So many times the saying is true, "Like father, like son." How parents are dependent on God-given understanding, knowledge and wisdom to bring up their children for the Lord. How much we need the right counsel. There is no better handbook in the world for bringing up children than the Bible. There is no better practice than reading the Bible each day to the children, and letting them read it. It is a light to them and a lamp. There is no greater knowledge for our children than the knowledge of God. All parents surely want their children to be blessed after them. What wonderful godly influence mothers have as well as fathers. Does any reader need to adjust some priorities? The highest ambition of any Christian parent should be to bring up their children for God. When they are taught to "seek first the kingdom of God and His righteousness", then, "all these things shall be added to them" (see Matthew 6:33). We have five children, two daughters-in-law, three sons-in-law, and sixteen grandchildren. We are not a criteria, but can acknowledge the mercy and grace of God in blessing them and seeing them seeking to live for God. All the grandchildren are not saved yet, but they will be. God's promises are true.

Solomon – a king

Solomon is not only the author of three of the books in the Bible but he was a king. He speaks of the "wrath of a king."

> "The wrath of a king is like the roaring of a lion;
> Whoever provokes him to anger sins against his own life."   (v. 2)

The judgment of a king

"A king who sits on the throne of judgment
Scatters all evil with his eyes." (v. 8)

The sifting and punishment of a king

"A wise king sifts out the wicked,
And brings the threshing wheel over them." (v. 26)

The mercy, truth and lovingkindness of a king

"Mercy and truth preserve the king,
And by lovingkindness he upholds his throne." (v. 28)

We have a heavenly King. Not only is He the God of love, but also the God of wrath – righteous anger against sin.

"He who believes in the Son has everlasting life; and he who does not believe the Son shall not see life, but the wrath of God abides on him." (John 3:36)

God is also the God of judgment. Paul said:

"For we shall all stand before the judgment seat of Christ. For it is written:

'As I live, says the LORD,
Every knee shall bow to Me,
And every tongue shall confess to God.'

So then each of us shall give account of himself to God."
(Romans 14:10–12)

One day, too, there will be sifting, a separating of believer and unbeliever. If men should rightly fear a human king, how much more the heavenly King?

But as Solomon spoke on the mercy, truth and lovingkindness of an earthly king, how much more is the mercy truth and lovingkindness of our heavenly King? Mercy in sending Jesus to die for our sins that we might be forgiven. Truth personified in Jesus, who could say:

> "I am the way, the truth, and the life. No one comes to the Father except through Me."   (John 14:6)

The abundance of His lovingkindness of which David could pray:

> "Remember, O Lord, Your tender mercies and
>   lovingkindnesses."   (Psalm 25:6)

> "How precious is Your lovingkindness, O God,
> Therefore the children of men put their trust
>   under the shadow of Your wings."   (Psalm 36:7)

> "Your lovingkindness is better then life."   (Psalm 63:3)

O Yes, our King is King of kings and Lord of lords. He is our righteousness. He is our salvation. He is our deliverer. He is our God. He is our Lord. He is our very present help in time of need. Let us live for Him and love Him.

Application

This chapter has covered many subjects: wine; deception; strife; laziness; counsel; understanding; unrighteous trade; value of knowledge; integrity; mercy; truth.

It has mentioned different people: drunkards, kings, fools, sluggards, parents, children, young men, old men, trades' people, talebearers.

The important questions are:

- What has God said to me?
- How should I respond to what He has said?
- What can I praise Him for?
- Are there sins I should confess?
- Are there needs I should bring before Him?

- Are there people I should pray for – my children, grand-children?
- Are there any adjustments I should make?

Thank God for His mercy, His truth, His lovingkindness.
Pray.

---

*If any of you lacks wisdom, let him ask of God, who gives to all liberally
and without reproach, and it **will** be given to him* (James 1:5).

Chapter 21

1. The king's heart is in the hand of the LORD, like the rivers of water; He turns it wherever He wishes.
2. Every way of a man is right in his own eyes, but the LORD weighs the hearts.
3. To do righteousness and justice is more acceptable to the LORD than sacrifice.
4. A haughty look, a proud heart, and the plowing of the wicked are sin.
5. The plans of the diligent lead surely to plenty, but those of everyone who is hasty, surely to poverty.
6. Getting treasures by a lying tongue is the fleeting fantasy of those who seek death.
7. The violence of the wicked will destroy them, because they refuse to do justice.
8. The way of a guilty man is perverse; but as for the pure, his work is right.
9. Better to dwell in a corner of a housetop, than in a house shared with a contentious woman.
10. The soul of the wicked desires evil; his neighbor finds no favor in his eyes.
11. When the scoffer is punished, the simple is made wise; but when the wise is instructed, he receives knowledge.
12. The righteous God wisely considers the house of the wicked, overthrowing the wicked for their wickedness.
13. Whoever shuts his ears to the cry of the poor will also cry himself and not be heard.
14. A gift in secret pacifies anger, and a bribe behind the back, strong wrath.
15. It is a joy for the just to do justice, but destruction will come to the workers of iniquity.
16. A man who wanders from the way of understanding will rest in the assembly of the dead.
17. He who loves pleasure will be a poor man; he who loves wine and oil will not be rich.

18. The wicked shall be a ransom for the righteous, and the unfaithful for the upright.
19. Better to dwell in the wilderness, than with a contentious and angry woman.
20. There is desirable treasure, and oil in the dwelling of the wise, but a foolish man squanders it.
21. He who follows righteousness and mercy finds life, righteousness, and honor.
22. A wise man scales the city of the mighty, and brings down the trusted stronghold.
23. Whoever guards his mouth and tongue keeps his soul from troubles.
24. A proud and haughty man – "Scoffer" is his name; he acts with arrogant pride.
25. The desire of the lazy man kills him, for his hands refuse to labor.
26. He covets greedily all day long, but the righteous gives and does not spare.
27. The sacrifice of the wicked is an abomination; how much more when he brings it with wicked intent!
28. A false witness shall perish, but the man who hears him will speak endlessly.
29. A wicked man hardens his face, but as for the upright, he establishes his way.
30. There is no wisdom or understanding or counsel against the LORD.
31. The horse is prepared for the day of battle, but deliverance is of the LORD.

Again in this chapter Solomon mentions different people. He contrasts the righteous and the wicked; the guilty and the pure; the lazy and the diligent; the false and the true; the foolish and the wise. He also mentions different subjects: righteousness; justice; pride; lying; poverty and pleasure; contention. As we read these words of wisdom we are obviously faced with a choice and a question: "What kind of person do I want to be?"

He delights, as we should, to declare the greatness of God. He himself is a king and admits:

> "The king's heart is in the hand of the LORD.
> Like the rivers of water;
> He turns it wherever He wishes."   (v. 1)

What an amazing statement. The hearts of rulers are in His hand. He turns their hearts wherever He wills. Nothing is outside God's sovereign control. God allows leaders either for blessing or for judgment. Daniel reminds us:

> "He [God] changes the times and the seasons;
> He removes kings and raises up kings;
> He gives wisdom to the wise
> And knowledge to those who have understanding.
> He reveals deep and secret things;
> He knows what is in the darkness,
> And light dwells with Him."   (Daniel 2:21–22)

Paul reminds us what we should do as far as those in authority are concerned:

> "I exhort first of all that supplications, prayers, intercessions, and giving of thanks be made for all men, for kings and all who are in authority, that we may lead a quiet and peaceable life in all godliness and reverence. For this is good and acceptable in the sight of God our Savior, who desires all men to be saved and to come to the knowledge of the truth."   (1 Timothy 2:1–4)

Do you do this? God raises up; God puts down. Where is Hitler, Mussolini, Stalin, Amin, Mao? In our lifetime we have witnessed the rise and fall of rulers and dictators, but God lives eternally supreme as King of kings and Lord of lords. Yes, we can say with Daniel, "Blessed be the name of God forever and ever" (Daniel 2:20).

The hand of the Lord

What a great expression: "in the hand of the LORD." This expression is often used in Scripture signifying a number of things:

- *Blessing.* We read, "the good hand of my God upon me" (Nehemiah 2:8). Remember the prayer of Jabez:

  > "Oh, that You would bless me indeed, enlarge my territory, that Your hand would be with me, and that you would keep me from evil."   (1 Chronicles 4:10)

- *Teaching*. Job said: "I will teach you about the hand of God" (Job 27:11). He will guide us in what we need to know as we seek to follow Him.

- *Salvation*:

   "The LORD's hand is not shortened,
   That it cannot save."   (Isaiah 59:1)

- *Safety*:

   "Humble yourselves under the mighty hand of God."

                                                             (1 Peter 5:6)

- *Power*. After the miracle of the children of Israel passing over the Jordan, Joshua declares:

   "That all the peoples of the earth may know the hand of the LORD, that it is mighty, that you may fear the LORD your God forever."   (Joshua 4:24)

What a wonderful place to be, "in the hand of the LORD," knowing His protection, power, provision, presence, direction, salvation, teaching. When our lives are submitted to Him day by day, trusting in Him, there is no safer place on earth: "that Your hand would be with me."

The Lord weighs the hearts

In a previous chapter Solomon said, "the LORD weighs the spirits" (16:2). He not only knows what we do, but why we do it. He knows the motives behind our actions. Remember the story of Belshazzer's feast when God wrote on the wall. God had weighed this wicked king's life in His balance, and the interpretation of the writing was, "You have been weighed in the balances, and found wanting" (Daniel 5:27). We can impress men, but it is not man's approval we should seek, but God's. The Lord Jesus did everything that God might be glorified. His motives were pure, therefore all His actions were right and righteous. Job cried:

   "Let me be weighed on honest scales,
   That God may know my integrity."   (Job 31:6)

God sees everything, and His verdict is always right. In verse 12 we read:

> "The righteous God wisely considers the house
>   of the wicked,
> Overthrowing the wicked for their wickedness."

And in verse 3:

> "To do righteousness and justice
> Is more acceptable to the LORD than sacrifice."

God does not initially look at what we bring to Him, but at the heart that brings it. In verse 30 we read:

> "There is no wisdom or understanding
> Or counsel against the LORD."

Nothing can prevail against God. Men may try to fight against God; deny Him; blaspheme Him; but they can never win. How puny man is. How great and gloriously wonderful, majestic, and all powerful is our God.

Eventually everyone who has ever lived will stand before Him. There will be a verdict on every life. It will be a righteous verdict: "Shall not the Judge of all the earth do right?" (Genesis 18:25). He is the *Righteous God*. As the old saying puts it:

> "Only one life, 'twill soon be past and only what's done for Christ
> will last."

Yes, the Lord knows the heart. The Lord weighs the heart.

How wonderful to be on His side. In Him is absolute safety. Solomon closes this chapter by declaring:

> "The horse is prepared for the day of battle,
> But *deliverance* is of the LORD."   (v. 31, emphasis added)

His father David wrote:

> "Some trust in chariots, and some in horses;
> But we will remember the name of the LORD our God."
>
> (Psalm 20:7)

How great is our God, as the hymn writer put it:

> "How great is our God, How great in His Name,
> How great is our God, forever the same.
> He rolled back the waters of the mighty Red Sea,
> And He said, 'I'll never leave you, put your trust in Me.'"
>
> (Author unknown)

The Lord knows, the Lord weighs, the Lord delivers. Blessed be the name of the Lord. Amen.

Choosing the way to live our lives

Here again in this chapter we are encouraged to live to please God, with all His encouragements of blessing and protection when we do. He shows us the right way, and warns us about the wrong way. We all have a choice of how we want to live. What a responsibility!

That choice affects our lives, the lives of family and friends; affects our future and affects our eternal destiny. The way we live is affected by the choices we make. When we reflect on our lives we can see that how we lived, where we lived, was determined by our own decisions. That remembrance may bring regret, or may bring thankfulness. However, we cannot retrace our steps, but we can now make new choices, or continue in the way we are. In our reflections we may say, "Oh, if only . . ." If only I had not made that choice; if only I had not formed that relationship; if only I had not made that mistake; if only I had not sinned that sin; if only I had chosen another way. Some may reflect with gratitude to God and agree with the sentiments of the hymn writer Frances van Alstyne:

"All the way my Savior leads me,
What have I to ask beside?
Can I doubt His tender mercy,
Who through life has been my guide?
Heavenly peace, divinest comfort,
Here by faith in Him to dwell,
For I know whate'er befalls me,
Jesus doeth all things well."

Yes, when we walk in His ways, we know His direction, His blessing, and His peace. We are told in this chapter about certain ways.

The way that seems right to a man (v. 2)

The way that seems right may not be right. Twice in previous chapters Solomon wrote:

"There is a way that seems right to a man,
But its end is the way of death."   (14:12; 16:25)

So the way that seems right may not be right at all. We all start off on the wrong way. Isaiah said:

"All we like sheep have gone astray;
We have turned, every one, to his own way."   (Isaiah 53:6)

Jeremiah rightly said:

"O LORD, I know the way of man is not in himself;
It is not in man who walks to direct his own steps."
                                          (Jeremiah 10:23)

What absolute folly it is to live the one life we have without God. He knows the way we should take. Jesus came not only to show us the way but to be the way:

"I am the way, the truth, and the life. No one comes to the Father except through Me."   (John 14:6)

Man's way may seem right, but without God it is not right. How wonderful that God has made provision through the Lord Jesus to bring man to the right way, God's way, and His enablement to keep us in His way all the days of our lives.

There is the way of religious observance

In Jesus' day, He was continually condemned by religious people, the scribes and the Pharisees. Theirs was an outward religion, the observance of things, of rules, which appeared to man to be right, and satisfied their own egos, but their hearts had never been changed. They were seeking the approval and praise of men, rather than the blessing and approval of God. Many people today try and find their security in religion, but if Jesus Christ is not the center, with trust in His redeeming work and the knowledge of sins forgiven, that religion is vain, and the end thereof is the way of death.

The way of the unrighteous

We are given a description of the way of the unrighteous, and of their character and behavior. Theirs is the way of:

Pride

> "A haughty look, a proud heart,
> And the plowing of the wicked are sin." (v. 4)

> "A proud and haughty man – 'Scoffer,' is his name;
> He acts with arrogant pride." (v. 24)

Pride is a sin especially abhorrent to God. Pride sets itself against the very being and sovereignty of God. It is spoken of as an abomination to the Lord. James tells us that:

> "God resists the proud,
> But gives grace to the humble." (James 4:6)

Pride is manifested in looks, in boastful words, in an independent spirit, in self-confidencee and self-conceit. Three times the Lord Jesus repeated a solemn warning, "Whoever exalts himself will be humbled" (Matthew 23:12; Luke 14:11; 18:14). Pride is the cause of all strife and contention:

> "By pride comes nothing but strife."   (13:10)

Lying

> "Getting treasures by a lying tongue
> Is the fleeting fantasy of those who seek death."   (v. 6)

We are living in a day when it is increasingly difficult to trust people and to rely on their promises. Like pride it is one of the things that God hates:

> "Lying lips are an abomination to the LORD."   (12:22)

Paul's exhortation to the Ephesians was:

> "Therefore, putting away lying, 'Let each one of you speak truth with his neighbor.'"   (Ephesians 4:25)

The way of the unrighteous is also the way of:

- *Violence*:
  > "The violence of the wicked will destroy them."   (v. 7)
- *Contention*: conflict; argument; strife; division (vv. 9, 19).
- *Scoffing*: mocking the things that are right, and the righteous (v. 24).
- *Pleasure seeking that leads to poverty*:
  > "He who loves pleasure will be a poor man."   (v. 17)
- *Laziness*:
  > "The desire of a lazy man kills him,
  > For his hands refuse to labor."   (v. 25)

The way of the unrighteous is the way of destruction

Yes, there is an end that "is the way of death":

> "There is a way that seems right to a man,
> But its end is the way of death."   (14:12)

"The righteous God wisely considers the house of the wicked,
Overthrowing the wicked for their wickedness." (v. 12)

"Destruction will come to the workers of iniquity." (v. 15)

"A false witness shall perish." (v. 28)

How honest Scripture is. How faithful God is to warn of the wrong
way and show us the right way. What folly to choose destruction
instead of life, misery instead of happiness, Hell instead of Heaven.
May we have the fear of the Lord which is to hate evil.

The way of righteousness

Thank God there is a way of righteousness. As in other chapters of
Proverbs there are continual contrasts. We have just seen something of the way of the unrighteous; now we look at the way of the
righteous as described in this chapter. The desire of our Good
Shepherd is to "lead us in the paths of righteousness for His name's
sake" (Psalm 23:3). Righteousness and holiness are often linked
together. Righteousness is the fulfillment of God's law; holiness is
conformity to God's character. Someone has put it this way:

As a condemned sinner we receive the "gift of righteousness."
As a member of Christ's household we become "the servants of
righteousness."
As a scholar in Christ's school we receive the "word of
righteousness."
As travelers we are led in the "paths of righteousness."
As guests in His house we are clothed with "the robe of
righteousness."
As worshipers we offer "the sacrifice of righteousness."
As planted by the Lord we grow up as "trees of righteousness."
As soldiers, fighting the good fight of faith we put on
"the armour of righteousness, and the breastplate of
righteousness."
And we look to that coming day when He will give to His
faithful servants "a crown of righteousness."

Here are some of the characteristics of the righteous in this chapter.

Diligence

> "The plans of the diligent lead surely to plenty."   (v. 5)

The righteous will wish to serve God with all their heart, working while it is still day and not doing things for man's approval, but God's.

Purity

> "As for the pure, his work is right."   (v. 8)

His work will be a reflection of his heart, his character. His motive will be pure and His words will be pure. In a previous chapter Solomon writes:

> "The words of the pure are pleasant."   (15:26)

Wisdom

> "When the wise is instructed, he receives knowledge."   (v. 11)

Yes, wise people will be righteous people, and righteous people will be wise people. How wonderful that God's wisdom is available to all who will ask for it and by faith receive it. Never forget the wonderful promise in James 1:5:

> "If any of you lacks wisdom, let him ask of God, who gives to all liberally and without reproach, and it will be given to him."

Put it on your daily prayer list. Wise people will act wisely; wise people will act righteously.

Justice

> "It is a joy for the just to do justice."   (v. 15)

Justice is honest, impartial, fair, moral, principled, upright. Situations will be assessed rightly, and there will be no unfairness or favoritism. I like what this verse says: "it is a *joy* for the just to do justice" – not merely a moral duty but a pleasurable experience.

Liberality

> "The righteous gives and does not spare." (v. 26)

Paul told the Corinthians that "God loves a cheerful giver" (2 Corinthians 9:7). There is no meanness with God. We just quoted from James that God "gives to all men liberally." Many years ago a well known Scottish minister by the name of John McNeil once described a cheerful giver as a man who turns round in church and says, "Hallelujah, here comes the collection plate."

Security

> "As for the upright, he establishes his way." (v. 29)

His way is firm, secure. There is always security in righteousness. The security of a clear conscience. The security of a right relationship with God. The security of integrity. The security of a life laid on the right foundation. The security of the promises of God. The security in the knowledge that when you do right, God is with you.

Right speech

> "Whoever guards his mouth and tongue
> Keeps his soul from troubles." (v. 23)

A righteous person will want to say the right things. But right words come from a right heart. As Jesus said, "Out of the abundance of the heart the mouth speaks" (Matthew 12:34).

What power there is in words. How we can bless, and how we can hurt. How we can discourage, and how we can encourage. How we can cheer, and how we can depress. Let's be those who guard our tongues and thus avoid trouble.

Application

What a lot of ground can be covered in a short chapter. Again let me say the important thing is to apply truth to our hearts, and conduct.

Let us *praise God*:

- For His love, power and wisdom.
- That He is the one who enthrones kings and rulers and also dethrones them.

Let us *thank God*:

- That He is truly the Righteous God.
- That He is our deliverer: "Deliverance is of the LORD" (v. 30).
- For His love in showing us His way.

Let us *pray*:

- For His wisdom available to us for the asking.
- That we will be kept from evil.
- That we we will be free from:
  - Pride.
  - Lying.
  - Contention.
  - Being lovers of pleasure.
  - Laziness.
  - Ignoring the poor.
  - Wanting our own way instead of God's way.
- Rather, that we will be:
  - Diligent.
  - Pure.
  - Wise.
  - Liberal.
  - Just.

Praise. Thank. Pray.

---

*If any of you lacks wisdom, let him ask of God, who gives to all liberally and without reproach, and it **will** be given to him* (James 1:5).

Chapter 22

1. A good name is to be chosen rather than great riches, loving favor rather than silver and gold.
2. The rich and the poor have this in common, the LORD is the maker of them all.
3. A prudent man foresees evil and hides himself, but the simple pass on and are punished.
4. By humility and the fear of the LORD are riches and honor and life.
5. Thorns and snares are in the way of the perverse; he who guards his soul will be far from them.
6. Train up a child in the way he should go, and when he is old he will not depart from it.
7. The rich rules over the poor, and the borrower is servant to the lender.
8. He who sows iniquity will reap sorrow, and the rod of his anger will fail.
9. He who has a generous eye will be blessed, for he gives of his bread to the poor.
10. Cast out the scoffer, and contention will leave; yes, strife and reproach will cease.
11. He who loves purity of heart and has grace on his lips, the king will be his friend.
12. The eyes of the LORD preserve knowledge, but He overthrows the words of the faithless.
13. The lazy man says, "There is a lion outside! I shall be slain in the streets!"
14. The mouth of an immoral woman is a deep pit; he who is abhorred by the LORD will fall there.
15. Foolishness is bound up in the heart of a child; the rod of correction will drive it far from him.
16. He who oppresses the poor to increase his riches, and he who gives to the rich, will surely come to poverty.

17. Incline your ear and hear the words of the wise, and apply your heart to my knowledge;

18. For it is a pleasant thing if you keep them within you; let them all be fixed upon your lips,

19. So that your trust may be in the LORD; I have instructed you today, even you.

20. Have I not written to you excellent things of counsels and knowledge,

21. That I may make you know the certainty of the words of truth, that you may answer words of truth to those who send to you?

22. Do not rob the poor because he is poor, nor oppress the afflicted at the gate;

23. For the LORD will plead their cause, and plunder the soul of those who plunder them.

24. Make no friendship with an angry man, and with a furious man do not go,

25. Lest you learn his ways and set a snare for your soul.

26. Do not be one of those who shakes hands in a pledge, one of those who is surety for debts;

27. If you have nothing with which to pay, why should he take away your bed from under you?

28. Do not remove the ancient landmark which your fathers have set.

29. Do you see a man who excels in his work? He will stand before kings; he will not stand before unknown men.

It is so good that you are continuing in the study of this wonderful book. of Proverbs. It is the book of wisdom, authored by God and written by King Solomon. Let me encourage you with the reminder that the main purpose of our reading the Word of God is that we might know Him, His ways and His will for us.

Some years ago, being in a poetic mood, I wrote these lines expressing the value and purpose of the Word of God. May it be our desire and prayer as we go to Proverbs 22 today:

> My God, I thank You for Your Word,
> That comes like medicine or a sword,
> To change my life that I may be
> In greater likeness unto Thee.

Speak how You will, that is Your choice,
In thunders peal or still small voice,
Your Word is truth, Your Word is light,
To show me how to live aright.

Reveal Yourself, that is my plea,
Reveal Yourself, O God, to me,
Show me Your will, show me Your ways,
That I may serve You all my days.

"Let there be light," You once did cry,
And brilliant radiance filled the sky,
Command again that light to me,
That I may more Your glory see.

You Living Word, I praise Your name,
You are forevermore the same,
You spoke to prophet, priest and king,
Then speak to me, Your word do bring.

I thirst for You, My God, My Lord,
And open up Your sacred Word,
I come to drink, I come to feed,
Then meet my very deepest need.

Come, Holy Ghost, come, heavenly dove,
Show me my Lord, the one I love,
And speak to me that I may say,
"Yes . . . God spoke to me today."

Amen.

When Solomon wrote this chapter he realized the importance of the counsel he was giving, and that it was a *"today"* word, up to date, relevant. It was not only good advice, but the best, excellent advice:

"I have instructed you today, even you.
Have I not written to you excellent things
Of counsels and knowledge,
That I may make you know the certainty of the words of truth?"

(vv. 19–21)

So also these words come to you and me personally, today –
excellent things. Therefore they deserve our close attention. So let's
look at the "excellent things," the "words of truth."

The excellence of a good name

> "A good name is to be chosen rather than great riches,
> Loving favor rather than silver and gold."   (v. 1)

How different God's value system is to man's. A good name, a
good reputation, is something to be chosen, and is of greater value
than great riches. A good name is the result of a good life, a
good character. You cannot have a good name without being a good
person, a righteous person. Several people in Scripture are described
as being good.

David spoke of a friend of his, "Ahimaaz ... a good man, and
comes with good news" (2 Samuel 18:27).

After Jesus was crucified there was a man called Joseph of
Arimathea who went to Pilate and asked for the body of Jesus, that
he might bury Him in his own tomb. He is described as "a good and
just man" (Luke 23:50).

One of Paul's companions, Barnabas, is described as "a good
man, full of the Holy Spirit and of faith" (Acts 11:24).

Think of men and women you know, and some of them I am
sure you would describe similarly: a good man or a good lady. What
do people say about you? Really good people do not want that
title for their glory, but for the glory of God. Jesus made Himself
of "no reputation" that all the praise, glory and credit may go to
the Father. Here are some of the biblical characteristics: of a "good
man."

- *His steps are ordered by the Lord.*

  > "The steps of a good man are ordered by the LORD,
  > And He delights in his way."   (Psalm 37:23)

  A good man desires to walk in the will of God.

- *He is gracious.*

  > "A good man deals graciously and lends;
  > He will guide his affairs with discretion."   (Psalm 112:5)

  A good person is a person of integrity.

- *He is contented.*

  > "A good man will be satisfied from above."   (Proverbs 14:14)

  His greatest desire is relationship and fellowship with God.

- *His life is a life of goodness.* Jesus said:

  > "A good man out of the good treasure of his heart brings forth
  > good things."   (Matthew 12:35)

  A good person has a good heart.

- *A good person has God's commendation.*

  > "A good man obtains favor from the LORD."   (12:2)

  Verse 1 in this chapter calls it "loving favor." There is no favor
  on earth, like God's favor; God's "well done good and faithful
  servant."

It takes time to establish a good name, and sadly a good name can
be lost through sin and foolish actions. Solomon was a good man,
but at the end of his life he sinned against God by taking foreign
wives and encouraging them in their idolatry. How dependent we
are on the Lord. He can keep us from falling, as Paul wrote to the
Philippians:

> "being confident of this very thing, that He who has begun a good
> work in you will complete it until the day of Jesus Christ."
>
> (Philippians 1:6)

Let's choose a good name.

The excellence of humility and the fear of the Lord

> "By humility and the fear of the LORD
> Are riches and honor and life."   (v. 4)

The key to riches, honor and life is given to us in this verse.

What an important couplet: humility and the fear of the Lord –
the knowledge and acknowledgment of our nothingness apart from
God, and the reverential acknowledgment of God's greatness. We
have seen in previous chapters the importance and frequent
repetition of the phrase "the fear of the LORD." We have seen it is
the beginning of knowledge; it is the beginning of wisdom. This
wisdom is God-given to all who will ask and receive, as again we are
reminded of James' words:

> "If any of you lacks wisdom, let him ask of God, who gives to all
> liberally and without reproach, and it will be given to him."
>
> (James 1:5)

A good man or woman will be humble and reverence God, giving
Him first place. The most learned men are usually well known for
their humility. The greatest person who ever lived on the earth,
Jesus, "humbled Himself and became obedient to the point of
death, even the death of the cross" (Philippians 2:8). The fear of the
Lord is manifested in our obedience to God. Remember when
Abraham obeyed God and put Isaac on the altar on Mount Moriah,
and as his hand was lifted with the knife to slay His son, God's voice
came:

> "Abraham, Abraham … Do not lay your hand on the lad, or do
> anything to him; for now I know that you fear God, since you have
> not withheld your son, your only son from Me."
>
> (Genesis 22:11–12)

What a wonderful God-given recipe for blessing: humility – freedom
from pride, self-conceit, self-seeking and presumption – and a holy
reverence and love for God. These are *excellent things*.

The excellence of knowledge and wisdom

How many times in Proverbs we are encouraged to be people of
knowledge, understanding and wisdom. We are told in verse 18
of this chapter that knowledge "is a pleasant thing" if we keep it
within us, and in verse 19 we see that one of main purposes of

knowledge is that we trust the Lord. The more knowledge and understanding we have of Him, the more we know Him, and the more we know the perfection of His character, the more we trust Him. He also mentions the purpose of knowledge is that we may "know the certainty of the words of truth," so that we will speak the words of truth (v. 21). This reminds us of the heartcry of Paul, "that I may know Him" (Philippians 3:10). Everything about God is excellent. The psalmist speaks of the excellence of His name; the excellence of His lovingkindness; the excellent of His greatness. Oh yes, Great is the Lord, and greatly to be praised.

At the end of the chapter we are encouraged to excel in all that we do. The excellent God does excellent things, and deserves that we do things excellently. Verse 29 states:

> "Do you see man who excels in his work?
> He will stand before kings;
> He will not stand before unknown men."

Paul exhorted the Corinthians to seek to excel in all that they did:

> " . . . whatever you do, do all to the glory of God."
>
> (1 Corinthians 10:31)

So let us seek:

- The excellence of a good name.
- The excellence of humility and the fear of the Lord.
- The excellence of the knowledge and wisdom of God.

Let us continue to see and embrace *excellent things* in this chapter.

The excellence of prudence

> "A prudent man foresees evil and hides himself,
> But the simple pass on and are punished."   (v. 3)

The word "prudence" means "discretion, foresight, caution."
Proverbs 8:12 tells us:

> "I, wisdom, dwell with prudence,
> And find out knowledge and discretion."

Prudence does not make hasty decisions to be regretted later. It
considers the future as well as the now. The behavior of a prudent
person is described in Proverbs:

> "A prudent man conceals knowledge."   (12:23)

That is, he does not boast about what he knows.

> "Every prudent man acts with knowledge."   (13:16)

There is purpose behind what he does. He is not thoughtless but
thoughtful.

> "The prudent are crowned with knowledge."   (14:18)

A prudent person will take correction in the right way:

> "He who receives correction is prudent."   (15:5)

David was called a prudent man. That was manifested in his
behavior before King Saul, who treated him so badly. It is said of
David, that he "behaved wisely in all his ways" (1 Samuel 18:14).
Prudence causes us to to do the right thing, at the right time, in the
right way, with the right motive.

The excellence of a pure heart

> "He who loves purity of heart
> And has grace on his lips,
> The king will be his friend."   (v. 11)

Gracious words will come from a pure heart. Luke 4:22 says, "all . . .
marveled at the gracious words which proceeded out of His
mouth." Isn't this a lovely statement about Jesus? Gracious words

from the purest of hearts. How excellent. Remember the question of the psalmist and the answer:

> "Who may ascend into the hill of the Lord?
> Or who may stand in His holy place?
> He who has clean hands and a pure heart,
> Who has not lifted up his soul to an idol,
> Nor sworn deceitfully." (Psalm 24:3–4)

And the oft quoted words of Jesus:

> "Blessed are the pure in heart,
> For they shall see God." (Matthew 5:8)

How wonderful that God has made everything available to enable us to have pure hearts:

- *The blood of Jesus* to cleanse us from all sin.
- *The Holy Spirit* whose fullness will enable us to be pure.
- *The Word of God*:

    > "The words of the Lord are pure words." (Psalm 12:6)

    Jesus said:

    > "You are already clean becuase of the word which I have spoken to you." (John 15:3)

- *Trials, testings and difficult circumstances* to purify us and remove the dross from the silver.
- *The knowledge of future judgment*: one day we must all stand before the Judgment seat of Christ to give an account of how we lived.

Let's ask God to give us a love of purity, resulting in our words being gracious and our lives bringing joy and pleasure to the heart of our Lord Jesus Christ.

Hindrances to excellence

As we are encouraged in the excellent things, we are also taught the things that hinder. They are described by types of people and also by actions. As we accept the good, so we should refuse the evil. We are warned about:

The perverse

"Perverse" means "to be obstinate, self-willed, contrary, willful."

> "Thorns and snares are in the way of the perverse,
> He who guards his soul will be far from them."   (v. 5)

In other chapters we read about perverse lips; a perverse heart; perverse ways; a perverse tongue. Being perverse is the opposite to being prudent.

A perverse person is also described in this chapter as one who "sows iniquity" and "will reap sorrow" (v. 8).

Scoffers, mockers, and those who cause trouble

> "Cast out the scoffer and contention will leave;
> Yes, strife and reproach will cease."   (v. 10)

Laziness

> "The lazy man says, 'There is a lion outside!
> I shall be slain in the streets!'"   (v. 13)

Any excuse not to work hard.

Oppressing the poor

We are also warned about how wrong it is to oppress the poor: it will lead to poverty

> "He who oppresses the poor to increase his riches,
> And he who gives to the rich, will surely come to poverty."
>   (v. 16)

The company of angry and furious people

We are also counseled to avoid the company of angry and furious people, in case something rubs off and we become like them:

"Make no friendship with an angry man,
And with a furious man do not go.
Lest you learn his ways
And set a snare for your soul." (vv. 24–25)

Then we are given for our protection a list of *do nots*:

"Do not rob the poor because he is poor." (v. 22)

"Do not be one of those who shakes hands in a pledge,
One of those who is surety for debts." (v. 26)

"Do not remove the ancient landmark
Which your fathers have set." (v. 28)

This referred to property boundaries that marked the rightful owner. It also applies to our not lowering the godly standards that have been laid down by our righteous forebears. We are living in day of increased lowering of righteous standards. God set some of these standards by giving us the Ten Commandments. Man may try to alter these boundaries but God never has and never will.

How important in the light of this that we obey verse 6:

"Train up a child in the way he should go,
And when he is old he will not depart form it."

Set righteous boundaries.

Application

Just as we have been encouraged to accept and embrace the *excellent things* let us also reject the evil things: perversity, iniquity, laziness, the company of angry and furious people, oppressors of the poor, standing surety for debts, lowering righteous standards. These are all for our good and the blessing of others. Look at verse 18 again:

"For it is a pleasant thing if you keep them within you,
Let them all be fixed upon your lips."

Again the choice is ours: we can choose a good name; a pure heart; diligence, the excellent things; or we can reject and refuse all that would hinder a God-pleasing life

The excellence of God and Jesus

Having looked at some of the excellent things in this chapter, our considerations would be incomplete if we did not mention the the excellence of our God and His Son Jesus Christ. We have been reminded that because of the greatness of God, He is to be feared, reverenced, respected, worshiped and obeyed:

> "By humility and the fear of the LORD
> Are riches and honor and life."   (v. 4)

We are also reminded of the wonder and power and glory of the Great Creator God:

> "The rich and the poor have this in common,
> The LORD is the maker of them all."   (v. 2)

When God created the heavens and the earth, everything was excellent, perfect:

> "Then God saw everything that He had made, and indeed it was
> very good."   (Genesis 1:31)

Everyone who lives is indebted to God for the very breath he breathes. Job said, "the breath of the Almighty gives me life" (Job 33:4).

We are also reminded in this chapter of the excellence of God's protection:

> "The eyes of the LORD preserve knowledge,
> But He overthrows the words of the faithless."   (v. 12)

We are encouraged to love the things that God loves and hate the things that God hates. We should desire the excellent, and discard the wrong. God loves the excellent and hates sin.

> "The mouth of an immoral woman is a deep pit,
> He who is abhorred of the LORD will fall there."   (v. 14)

We have also seen in this chapter that Solomon wrote excellent things about God and His ways that we may trust in Him. Excellent things come from an excellent God. His excellence was acknowledged by those who loved Him and followed Him. Here are a few examples:

- *Moses and the children of Israel.* After the mighty deliverance God gave the children of Israel in parting the Red Sea and destroying Pharaoh's army, Moses and the children of Israel unitedly sang a song to the Lord. It is hymn number 1 in the Bible, Exodus 15, and in it they exclaimed:

  > "In the *greatness of Your excellence*
  > You have overthrown those who rose against You."
  >
  > (Exodus 15:7, emphasis added)

  Oh yes, our God is *great in excellence.*

- *Psalm 150.* The last psalm is a psalm of praise and includes:

  > "Praise Him for His mighty acts;
  > Praise Him according to *His excellent greatness!*"
  >
  > (Psalm 150:2, emphasis added)

- *Psalm 8.* With a heart full of gratitude David sings:

  > "O LORD, our LORD,
  > How *excellent is Your name in all the earth.*
  > Who have set Your glory above the heavens!"
  >
  > (Psalm 2:1, emphasis added)

- *Psalm 36:*

  > "How *excellent is thy lovingkindness,* O God! therefore the children of men put their trust under the shadow of thy wings."
  >
  > (Psalm 36:7, KJV, emphasis added)

And how gloriously excellent is our Lord Jesus Christ, surpassing all. The writer to the Hebrews in his opening words is caught up with the wonders of Jesus:

> "... heir of all things through whom also He made the worlds; who being the brightness of His glory and the express image of His person, and upholding all things by the word of His power ... sat down at the right hand of the Majesty on high, having become so much better than the angels, as He has by inheritance obtained *a more excellent name than they.*" (Hebrews 1:3–4, emphasis added)

But more than this, the writer to the Hebrews goes on to say that compared to all the great ministries of His servants – of Moses, and so many others – Jesus "has obtained *a more excellent ministry*" (Hebrews 8:6, emphasis added).

And again, without apology, we say "Amen" to the psalmist's words:

> "Praise Him according to His *excellent greatness!*"
> (Psalm 150:2, emphasis added)

Yes, He excels over all. He is excellent and has done, and will continue to do, excellent things. Lord of lords, King of kings. I find no fault in this Man.

How wonderful is the grace of God in bringing us into relationship with Him through our Lord Jesus Christ. He has given us and makes available to us the greatest riches anyone can possess. The riches and excellence of eternal life, All the total riches of the world could not purchase the salvation of one single soul.

> "He who believes in the Son has everlasting life."   (John 3:36)

What a hope for every follower of Jesus that one day we will see His excellence, we will see His glory, we will live forever in perfect surroundings. We will love and serve Him as we should. We will be like Him.

> "And everyone who has this hope in Him purifies himself, just as He is pure."   (1 John 3:3)

Application

Let us evidence our love for Him by applying these truths we have shared from this chapter:

- Let us choose to have a good name so that His name might be glorified.
- Let us be prudent in what we do, acting with wisdom and thoughtfulness.
- Let us walk humbly with God, continually reverencing Him and giving Him first place.
- Let us be bountiful givers, with the promised blessing: "he who sows bountifully will also reap bountifully" (2 Corinthians 9:6).
- Let us seek knowledge, understanding and truth.
- Let us trust the Lord in all that we do, committing our ways and works to Him.
- Let us have hearts that consider and help the poor.
- Let us excel in everything we do; doing our best, not for self-satisfaction, or to seek the approval of men, but for His praise and glory.

Let us ask the Lord to help us.

Prayer

Father God, we praise You for Your greatness, Your excellence, the wonders of Your creative and keeping power. Great is the Lord and greatly to be praised. Thank You for the so many ways You have proved to us that You are a God who is so continually trustworthy. Thank You for the teachings of Your Word. Please help us and enable us to apply these truths to our lives, that we may be enabled by the power of Your Holy Spirit, and for Your glory, to excel in all that we do. In Jesus' Name. Amen.

---

*If any of you lacks wisdom, let him ask of God, who gives to all liberally and without reproach, and it **will** be given to him* (James 1:5).

Chapter 23

1. When you sit down to eat with a ruler, consider carefully what is before you;
2. And put a knife to your throat if you are a man given to appetite.
3. Do not desire his delicacies, for they are deceptive food.
4. Do not overwork to be rich; because of your own understanding, cease!
5. Will you set your eyes on that which is not? For riches certainly make themselves wings; they fly away like an eagle toward heaven.
6. Do not eat the bread of a miser, nor desire his delicacies;
7. For as he thinks in his heart, so is he. "Eat and drink!" he says to you, but his heart is not with you.
8. The morsel you have eaten, you will vomit up, and waste your pleasant words.
9. Do not speak in the hearing of a fool, for he will despise the wisdom of your words.
10. Do not remove the ancient landmark, nor enter the fields of the fatherless;
11. For their Redeemer is mighty; He will plead their cause against you.
12. Apply your heart to instruction, and your ears to words of knowledge.
13. Do not withhold correction from a child, for if you beat him with a rod, he will not die.
14. You shall beat him with a rod, and deliver his soul from hell.
15. My son, if your heart is wise, my heart will rejoice – indeed, I myself;
16. Yes, my inmost being will rejoice when your lips speak right things.
17. Do not let your heart envy sinners, but be zealous for the fear of the LORD all the day;!
18. For surely there is a hereafter, and your hope will not be cut off.
19. Hear, my son, and be wise; and guide your heart in the way.
20. Do not mix with winebibbers, or with gluttonous eaters of meat;
21. For the drunkard and the glutton will come to poverty, and drowsiness will clothe a man with rags.

22. Listen to your father who begot you, and do not despise your mother when she is old.

23. Buy the truth, and do not sell it, also wisdom and instruction and understanding.

24. The father of the righteous will greatly rejoice, and he who begets a wise child will delight in him.

25. Let your father and your mother be glad, and let her who bore you rejoice.

26. My son, give me your heart, and let your eyes observe my ways.

27. For a harlot is a deep pit, and a seductress is a narrow well.

28. She also lies in wait as for a victim, and increases the unfaithful among men.

29. Who has woe? Who has sorrow? Who has contentions? Who has complaints? Who has wounds without cause? Who has redness of eyes?

30. Those who linger long at the wine, those who go in search of mixed wine.

31. Do not look on the wine when it is red, when it sparkles in the cup, when it swirls around smoothly;

32. At the last it bites like a serpent, and stings like a viper.

33. Your eyes will see strange things, and your heart will utter perverse things.

34. Yes, you will be like one who lies down in the midst of the sea, or like one who lies at the top of the mast, saying:

35. "They have struck me, but I was not hurt; they have beaten me, but I did not feel it. When shall I awake, that I may seek another drink?"

Introduction

How "down to earth" this book is. It deals with life and the circumstances of life that face us. Again it warns us of dangers, and advises us how to live the right way. Although many things are mentioned, there is one purpose behind them, and that is that we have a quality of life and living, without hurting ourselves or others. There is a variety of things mentioned in this chapter:

- Eating and drinking.
- The importance of knowledge, wisdom and instruction.
- Bringing up children.

- Parental concerns and parental joys.
- Warnings and encouragements
- Time and eternity.

How to conduct yourself while being entertained

We may not receive many, or any, invitations to wine and dine with important people, but the teaching in this book covers all of society from the rich to the poor; from the mighty to the humble. Solomon encourages us always to be disciplined. He refers to a person being asked to a feast with magnificent food and delicacies, and counsels to behave wisely. Not to behave like a glutton, and not to envy the rich man's life-style.

He also mentions dining with a person he describes as a miser. There is an outward show of hospitality and kindness but the host is mean and resents even what you are eating. He encourages one to "eat and drink" but he doesn't mean it. He is heartless, his heart is not with you. He can't help it, that is his character: "as he thinks in his heart, so is he" (v. 7). That statement refers to all of our actions. What we do and think is a manifestation of what we are. These two illustrations of feasts reveal not only the heart of the host, but the heart of the guests. A heart of greed, and a heart of liberality, a heart of meanness disguised by hypocritical talk.

The heart

In this chapter the heart is mentioned a number of times:

- As one thinks in the heart, so is he (v. 7).
- His heart is not with you (v. 7).
- Apply your heart to instruction (v. 12).
- A wise heart (v. 15)
- A rejoicing heart (v. 15).
- A heart that envies (v. 17).
- Guide your heart in the right way (v. 19).

And then the writer makes this plea to his son, which God our Father makes to us: *"My son, give me your heart"* (v. 26, emphasis added). That is where the Christian life begins. It begins in the heart. We hear the invitation of our Blessed Lord Jesus saying to us:

> "Behold, I stand at the door and knock. If anyone hears My voice and opens the door, I will come in to him and dine with him, and he with Me." (Revelation 3:20)

And if you are a Christian that is what you did. You opened your heart to Jesus. He said, "Give Me your heart." And you did. If you have never done that, you can. A nail-pierced hand – the marks of the cross, the price paid for our salvation – seeks entry into your life. He waits for your response to His request. It is your heart He seeks, that is your whole life. Our hearts are naturally sinful, but He can cleanse them by His own precious blood. Our hearts want our own way, but He can lead us in His way. Does He have your heart, all of your heart? "My son, daughter give Me your heart." I love the simplicity of the words of an old chorus:

> Into my heart, into my heart,
> Come into my heart, Lord Jesus,
> Come in today, come in to stay,
> Come into my heart, Lord Jesus.

All we do is a revelation of our hearts, and who is in control of them.

Do not overwork to be rich

We are encouraged to work and be diligent in all that we do, but here we are exhorted not to overwork with the purpose of being rich. The word "workaholic" is used today to describe a person who is obsessed with their profession or work above every thing else. How such a one suffers for this unbalanced attitude to life, and how others suffer through neglect. If the person is a father, the marriage suffers, the family suffers, health suffers, all for what? Riches? They disappear. They do not satisfy. They "make themselves wings; they fly away like an eagle toward heaven" (v. 5). The biography of rich and wealthy people who have set their hearts on riches is generally one of unhappiness, dissatisfaction, misery. I remember reading of one wealthy man who said he would give a million pounds to be able to eat a meal without pain. Another very rich man said, "I walk up and down thinking I am happy, but I am not." I was just reading yesterday about a man who won over three million pounds in the lottery three years ago, but is now penniless, divorced and unhappy. Thank God for the true riches: the riches of God's salvation; the riches of God's blessing; the riches of God's presence; the riches of God's promises. These riches do not fly away, but are eternal. What good advice that is. Do no overwork to be rich. Thank God for one of His great and precious promises:

> "My God shall supply all your need according to His riches in glory by Christ Jesus. Now to our God and Father be glory forever and ever. Amen."   (Philippians 4:19–20)

Some "do nots"

In these opening verses there are a few "do nots":

- Do not desire a rich man's delicacies.
- Do not eat the bread of a miser.
- Do not overwork to be rich.

The dangers of drink

Remembering that this chapter was written nearly 3,000 years ago, how relevant is its message. Much of this chapter is taken up with the subject of alcohol. We have just seen the dangers and problems of a workaholic, now it is the alcoholic. This is being written by a loving father to his son. He is pleading with him to be wise and to guide and to guard his life against this particular danger. Yes, how applicable today when we are so often reminded of the lost hours at work; the burden on the health services, the broken marriages, broken homes and broken lives, resulting from the misuse of drink. He refers to winebibbers; drunkards; those who linger long at wine; those who search for mixed wine. He lists some of the adverse affects by asking the questions (v. 29):

- Who has woe?
- Who has sorrow?
- Who has contentions?
- Who has complaints?
- Who has wounds without cause?
- Who has redness of eyes?

These result in:

- Hallucinations – seeing strange things (v. 33).
- Speaking stupid, perverse things (v. 33).

Alcoholics are captive to the habit, slaves to it. Alcohol controls their lives. It brings people to poverty, it fills them with drowsiness and it makes them insensitive:

> "They have struck me, but I was not hurt;
> They have beaten me but I did not feel it."   (v. 35)

Unaware of their great danger, like someone high up on a ship's mast, their waking thought is, "Where can I get another drink?"

We see the results of this almost every day in the streets of our cities. No alcoholic ever thought he would be one. Every alcoholic started off with one drink. Its true character is revealed in this chapter: "it bites like a serpent, and stings like a viper" (v. 32). It is a *killer*. Solomon's advice is:

> "Do not mix with winebibbers . . .
> Listen to your father who begot you,
> And do not despise your mother."   (vv. 20, 22)

Like all parents they want to be proud of their children:

> "The father of the righteous will greatly rejoice,
> And he who begets a wise child will delight in him."
> Let your father and your mother be glad,
> And let her who bore you rejoice."   (vv. 24–25)

The danger of immorality

Sometimes drink and immorality are linked. Solomon warns:

> "A harlot is a deep pit,
> And a seductress is a narrow well [or pit].
> She also lies in wait as for a victim,
> And increases the unfaithful among men."   (vv. 27–28)

How many men have had too much to drink resulting in immorality and unfaithfulness, and all the subsequent problems? Truly, as the Bible says, "the way of the unfaithful is hard" (13:15) and "the wages of sin is death" (Romans 6:23).

Their redeemer is strong

> "For their Redeemer is mighty;
> He will plead their cause against you."   (v. 11)

How great and powerful is our God who can liberate the captive, save the sinner, forgive all the past and empower people to live a life of freedom. Isn't that a great statement in verse 11? The context is God's care for the fatherless and he states, "Their Redeemer is mighty." Praise God, there is a Redeemer; One who has paid the price to buy us out of the slave market of sin, and give us a new life. He is strong. Job said:

> "For I know that my Redeemer lives,
> And He shall stand at last on the earth."   (Job 19:25)

We have seen the problems of workaholics, alcoholics and the immoral, but the Word that reveals the problem is the same Word who reveals the answer. Isaiah reminds us:

> "The LORD of hosts is His name;
> And your Redeemer is the Holy One of Israel;
> He is called the God of the whole earth."   (Isaiah 54:5)

Oh yes, our Redeemer is strong. He brings us His liberating truth. Solomon advises his son in this chapter:

> "Buy the truth [that is, do all you can to get it], and do not sell it
>   [that is, don"t pay any price to lose it],"
> Also wisdom and instruction and understanding." (v. 23)

Again he gives the answer: the fear of the Lord:

> "Be zealous for the fear of the LORD all the day." (v. 17)

Give God first place, reverence and obey Him.

> "The fear of the LORD is to hate evil." (8:13)

Discipline children

Just as Solomon is advising his son he also advises us:

> "Do not withhold correction from a child,
> For if you beat him with a rod, he will not die.
> You shall beat him with a rod,
> And deliver his soul from hell." (vv. 13–14)

There is no suggestion of cruelty in this statement, but love. Right and just correction is an evidence of love:

> "As many as I love, I rebuke and chasten." (Revelation 3:19)

This is not the philosophy of today, and how we are reaping the consequences. School teachers are often in fear of their pupils. Crime among children and young people is on the increase. Loving parental discipline has often been lacking. It is better to correct now that weep later.

If you are a parent, one of the good things to do is to read a chapter of Proverbs to your children every day. My parents did that, and I am grateful. I did it with my children and they are grateful. They are doing it with their children and they will be grateful.

There is such a great need for right, true, and just standards to be set. Children must be taught what is right and what is wrong, and God lays that responsibility initially with parents. It is not too late to start if your children are still with you. You, parent, I am sure would echo the words we have just repeated:

> "Let your father and your mother be glad,
> And let her who bore you rejoice."   (v. 25)

As we saw in chapter 22:

> "Train up a child in the way he should go,
> And when he is old he will not depart from it."   (22:6)

Why not just pause now and offer a prayer for your children, and perhaps your grandchildren. God hears.

The "dos" and the "do nots"

We have been advised in this chapter to do certain things, and also not to do certain things.

The "dos"

- When you sit down with a ruler consider carefully what is before you (v. 1).
- Apply your heart to instruction and knowledge (v. 12).
- Be in the fear of the Lord all day long (v. 17).
- Hear, be wise, guide your heart in the way (v. 19).
- Listen to your father (v. 22).
- Buy the truth (v. 23).
- Let your father and mother be glad and rejoice (v. 25).
- Give me your heart (v. 26).

The "do nots"

- Do not desire a rich man's delicacies (v. 3).
- Do not overwork (v. 4).
- Do not eat the food of a miser (v. 6).

- Do not speak in the hearing of a fool (v. 9).
- Do not remove the ancient landmark (v. 10).
- Do not withhold correction from a child (v. 13).
- Do not let your heart envy sinners (v. 17).
- Do not mix with winebibbers (v. 20).
- Do not despise your mother when she is old (v. 22).
- Do not sell truth (v. 23).
- Do not look on the wine when it is red, sparkles in the cup, swirls smoothly (v. 31).

These instructions, when obeyed, will bring blessing, and their reward. However, we are also encouraged not to concentrate only on our life here, but on our hereafter.

The hereafter

"For surely there is a hereafter,
And your hope will not be cut off."   (v. 18)

What an excellent reminder. There is not only a here, but there is a hereafter. The truth is that what we do here will affect what we will do in the future. Jesus encouraged His followers to, "lay up for yourselves treasures in heaven" (Matthew 6:20). For everyone who has ever lived, and for you, and me, there is a hereafter, an eternity.

I remember years ago reading about a large poster which was put on a billboard outside a busy railway station. Thousands saw it every day. In large letters there was one large word, "ETERNITY." There was such a protest about it they were forced to take it down. It was a disturbing thought. People would rather not be told or be reminded of the truth of the hereafter. But it is true. There is an eternity, a forever and forever. For the Christian seeking to please God, that is a glorious hope. It is a light that shines in the darkness so many times. If we die before Jesus returns, one day we will be resurrected and spend eternity with Him. If we are living when He returns we will be caught up together with Him and forever be with the Lord. That truth is not a vague hope, but a certain hope.

Our time on earth is so comparatively short compared to an unending eternity. It is here we can love Him and serve Him. What we do here, and how we live here, is so very important. "Surely there is a hereafter." What are your thought about that? Can we say in honesty, "Even so, come, Lord Jesus" (Revelation 22:20)? How important it is that we are living for Him today, being ready for when He comes, or He takes us home.

Thank God for His grace which has supplied everything we need to be right with God. It is *here*:

- We can confess our sins and be forgiven.
- We can be totally committed to Him.
- We can get to know Him better.
- We can give to Him.
- We can serve Him.
- We can be reconciled one to another.

Yes, it is *here*, and there is a *hereafter*. The important thing to do is what Mary, the mother of Jesus, said: "Whatever He says to you, do it" (John 2:5).

Again, let us apply and pray in this teaching.

Pray.

---

*If any of you lacks wisdom, let him ask of God, who gives to all liberally and without reproach, and it **will** be given to him* (James 1:5).

Chapter 24

1. Do not be envious of evil men, nor desire to be with them;
2. For their heart devises violence, and their lips talk of troublemaking.
3. Through wisdom a house is built, and by understanding it is established;
4. By knowledge the rooms are filled with all precious and pleasant riches.
5. A wise man is strong, yes, a man of knowledge increases strength;
6. For by wise counsel you will wage your own war, and in a multitude of counselors there is safety.
7. Wisdom is too lofty for a fool; he does not open his mouth in the gate.
8. He who plots to do evil will be called a schemer.
9. The devising of foolishness is sin, and the scoffer is an abomination to men.
10. If you faint in the day of adversity, your strength is small.
11. Deliver those who are drawn toward death, and hold back those stumbling to the slaughter.
12. If you say, "Surely we did not know this," does not He who weighs the hearts consider it? He who keeps your soul, does He not know it? And will He not render to each man according to his deeds?
13. My son, eat honey because it is good, and the honeycomb which is sweet to your taste;
14. So shall the knowledge of wisdom be to your soul; if you have found it, there is a prospect, and your hope will not be cut off.
15. Do not lie in wait, O wicked man, against the dwelling of the righteous; do not plunder his resting place;
16. For a righteous man may fall seven times and rise again, but the wicked shall fall by calamity.
17. Do not rejoice when your enemy falls, and do not let your heart be glad when he stumbles;
18. Lest the LORD see it, and it displease Him, and He turn away His wrath from him.
19. Do not fret because of evildoers, nor be envious of the wicked;

20. For there will be no prospect for the evil man; the lamp of the wicked will be put out.

21. My son, fear the LORD and the king; do not associate with those given to change;

22. For their calamity will rise suddenly, and who knows the ruin those two can bring?

23. These things also belong to the wise: it is not good to show partiality in judgment.

24. He who says to the wicked, "You are righteous," him the people will curse; nations will abhor him.

25. But those who rebuke the wicked will have delight, and a good blessing will come upon them.

26. He who gives a right answer kisses the lips.

27. Prepare your outside work, make it fit for yourself in the field; and afterward build your house.

28. Do not be a witness against your neighbor without cause, for would you deceive with your lips?

29. Do not say, "I will do to him just as he has done to me; I will render to the man according to his work."

30. I went by the field of the lazy man, and by the vineyard of the man devoid of understanding;

31. And there it was, all overgrown with thorns; its surface was covered with nettles; its stone wall was broken down.

32. When I saw it, I considered it well; I looked on it and received instruction:

33. A little sleep, a little slumber, a little folding of the hands to rest;

34. So shall your poverty come like a prowler, and your need like an armed man.

Introduction

The people described in this chapter have differing lifestyles and behavior. The contrasts are meant to make it easier for us to see what kind of people we want to be. The examples encourage us to be:

- Wise.
- Righteous.

Or, by contrast:

- Evildoers.
- Fools.
- Scoffers.
- Wicked.
- Slothful, lazy.

The contrasts in behavior are:

- Wisdom, understanding and knowledge.
- Strength.
- Precious and pleasant riches.
- Wise counsel.
- Compassion.

In comparison to:

- Violence.
- Trouble-making.
- Plotting evil.
- Adversity.
- Foolishness.
- Envy.
- Calamity.
- Partiality.
- Poverty.

What an encouragement there is in this chapter to all those, who like Solomon, choose wisdom. There are so many nuggets of gold in Proverbs with concise statements which overflow with truth. For example verses 3 and 4 in this chapter:

> "Through wisdom a house is built,
> And by understanding it is established;
> By knowledge the rooms are filled
> With all precious and pleasant riches."

Day by day we are all building something: our bodies, our reputations, our families, our work or business, our churches. We are building, not only for the present but also for the future. The

finest ingredients for all kinds of building are those frequently
quoted things: wisdom, understanding and knowledge.

Through wisdom a house is built

Wisdom is the ability to apply to our lives and actions the things we
know and understand. Wisdom is valuable because:

It is God-given

> "The LORD gives wisdom;
> From His mouth come knowledge and understanding."   (2:6)

It is of great value

> "Wisdom is the principal thing;
> Therefore get wisdom.
> And with all your getting, get understanding."   (4:7)

> "Wisdom is better than rubies."   (8:11)

> "How much better to get wisdom than gold!"   (16:16)

> "Wisdom is better than weapons of war."   (Ecclesiastes 9:18)

Wisdom starts with the fear of the Lord

> "The fear of the LORD is the beginning of wisdom."   (9:10)

> "The fear of the LORD is the instruction of wisdom."   (15:33)

> "My son, fear the LORD."   (v. 21)

The evidence of truly fearing the Lord:

- We reverence and respect Him for who He is.
- We hate evil.
- We realize our total dependence on Him.
- We love His Word and desire to know and do His will.
- We love God. Jesus said: "If you love Me, keep My command-
  ments" (John 14:15).
- We desire all we do to bring glory to God.

So be encouraged. Build right and with the right materials: wisdom, understanding and knowledge. Build with the Master Builder, God Himself. That is the wonderful thing about the Bible. It contains the Master Builder's instructions. It is not only a handbook, but a heart book. The wisdom that created the world, and upholds it, is what God has made available to us for the asking and receiving. What a God!

By understanding it is established

Wisdom builds. Understanding establishes, makes firm, consolidates, makes secure and sustains. The meaning of "understanding" is "to perceive the meaning of things." It is insight, perception and intelligence. Again, "the fear of the LORD is the beginning of understanding" (9:10). Like wisdom it is to be sought, it is something to get:

"Apply your heart to understanding." (2:2)

"Lift up your voice for understanding." (2:3)

'In all your getting, get understanding." (4:7)

What is understanding?
See this wonderful biblical answer:

"The knowledge of the Holy One is understanding." (9:10)

The more we increase in the knowledge of God, the more we will understand. He is the source of all true understanding.

It is knowing the will of God

"Therefore do not be unwise, but understand what the will of the Lord is." (Ephesians 5:17)

It is receiving revelation of truth

"The eyes of your understanding being enlightened; that you may know what is the hope of His calling, what are the riches of the glory of His inheritance in the saints, and what is the exceeding greatness of His power toward us that believe."

(Ephesians 1:18–19)

It is departing from evil

"Behold, the fear of the Lord, that is wisdom,
And to depart from evil is understanding."   (Job 28:28)

It is God-given
Paul writing to Timothy said:

"... may the Lord give you understanding in all things."

(2 Timothy 2:7)

And God said to Solomon:

"... I have given you a wise and understanding heart."

(1 Kings 3:12)

Remember what Jesus did to the two on the Emmaus road:

"He opened their understanding, that they might comprehend the Scriptures."   (Luke 24:45)

How to obtain understanding

- Ask for it like Solomon:

  "Give to your servant an understanding heart."   (1 Kings 3:9)

- Do not depend on your own understanding:

  "Trust in the LORD with all your heart,
  And lean not on your own understanding."   (3:5)

- Meditate in God's Word. David said:

  "I have more understanding than all my teachers,
  For Your testimonies are my meditation."   (Psalm 119:99)

  "The entrance of your words gives light
  It gives understanding to the simple."   (Psalm 119:130)

The results of understanding

- Happiness:

    "Happy is the man . . . who gains understanding."   (3:13)

- We are guarded in what we say:

    "A man of understanding holds his peace."   (11:12)

- We will find good:

    "He who keeps understanding will find good."   (19:8)

Let us borrow Solomon's prayer:

O Lord, my God, give to your servant an understanding heart.

The results of building with wisdom

As we continue to look at this analogy of the house built by wisdom, established by understanding, and knowledge, filling all the rooms with precious and pleasant riches, we are reminded of the wonder of the Lord Jesus entering our lives. Our life is like a house. Paul refers to it as "the temple of the living God" (2 Corinthians 6:16).

How did, and how does, Jesus enter our lives? Revelation 3:20 reminds us that He stands at the door of our lives and knocks, seeking admission. When we hear His voice and obey it by acknowledging and repenting of our sins, believing that He died for our sins, and rose again from the dead, He comes through the opened door to dwell within. He comes into the entry hall. He does not come to visit us, He comes to take possession. When we are saved we confess Him as Lord, that is, Master. We yield the totality of our lives to Him. The house is His. There is the sitting room where we can sit with Him and enjoy His company. There is the dining room where we can feed on His Word. There is the kitchen where we can serve Him by serving others. There is the bedroom where we hear Him say, "Come to Me, all you who labor and are heavy laden, and I will give you rest" (Matthew 11:28). He wants the house to be filled with His presence. How is it filled? It is filled with the knowledge of Himself; the knowledge of His Word;

the knowledge of His will; the knowledge of his "exceedingly great and precious promises" (2 Peter 1:4). When He has entered our lives, our chief pursuit in life should be to know Him. No wonder Paul cries out:

> "Oh, the depth of the riches both of the wisdom
>   and knowledge of God!"   (Romans 11:33)

Here is the greatest treasure man can have. Here are the true riches. This knowledge is so costly. Before we could know the riches of the knowledge of God, Jesus had to die, to shed His precious blood. His great desire for us was that we might know God. He said:

> "This is eternal life, that they may know You, the only true God,
>   and Jesus Christ whom You have sent."   (John 17:3)

Again the starting point is the same as for wisdom and understanding:

> "The fear of the LORD is the beginning of knowledge."   (1:7)

To know God, it is essential to reverence Him, love and obey Him. What is the result?

> " . . . the rooms are filled
> With all precious and pleasant riches."   (v. 4)

A house can be filled with precious things and yet not be pleasant. One can visit museums and art galleries and look on priceless objects, and yet there is no particular pleasantness in the building. God wants our lives to be both precious and pleasant. Remember these two words "precious" and "pleasant" are mentioned in Psalm 133, speaking of unity:

> "Behold, how good and how pleasant it is
> For brethren to dwell together in unity!
> It is like the precious oil upon the head."   (Psalm 133:1–2)

What is the point in our homes being beautifully furnished with all modern conveniences if strife, contention and bad relationships are present in the home? When we pursue the knowledge of God we will have that which is both precious and pleasant. Here are some of the precious things:

- The Word of God (1 Samuel 3:1, KJV).
- Wisdom: "more precious than rubies" (3:15).
- Faith: "more precious than gold" (1 Peter 1:7).
- The blood of Jesus: "redeemed . . . with the precious blood of Christ" (1 Peter 1:18–19).
- Jesus Himself: "to you who believe, He is precious" (1 Peter 2:7).
- Our souls: "What will it profit a man if he gains the whole world, and loses his own soul?" (Mark 8:36).
- The promises of God: "exceedingly great and precious promises" (2 Peter 1:4).
- The death of saints:

    "Precious in the sight of the LORD
    Is the death of His saints."   (Psalm 116:15)

    " 'Blessed are the dead who die in the Lord from now on.' 'Yes,' says the Spirit, 'that they may rest from their labors, and their works follow them.' "
                                                          (Revelation 14:13)

Yes, let us resolve to build with wisdom, be established by understanding, and filled with the knowledge of God.

This chapter continues to encourage us in these truths:

    "A wise man is strong,
    Yes, a man of knowledge increases strength."   (v. 5)

    "By wise counsel you will wage your own war,
    And in a multitude of counselors there is safety."   (v. 6)

Solomon states what some of the evidence of being wise will be:

- Not showing partiality in judgment (v. 23).
- Not calling wicked people righteous (v. 24).

- Rebuking the wicked (v. 25).
- Giving the right answer (v. 26).
- Being diligent in doing work in the right order (v. 27).
- Not witnessing falsely against a neighbor (v. 28).

Another picture

Also in this chapter there is a complete contrast to a house being built with wisdom, understanding and knowledge. Solomon was out walking and came to a vineyard owned by a man who he describes as "devoid of understanding" (v. 30).

It was overgrown with thorns, covered with nettles, and its walls were broken down (v. 31). Solomon looked, considered, and learned a lesson (v. 32). Here was a garden that could be producing grapes, giving an income, blessing others, but it was in ruins producing nothing.

What was the reason? Laziness, ease, lack of diligence, missed opportunities.

This reminds us of a question James asked in his epistle, "What is your life?" (James 4:14). Is it like the house, or the broken down vineyard? What has life produced? Precious and pleasant things, or thorns, nettles, broken down walls? Let's, to use Peter's words: "Be even more diligent to make your call and election sure" (2 Peter 1:10). He has made available to us His wisdom, understanding and knowledge. He wants us to be "a fruitful vine" as a result of our abiding in Him, and His Word abiding in us.

It is never too late to start, and never too late to start again. Let's all build for the Kingdom of God. Anything less than that is unfulfilling and poverty-stricken. God wants us to be rich towards Him, wise people, understanding people, knowledgeable people. Jesus said:

> "I must work the works of Him who sent Me while it is day; the night is coming when no one can work."   (John 9:3)

There is no retirement policy in God's kingdom.

> "As your days, so shall your strength be."   (Deuteronomy 33:25)

Listen again to the words of Jesus Himself:

> "I am the vine, you are the branches. He who abides in Me, and I in him, bears much fruit; for without Me, you can do nothing . . . If you abide in Me, and My words abide in you, you will ask what you desire, and it shall be done for you." (John 15:5, 7)

What do you desire? Shall we repeat the previous request:

> "Give me an understanding heart," Amen?

The requirement of knowledge

In the glorious quest for the knowledge of God, there are certain requirements.

Diligence

God is a rewarder of those who diligently seek Him. It is fairly true to say that we can know God as much as want to. It takes both resolve and discipline.

Continuance

We would all admit to our need of the knowledge of God, and sometimes we respond to the challenge to do this, and start. But it is persistence that is important:

> "Then shall we know, if we follow on to know the LORD." (Hosea 6:3, KJV)

> "Grow in the grace and knowledge of our Lord and Savior Jesus Christ." (2 Peter 3:18)

> "That you may walk worthy of the Lord, fully pleasing Him, being fruitful in every good work and *increasing in the knowledge* of God." (Colossians 1:10, emphasis added)

Revelation

> "That the God of our Lord Jesus Christ, the Father of glory, may give to you the spirit of wisdom and *revelation in the knowledge* of Him." (Ephesians 1:17, emphasis added)

Obedience to revealed truth

"If anyone wills to do His will, he shall know concerning the doctrine, whether it is from God or whether I speak on My own authority."   (John 7:17)

Humility

"The humble He teaches His way."   (Psalm 25:9)

Hunger and thirst

"Blessed are those who hunger and thirst for righteousness,
For they shall be filled."   (Matthew 5:6)

The Holy Spirit

"When He, the Spirit of truth, has come, He will guide you into all truth."   (John 16:13)

Getting beyond the milk stage

"Whom will He teach knowledge?
And whom will He make to understand the message?
Those just weaned from milk?
Those just drawn from the breasts?"   (Isaiah 28:9)

"I brethren, could not speak to you as to spiritual people but as to carnal, as to babes in Christ. I fed you with milk and not with solid food."   (1 Corinthians 3:1–2)

The means of acquiring knowledge

We can acquire knowledge through the following means:

- The Word of God.
- Prayer.
- Ministries.
- Our own experience.
- Experience of others.
- The still small voice.
- The gifts of the Spirit.

- Creation:

    > "The heavens declare the glory of God;
    > And the firmament shows His handiwork." (Psalm 19:1)

- Dreams and visions.

Let's use all the means He makes available to us.

"Dos" and "do nots"

It is always important when you read the Word of God to note what God tells us to do, and what He says He will do. Let's look at the instructions in this chapter. There are lists of "dos" and of "do nots." Here they are:

The "Dos"

- Build with wisdom, understanding and knowledge (vv. 3–4).
- Make sure your life and home are filled with precious and pleasant things (v. 4).
- Accept wise counsel (v. 6).
- Deliver, help those who are going in the wrong way (v. 11).
- Fear the Lord (v. 21).

The "do nots"

This list shows the things that would hinder us from being wise, understanding, and doing the will of God:

- Do not be envious of wicked men, or desire to be with them (v. 1).
- Do not faint in the day of adversity (v. 10).
- Do not do anything against the home of the righteous (v. 15).
- Do not rejoice when your enemy falls, or stumbles; that would displease the Lord (v. 17).
- Do not fret because of evildoers (v. 19).
- Do not associate with people with a rebellious spirit (v. 21).
- Do not falsely witness against your neighbor (v. 28).
- Do not take vengeance, doing to others what they did to you (v. 29).
- Do not be lazy, and neglect your work or your life (vv. 31–34).

Application

As we conclude this brief time of sharing God's Word, the questions remain the same:

- What has God said to me?
- What do I have to praise Him and thank Him for?
- Am I continually seeking to know God more?
- Are there any adjustments that need to be made?
- Is there anyone I should pray for in the light of these scriptures?

Prayer

> Thank You, Father, that You are always a very present help in time of need. We acknowledge there is not one moment in our lives when we do not need You. Please help me to be a person of wisdom, understanding and knowledge, and help me to build my life, my home, my family according to Your precious Word. Save me from a life of fruitlessness, and help me to abide in You, and let Your Word abide in me. Thank You for all Your goodness and mercy. Thank You for Your Word. Help me to be of help to others. In Jesus' Name. Amen.

---

*If any of you lacks wisdom, let him ask of God, who gives to all liberally and without reproach, and it **will** be given to him* (James 1:5).

Chapter 25

1. These also are proverbs of Solomon which the men of Hezekiah king of Judah copied:
2. It is the glory of God to conceal a matter, but the glory of kings is to search out a matter.
3. As the heavens for height and the earth for depth, so the heart of kings is unsearchable.
4. Take away the dross from silver, and it will go to the silversmith for jewelry.
5. Take away the wicked from before the king, and his throne will be established in righteousness.
6. Do not exalt yourself in the presence of the king, and do not stand in the place of the great;
7. For it is better that he say to you, "Come up here," than that you should be put lower in the presence of the prince, whom your eyes have seen.
8. Do not go hastily to court; for what will you do in the end, when your neighbor has put you to shame?
9. Debate your case with your neighbor, and do not disclose the secret to another;
10. Lest he who hears it expose your shame, and your reputation be ruined.
11. A word fitly spoken is like apples of gold in settings of silver.
12. Like an earring of gold and an ornament of fine gold is a wise rebuker to an obedient ear.
13. Like the cold of snow in time of harvest is a faithful messenger to those who send him, for he refreshes the soul of his masters.
14. Whoever falsely boasts of giving is like clouds and wind without rain.
15. By long forbearance a ruler is persuaded, and a gentle tongue breaks a bone.
16. Have you found honey? Eat only as much as you need, lest you be filled with it and vomit.
17. Seldom set foot in your neighbor's house, lest he become weary of you and hate you.

18. A man who bears false witness against his neighbor is like a club, a sword, and a sharp arrow.
19. Confidence in an unfaithful man in time of trouble is like a bad tooth and a foot out of joint.
20. Like one who takes away a garment in cold weather, and like vinegar on soda, is one who sings songs to a heavy heart.
21. If your enemy is hungry, give him bread to eat; and if he is thirsty, give him water to drink;
22. For so you will heap coals of fire on his head, and the LORD will reward you.
23. The north wind brings forth rain, and a backbiting tongue an angry countenance.
24. It is better to dwell in a corner of a housetop, than in a house shared with a contentious woman.
25. As cold water to a weary soul, so is good news from a far country.
26. A righteous man who falters before the wicked is like a murky spring and a polluted well.
27. It is not good to eat much honey; so to seek one's own glory is not glory.
28. Whoever has no rule over his own spirit is like a city broken down, without walls.

Although this chapter was copied three hundred years after being written, there is no mistaking Solomon's style. Here are still the pithy sayings and also the diverse people referred to as well as diverse subjects. The people referred to in this chapter are:

- Kings.
- Neighbors.
- Faithful messengers.
- Righteous people.
- The wicked.
- Boasters.
- False witnesses.
- Unfaithful men.
- Enemies.
- Contentious women.

The subjects mentioned are:

- Concealing and exposing knowledge.
- The human heart.
- Right words.
- Going to court.
- How to treat enemies.
- Good news.
- Moderation.
- Self-control.

It is also very important always to know what is written about.

God – the God of all knowledge

In verse 2 we read:

> "It is the glory of God to conceal a matter,
> But the glory of kings is to search out a matter."

Here is the wonderful attribute of God's character. He is omniscient; that is, He knows everything. God does not need to do what kings do, search out a matter, for He knows the answer to everything. God knows what to reveal and what to conceal. Moses wrote:

> "The secret things belong to the LORD our God, but those things which are revealed belong to us and to our children forever."
>
> (Deuteronomy 29:29)

Kings have to search for answers, and that is a good thing, their privilege, their glory, and if they are wise they will seek the answers from God. David, when king, realized that he couldn't understand his own heart so prayed:

> "Search me, O God, and know my heart,
> Try me, and know my anxieties."   (Psalm 139:23)

We can all have confidence in our God of all knowledge to reveal to us what we need to know. In life there are many situations which we may not understand, and raise questions from us. God is not obligated to explain to us everything He does or allows to happen to us. However, we can be absolutely confident that as long as we seek to walk with God, nothing will happen without a divine purpose, so we can trust Him. As Solomon told us previously:

> "*Trust* in the LORD with all your heart,
> And lean not to your own understanding;
> In all your ways acknowledge Him,
> And He *shall* direct your paths."   (3:5–6, emphasis added)

God is a rewarder

Later in this chapter we are encouraged to feed our enemies when they are hungry and give them water when they are thirsty, and the promise is given, "the LORD will reward you" (v. 22). We must never forget that once we were enemies of God and His ways, but through Christ He has redeemed and forgiven us and rewarded us with everlasting life. What a rewarder He is! He promises reward to:

- Those who are kind to their enemies (vv. 21–22).
- Those who diligently seek Him (Hebrews 11:6).
- Those who do their good deeds secretly; they will be rewarded openly (Matthew 6:4).
- Each according to his works, when Jesus comes back (Matthew 16:27).

What a wonderful God: God of all knowledge; God the rewarder.

"Dos" and "do nots"

In this chapter there is a list of instructions; things we should do, and things we should not do.

Take away the dross from silver (v. 4)

Solomon is speaking of removing all that would prevent the silver from being pure and shining. God speaks of Himself as "a refiner and a purifier of silver," who would purify His servants, "and purge them as gold and silver, that they may offer to the LORD an offering in righteousness" (Malachi 3:3). He uses this as an illustration for the king's court, that when the wicked are removed from the king's presence, "his throne will be established in righteousness" (v. 5).

The personal application is obvious. If we are going to be lights that shine for Jesus, we have to ensure that there are no impurities or dross in our lives to tarnish the shine. One of the beatitudes is:

> "Blessed are the pure in heart,
> For they shall see God."   (Matthew 5:8)

Solomon goes on in this chapter to mention some of that dross.

Pride

> "Do not exalt yourself in the presence of the king,
> And do not stand in the place of the great."   (v. 6)

Jesus said:

> "Whoever exalts himself will be humbled, and he who humbles himself will be exalted."   (Matthew 23:12)

Pride is a root sin. It is the cause of all strife and contention:

> "By pride comes nothing but strife."   (13:10)

It is pride that:

- Prevents men from seeking God:

  > "The wicked in his proud countenance does not seek God.
  > God is in none of his thoughts."   (Psalm 10:4)

- Binds people:

  > "Pride compasseth them about as a chain."   (Psalm 73:6, KJV)

- Deceives:

  > "The pride of your heart has deceived you."   (Obadiah 3)

- Leads to destruction:

  "Pride goes before destruction."   (16:18)

- Brings shame:

  "When pride comes, then comes shame."   (11:2)

What is God's counsel to us?

"Humble yourself under the mighty hand of God."   (1 Peter 5:6)

We have nothing wherein to boast save in the cross of our Lord Jesus Christ. Yes, pride is dross, is impure, is darkness. Let us borrow Paul's words:

"God forbid that I should boast except in the cross of our Lord Jesus Christ, by whom the world has been crucified to me, and I to the world."   (Galatians 6:14)

Wrong attitudes and behavior towards others

Solomon emphasizes the importance of our attitudes to our neighbors and others. Jesus said:

" 'You shall love the LORD your God with all your heart, with all your soul, with all your mind, and with all your strength.' This is the first commandment. And the second, like it, is this: 'You shall love your neighbor as yourself.' "   (Mark 12:30–31)

Wrong relationships are like dross in our lives, hindering our lights from shining before men.

Do not hastily go to court

Solomon shows how ill-advised it is to go to court instead of sitting down with your neighbor, and debating the problem. When this is not done, the result many times is that a person is put to shame, and loses his reputation. Paul also, points out how terrible it is for a Christian to go to court against another Christian:

"Dare any of you, having a matter against another, go to law before the unrighteous, and not before the saints?" (1 Corinthians 6:1)

The Word of God is so practical. It does happen that people have disputes and disagreements, and these should be dealt with in a proper way. Jesus gave clear instructions of what should happen when a Christian sins against another. Think of the problems that would have been solved if it had been put into practice.

"If your brother sins against you, go and tell him his fault between you and him alone. If he hears you, you have gained your brother. But if he will not hear, take with you one or two more, that by the mouth of two or three witnesses every word may be established. And if he refuses to hear them, tell it to the church. But if he refuses even to hear the church, let him be to you like a heathen and a tax collector." (Matthew 18:15–17)

How many times have you seen this in operation? What wisdom. Talk it over, and if there is no response take witnesses. If there is still no satisfactory conclusion, it becomes a church discipline matter.

Do not outstay your welcome

"Seldom set foot in your neighbor's house,
Lest he become weary of you and hate you." (v. 17)

In other words, be sensitive to others, as also he advises in verse 20: don't sing "songs to a heavy heart."

Do not bear false witness against your neighbor

"A man who bears false witness against his neighbor
Is like a club [a heavy sledge-hammer], a sword,
and a sharp arrow." (v. 18)

Of course, this is the ninth commandment:

"You shall not bear false witness against your neighbor."
(Exodus 20:16)

One of the great Christian testimonies should be that we love one another:

> "Love will cover a multitude of sins."   (1 Peter 4:8)

Peter asked Jesus:

> "Lord, how often shall my brother sin against me, and I forgive him? Up to seven times?" Jesus said to him, "I do not say to you, up to seven times, but up to seventy times seven." (Matthew 18:21–22)

False witness is dross. Avoid it.

Faithfulness and refreshment

What a lovely statement, "a faithful witness."

> "Like the cold of snow in time of harvest
> Is a faithful messenger to those who send him,
> For he refreshes the soul of his masters."   (v. 13)

How wonderful to be a refresher. Many times we need to be refreshed, encouraged, cheered. We do get weary, tired and disappointed, and we need to be rejuvenated, restored and revived. A faithful witness brings these. Paul confessed his need to be refreshed when he wrote to the church at Rome:

> "That I may come to you with joy by the will of God, and may be refreshed together with you."   (Romans 15:32)

He also mentioned some who had refreshed him:

- Onesiphorus:

  > "He often refreshed me, and was not ashamed of my chain."
  >   (2 Timothy 1:16)

- Stephanas, Forthunatus, Achaicus:

  > "They refreshed my spirit."   (1 Corinthians 16:18)

I am sure we can all think of people who always refresh us when we meet them. We can also think of others who depress rather than refresh! Thank God there are rivers of living water within us which can bless others. A little girl was once asked, "Why is it that everyone seems to love you?" She replied, "I don't know, unless it is because I love everybody." Let us resolve to be good neighbors, and refreshers. Amen?

The importance of words

In Proverbs we are often reminded of the importance of words. As we have seen, we can refresh or depress. We can build up or pull down. How important that we say the right word at the right time. What a lovely illustration of right words at the right time:

> "A word fitly spoken is like apples of gold
> In settings of silver." (v. 11)

How exquisite, attractive and precious. People wondered at the "gracious words" which proceeded from the mouth of the Lord Jesus: "No man ever spoke like this Man!" (John 7:46). Sometimes a word fitly spoke is a word of rebuke or correction, but look at verse 12:

> "Like an earring of gold and an ornament of fine gold
> Is a wise rebuker to an obedient ear." (v. 12)

To a wise person wishing to live to please the Lord, correction is invaluable. Wise rebuke will not be judgmental, or critical, but will be lovingly honest with the interest of the person at heart. An obedient ear will accept it, and will be willing to listen and accept advice. Those receiving correction will not be defensive, or self-justifying, or offended, but rather be grateful for the help. Rebuke is not pleasant, but remember the call in the first chapter of Proverbs:

> "Turn at my rebuke;
> Surely I will pour out my spirit on you;
> I will make my words known to you.

Because I have called and you refused,
I have stretched out my hand and no one regarded."   (1:23–24)

The result of refusal is calamity. In other chapters he says of rebuke:

"He who regards a rebuke will be honored."   (13:18)

"He who receives correction is prudent."   (15:5)

"The ear that hears the rebukes of life
Will abide among the wise."   (15:31)

"He who heeds rebuke gets understanding."   (15:32)

A solemn warning is given to those who continually refuse to accept rebuke:

"He who is often rebuked, and hardens his neck,
Will suddenly be destroyed, and that without remedy."   (29:1)

If we are ever called to rebuke anyone, how important it is that our own hearts and attitudes are right. Remember Paul's advice to the Galatian church:

"Brethren, if a man is overtaken in any trespass, you who are spiritual restore such a one in a spirit of gentleness, considering yourself lest you also be tempted."   (Galatians 6:1)

What a good statement in verse 15:

"A gentle tongue breaks a bone."

The bone speaks of that which is hard, and many times hardness is more responsive to gentleness than to sternness and severity. Try it! Remember God's dealings with Elijah the prophet. In reproving His servant He showed He could do it in the strong wind and the earthquake, but His effective rebuke was in "a still small voice" (see 1 Kings 19). Let us covet words that are "fitly spoken," gentle, refreshing, truthful, loving and righteous. David who personally experienced so much of the power and greatness of God, said to Him one day:

> "You have also given me the shield of Your salvation;
> Your right hand has held me up;
> *Your gentleness* has made me great."
>
> (Psalm 18:35, emphasis added)

"Gentleness" means "meekness, humility, ability to yield, patient, kind." Paul writing to Timothy said:

> "A servant of the Lord must not quarrel but be *gentle* to all, able to teach, patient, in humility correcting those who are in opposition."
>
> (2 Timothy 2:24–25)

Moderation

Moderation is inferred in the advice given in verse 16:

> "Have you found honey?
> Eat only as much as you need,
> Lest you be filled with it and vomit."

Excess always spoils. Some biographies in Scripture are spoiled by a little three letter word, *"but"*:

- *Solomon* himself:

  > "*But* King Solomon loved many foreign women . . ."
  >
  > (1 Kings 11:1, emphasis added)

- *Uzziah.* He was a great king and did many great things,

  > "*But* when he was strong his heart was lifted up, to his destruction . . ."   (2 Chronicles 26:16, emphasis added)

Paul wrote to he Philippians:

> "Let your moderation be known unto all men."
>
> (Philippians 4:5, KJV)

And in verse 28 of this chapter in Proverbs:

> "Whoever has no rule over his own spirit
> Is like a city broken down, without walls."

Application

Again one is amazed in how much, and how many subjects are dealt with in one chapter. Once more let me encourage you to note what God has said to you and respond to it. If we do our part, God will always do His.

Instructions

- Take away the dross from the silver (v. 4).
- Do not exalt yourself (v. 6).
- Do not hastily take your neighbor to court (v. 8).
- Let your words be fitly spoken (v. 11).
- Be obedient to reproof (v. 12).
- Be a faithful messenger (v. 13).
- Be a refresher (v. 13).
- Do not boast about what you give (v. 14).
- Be moderate (v. 16).
- Do not weary your neighbor (v. 17).
- Give bread and drink to your enemy (v. 21).
- Be steadfast (v. 26).
- Do not seek your own glory (v. 27).

Pray them in ... **work** them out.

---

*If any of you lacks wisdom, let him ask of God, who gives to all liberally and without reproach, and it **will** be given to him* (James 1:5).

Chapter 26

1. As snow in summer and rain in harvest, so honor is not fitting for a fool.
2. Like a flitting sparrow, like a flying swallow, so a curse without cause shall not alight.
3. A whip for the horse, a bridle for the donkey, and a rod for the fool's back.
4. Do not answer a fool according to his folly, lest you also be like him.
5. Answer a fool according to his folly, lest he be wise in his own eyes.
6. He who sends a message by the hand of a fool cuts off his own feet and drinks violence.
7. Like the legs of the lame that hang limp is a proverb in the mouth of fools.
8. Like one who binds a stone in a sling is he who gives honor to a fool.
9. Like a thorn that goes into the hand of a drunkard is a proverb in the mouth of fools.
10. The great God who formed everything gives the fool his hire and the transgressor his wages.
11. As a dog returns to his own vomit, so a fool repeats his folly.
12. Do you see a man wise in his own eyes? There is more hope for a fool than for him.
13. The lazy man says, "There is a lion in the road! A fierce lion is in the streets!"
14. As a door turns on its hinges, so does the lazy man on his bed.
15. The lazy man buries his hand in the bowl; it wearies him to bring it back to his mouth.
16. The lazy man is wiser in his own eyes than seven men who can answer sensibly.

17. He who passes by and meddles in a quarrel not his own is like one who takes a dog by the ears.

18. Like a madman who throws firebrands, arrows, and death, is the man who deceives his neighbor, and says, "I was only joking!"

20. Where there is no wood, the fire goes out; and where there is no talebearer, strife ceases.

21. As charcoal is to burning coals, and wood to fire, so is a contentious man to kindle strife.

22. The words of a talebearer are like tasty trifles, and they go down into the inmost body.

23. Fervent lips with a wicked heart are like earthenware covered with silver dross.

24. He who hates, disguises it with his lips, and lays up deceit within himself;

25. When he speaks kindly, do not believe him, for there are seven abominations in his heart;

26. Though his hatred is covered by deceit, his wickedness will be revealed before the assembly.

27. Whoever digs a pit will fall into it, and he who rolls a stone will have it roll back on him.

28. A lying tongue hates those who are crushed by it, and a flattering mouth works ruin.

The first part of this chapter is taken up with the subject of fools. Solomon continually uses contrasts to accentuate the value of the true and real thing. For example, he is here talking about fools who are the absolute opposite to wise people. He shows their behavior and attitude so that the conclusion should be, "Who would choose to be a fool?" This word "fool," is not used lightly or casually. Some in Scripture acknowledged their foolishness like King Saul. He had a hatred for David, hunted him down, seeking to kill him. One day when David had the opportunity of killing him, he refused to do so, and Saul realizing this cried out "I have played the fool" (1 Samuel 26:21).

Jesus told the story of the rich farmer who had had a great harvest, and planned in his heart to enlarge his barns, and said, "Soul, you have many goods laid up for many years; take your ease; eat drink and be merry." But God responded, "Fool! This night your soul will be required of you" (see Luke 12:16–21). The story has the obvious application for all of us: that it is folly to lay up treasure on earth, and not lay up treasure in heaven. Life is uncertain. We do not know what one day will bring forth. Scripture also makes it plain that men who deny the existence of God, irrespective of all their scholastic achievements are fools:

> "The fool has said in his heart,
> 'There is no God.' "   (Psalm 14:1)

The behavior of fools

Other scriptures describe fools thus:

> "The way of a fool is right in his own eyes."   (12:15)

> "A fool despises his father's instruction."   (15:5)

> "A fool has no delight in understanding."   (18:2)

> "He who trusts in his own heart is a fool."   (28:26)

> "A fool vents all his feelings."   (29:11)

> "The fool walks in darkness."   (Ecclesiastes 2:14)

> "A fool also multiplies words."   (Ecclesiastes 10:14)

Instructions and advice about fools in this chapter

Don't give honor to a fool

> "As snow in summer and rain in harvest,
> So honor is not fitting for a fool."   (v. 1)

Just as snow and rain in these seasons would be completely out of place, so is honor given to fools. Fools given honor will misuse it, and misinterpret it. They will give themselves the credit for what they do. They are self-dependent, and independent. They have no sense of need of God. Today we often see honor given to foolish people. They are the idols of today. Honor is heaped on them, yet so many times their personal lives are in a mess, and their behavior disgraceful. Honoring them is out of place.

A fool requires discipline

> "A whip for the horse,
> A bridle for the donkey,
> And a rod for the fool's back." (v. 3)

The only thing that brings some fools to their senses is punishment for their folly. Discipline is so necessary right from childhood. Today in some countries it is illegal to chastise your child. They know better than God, but what are the results in society? Authority is despised, correction is omitted, and crime, especially among young people is increasing, because correction is either forbidden or ignored.

A fool should be answered correctly

There are two statements made which at first seem contradictory, but are not:

> "Answer a fool according to his folly,
> Lest he be wise in his own eyes." (v. 5)

> "Do not answer a fool according to his folly,
> Lest you also be like him." (v. 4)

We should not reply to a fool in his foolish manner. A fool so many times is obstinate, self-opinionated and quick-tempered, but we must not behave in the same way when responding to him. Peter's instructions are:

> "not returning evil for evil or reviling for reviling."
> (1 Peter 3:9)

We must not in our own wisdom try to belittle him, but expose the foolishness of his behavior or words, sometimes with silence, sometimes countering lies with truth.

A fool is unreliable

You cannot trust a fool. Solomon puts it this way:

> "He who sends a message by the hand of a fool
> Cuts off his own feet and drinks violence.
> Like the legs of the lame that hang limp
> Is a proverb in the mouth of fools.
> Like one who binds a stone in a sling
> Is he who gives honor to a fool."   (vv. 6–8)

You cannot trust a fool to safely deliver a message. It is useless, like lame legs. It is also deadly. A sling and stone are instruments of hurting, wounding and killing.

A fool is insensitive to teaching and instruction

> "Like a thorn that goes into the hand of a drunkard
> Is a proverb in the mouth of fools."   (v. 9)

Just as a drunk man would be insensitive to a thorn in his hand, so truth is ineffective to a fool. Not only so, but even though sometimes being corrected, he will return to his own ways, as it is described so graphically:

> "As a dog returns to his own vomit,
> So a fool repeats his folly."   (v. 11)

It is not a change in conduct he needs, but a change of heart. Thank God, He alone can do that, and can transform fools into wise people. Unless a fool changes he will reap what he sows, and one day stand before God and give account.

Laziness

We have continually noticed in this book that there is much repetition of certain truths. This repetition has a purpose. We can be forgetful hearers; we can be starters and not finishers; our application of discipline can deteriorate. We need to be reminded. Remember Peter, in his second epistle, made no excuse for repetition, but said,

> "I will not be negligent to remind you always of these things, though you know and are established in the present truth."
>
> (2 Peter 1:12)

There is another reminder in this chapter of the folly of laziness and slothfulness. The lazy man is described in several ways:

As someone who finds an excuse for not working:

> "The lazy man says, 'There is a lion in the road!
> A fierce lion is in the streets!'"   (v. 13)

As someone with movement but no progress

> "As a door turns on its hinges,
> So does the lazy man on his bed."   (v. 14)

How sad; time passes but there is no advance. For the Christian, God's desire for us is to advance, to grow in the knowledge of our Lord and Savior Jesus Christ. The writer to the Hebrews lamented the fact that many Christians were still babes in Christ. Paul had the same complaint about the Corinthian believers. He wanted to give them meat but they could only take milk

As someone who does not use the means available to him

> "The lazy man buries his hand in the bowl;
> It wearies him to bring it back to his mouth."   (v. 15)

What a picture. It seems so ridiculous! There is bread set before him but he starves himself by not receiving what is set before him.

Ridiculous as that may sound, it can be an accurate picture of some Christians. God has given us bread, as He gave manna to the children of Israel. He supplied it, but they had to collect it. We have His Word, the Bible. We can have the Book and yet it can remain unopened, or we can grab a few verses without giving them thought and application. "It wearies him to bring it back to his mouth." He can't be bothered, so there he is: movement without progress; food without eating.

A someone who is self-deceived

> "The lazy man is wiser in his own eyes
> Than seven men who can answer sensibly."   (v. 16)

He still has a high opinion of himself. To him "ignorance is bliss." He ignores the counsel and advice of wiser men. He is self-satisfied as well as self-opinionated, and therefore self-deceived.

So what is the answer to laziness? How can we be saved from such a position? The answer to laziness is, of course, diligence, discipline, a desire to grow, and to increase in the knowledge of God; to be effective in His kingdom.

Strife, talebearing, contention

We are reminded of some more dangers: of meddling in other people's quarrels; talebearing; deception; hypocrisy. We face these things in life. How foolish to get unnecessarily involved in conflict.

> "He who passes by and meddles in a quarrel not his own
> Is like one who takes a dog by the ears."   (v. 17)

What heartache and heartbreak is caused by strife and contention. Remember when there was trouble between the herdsmen of Abraham and Lot. Abraham said to his nephew, "Please let there be no strife between you and me" (Genesis 13:8). What good advice. Jesus in teaching the Beatitudes said:

> "Blessed are peacemakers,
> For they shall be called sons of God."   (Matthew 5:9)

Many times in disputes we have to mind our own business. Give advice only when asked, otherwise situations can be worsened, like incendiaries:

> "Like a madman who throws firebrands, arrows and death . . .
> And says, 'I was only joking.'"   (vv. 18–19)

Who needs that kind of interference?

Talebearing

Again this sin is mentioned. What havoc, what contentions, what strife results from talebearing, gossip. God instructed Israel through Moses: "You shall not go about as a talebearer among your people" (Leviticus 19:16). How expressive are these words in this chapter:

> "Where there is no wood, the fire goes out;
> And where there is no talebearer, strife ceases.
> As charcoal is to burning coals, and wood to fire,
> So is a contentious man to kindle strife.
> The words of a talebearer are like tasty trifles,
> And they go down into the inmost body."   (vv. 20–22)

Let us resolve to be those who do not pass on these tasty trifles, but those who "seek peace and pursue it" (Psalm 34:14).

Let us heal and not hurt:

> "The words of a talebearer are as wounds."   (18:8, KJV)

The power of words

What havoc is wrought with the tongue. Remember James told us that if we can control our tongues we can control our whole body. Various tongues are mentioned in this chapter:

- The fool's tongue (v. 7).
- The meddling tongue (v. 17).
- The deceiving tongue (v. 19).
- The contentious tongue (v. 21).

- The talebearer's tongue (v. 22).
- The hating tongue (v. 24).
- The lying tongue (v. 28).
- The flattering tongue (v. 28).

Having been reminded of these dangers, the harm caused and the wounds inflicted, let us borrow David's prayer again.:

> "Let the words of my mouth and the meditation of my heart
> Be acceptable in Your sight,
> O Lord, my strength and my Redeemer."   (Psalm 19:14)

The greatness of God

There is only one mention of God in this chapter. In some versions it is not mentioned, but in the New King James Version from which we have been reading and quoting, verse 10 states:

> "The *great God* who formed everything
> Gives the fool his hire and the transgressor his wages."

How refreshing! Having looked at the things that are detrimental to ourselves and to others, we look to God and His greatness. How great is our God. The main thing in Christian living is to be enraptured with God and His beloved Son, Jesus, desiring to live for His glory, and to worship and serve Him.

He is God the great *Creator*, who formed and made all things:

> "The heavens declare the glory of God;
> And the firmament shows His handiwork."   (Psalm 19:1)

God spoke and things came into being:

- God said, "Let there be light," and there was light.
- God said, "Let there be a firmament," and there was a firmament.
- God called the dry land earth and the waters seas.
- God said, "Let the earth bring forth ..." And there came forth grass, herbs and fruit trees.

- God said, "Let there be lights in the firmament," and the sun, moon, and stars came forth.
- God said . . . and there came forth living creatures: birds, fish.
- God said, "Let us make man," and God created man in His own image.

Oh the greatness of God our Creator.

The contemplation of His greatness, and experience of His greatness brought forth worship and praise from His saints. Let's listen to some of them.

From David

> "Yours, O LORD, is the *greatness*,
> The power and the glory,
> The victory and the majesty;
> For all that is in heaven and in earth is Yours;
> Yours is the kingdom, O LORD,
> And You are exalted as head over all.
> Both riches and honor come from You,
> And You reign over all.
> In Your hand is power and might;
> In Your hand it is to make great
> And to give strength to all."
>
> (1 Chronicles 29:11–12, emphasis added)

When Nathan the prophet came to David, and told him that his son, Solomon, would build the temple after he himself had done much preparation for it, he declares:

> "You have done all this *greatness* . . . O LORD, there is none like You, nor is there any God besides You."
>
> (1 Chronicles 17:19–20, emphasis added)

So many times in the Psalms David expresses the *greatness* of God. Here is the key to the man whom God describes as "a man after His own heart" (1 Samuel 13:14). He was enraptured with the greatness and wonder of God.

"Oh, how *great is Your goodness*,
Which You have laid up for those who fear You,
Which You have prepared for those who trust You."

(Psalm 31:19, emphasis added)

"For You are *great*, and do *wondrous things*;
You alone are God." (Psalm 86:10, emphasis added)

He so appreciated God, even thinking about him:

"How precious also are Your thoughts to me, O God!
How *great* is the sum of them!" (Psalm 139:17, emphasis added)

From Moses

When God parted the Red Sea and then destroyed the Egyptians in it, Moses and the children of Israel gathered together and worshiped and praised God for the *excellence of His greatness*:

"In the *greatness of Your excellence*
You have overthrown those who rose against You;
You sent forth Your wrath;
It consumed them like stubble." (Exodus 15:7, emphasis added)

When Israel had sinned, Moses knew that this great God was great in mercy:

"The LORD is longsuffering and abundant in mercy, forgiving iniquity and transgression ... Pardon the iniquity of this people, I pray, according to the *greatness of Your mercy*, just as you have forgiven Your people, from Egypt even until now."

(Numbers 14:18–19, emphasis added)

From Isaiah

God speaking through His prophet, Isaiah, says:

" 'To whom will you liken Me,
Or to whom shall I be equal?' says the Holy One.
Lift up your eyes on high,
And see who has created these things,
Who brings out their host by number;

He calls them all by name,
By the *greatness of His might*
And the strength of His power;
Not one is missing."   (Isaiah 40:25–26, emphasis added)

From Paul

Paul prayed that His people would be aware and appreciate the greatness of God and His beloved Son, Jesus:

> "That the God of our Lord Jesus Christ, the Father of glory, may give to you the spirit of wisdom and revelation in the knowledge of Him, the eyes of your understanding being enlightened; that you may know what is the hope of His calling, what are the riches of the glory of His inheritance in the saints, and what is the *exceeding greatness of His power* toward us who believe, according to the working of His mighty power."   (Ephesians 1:17–19)

Application

Let us ensure our lives are free from all things (foolishness, laziness, strife, talebearing, contention) that would hinder the revelation of His *greatness*; that we may be engrossed with the knowledge of the greatness of God. Let us walk in the fear of the Lord, reverence Him, love Him, worship Him and serve Him. "Great is our God and greatly to be praised."

Prayer

> Yes, O God, You are great and greatly to be praised. We acknowledge with gratitude the greatness of your Creation; the greatness of Your character; the greatness of Your beloved Son, Jesus; the greatness of Your salvation; the greatness of Your love, grace, and mercy. Help us to be free from everything that would mar or hinder our pursuit of the knowledge of Yourself, and let the beauty of Jesus be seen in us. Amen.

---

*If any of you lacks wisdom, let him ask of God, who gives to all liberally and without reproach, and it **will** be given to him (James 1:5).*

Chapter 27

1. Do not boast about tomorrow, for you do not know what a day may bring forth.
2. Let another man praise you, and not your own mouth; a stranger, and not your own lips.
3. A stone is heavy and sand is weighty, but a fool's wrath is heavier than both of them.
4. Wrath is cruel and anger a torrent, but who is able to stand before jealousy?
5. Open rebuke is better than love carefully concealed.
6. Faithful are the wounds of a friend, but the kisses of an enemy are deceitful.
7. A satisfied soul loathes the honeycomb, but to a hungry soul every bitter thing is sweet.
8. Like a bird that wanders from its nest is a man who wanders from his place.
9. Ointment and perfume delight the heart, and the sweetness of a man's friend gives delight by hearty counsel.
10. Do not forsake your own friend or your father's friend, nor go to your brother's house in the day of your calamity; better is a neighbor nearby than a brother far away.
11. My son, be wise, and make my heart glad, that I may answer him who reproaches me.
12. A prudent man foresees evil and hides himself; the simple pass on and are punished.
13. Take the garment of him who is surety for a stranger, and hold it in pledge when he is surety for a seductress.
14. He who blesses his friend with a loud voice, rising early in the morning, it will be counted a curse to him.
15. A continual dripping on a very rainy day and a contentious woman are alike;

16. Whoever restrains her restrains the wind, and grasps oil with his right hand.
17. As iron sharpens iron, so a man sharpens the countenance of his friend.
18. Whoever keeps the fig tree will eat its fruit; so he who waits on his master will be honored.
19. As in water face reflects face, so a man's heart reveals the man.
20. Hell and Destruction are never full; so the eyes of man are never satisfied.
21. The refining pot is for silver and the furnace for gold, and a man is valued by what others say of him.
22. Though you grind a fool in a mortar with a pestle along with crushed grain, yet his foolishness will not depart from him.
23. Be diligent to know the state of your flocks, and attend to your herds;
24. For riches are not forever, nor does a crown endure to all generations.
25. When the hay is removed, and the tender grass shows itself, and the herbs of the mountains are gathered in,
26. The lambs will provide your clothing, and the goats the price of a field;
27. You shall have enough goats' milk for your food, for the food of your household, and the nourishment of your maidservants.

This chapter starts off by reminding us of the importance of now, and how there is no guarantee for tomorrow.

Do not boast about tomorrow

> "Do not boast about tomorrow,
> For you do not know what a day may bring forth."   (v. 1)

We can and should plan for tomorrow but there is no guarantee. The word "boast" means "to praise oneself," so we must not praise ourselves in what we are going to do tomorrow. Remember the advice given by James:

> "Come now, you who say, 'Today or tomorrow we will go to such and such a city, spend a year there, buy and sell, and make a profit'; whereas you do not know what will happen tomorrow. For what is your life? It is even a vapor that appears for a little time and then vanishes away. Instead you ought to say, 'If the Lord wills, we shall live and do this or that.'"   (James 4:13–15)

Remember the rich farmer boasted about his tomorrows, but died that night. The most important time in our lives is *now* – *today*. Inscribed in a very old cathedral clock are these words:

> Time past is gone, thou canst not it recall.
> Time future is not and can never be.
> Time present is the only time for thee.

Today

How the importance of *today* is emphasized in Scripture:

> "Therefore, as the Holy Spirit says:
>
> '*Today*, if you will hear His voice,
> Do not harden your hearts as in the rebellion.' "
>
> (Hebrews 3:7–8, emphasis added)

> "Exhort one another *daily*, while it is called '*Today*,' lest any of you be hardened through the deceitfulness of sin."
>
> (Hebrews 3:13, emphasis added)

Thank God:

> "Jesus Christ is the same yesterday, *today*, and forever."
>
> (Hebrews 13:8)

In making future plans let's always start with God – if the Lord wills – and desire that all we do and all we plan is in the will of God.

Do not boast about yourself

> "Let another man praise you, and not your own mouth;
> A stranger, and not your own lips." (v. 2)

What good advice. God's Word tells us to:

> "Humble [ourselves] under the mighty hand of God."
>
> (1 Peter 5:6)

We are encouraged to:

> "Be clothed with humility." (1 Peter 5:5)

Talking of humility, it has been said, "It is the first garment to be put on, and the last to be put off." And also, "Praise is a comely garment, but though you wear it another must put it on, or else it will never sit well on you." John the Baptist declared that he was unworthy even to unloose the Lord's sandals, but Jesus said of him, "among those born of women there is not a greater prophet" (Luke 7:28). The centurion said he was not worthy that Jesus should enter his house, yet the elders of Israel testified that he was worthy, and Jesus said of him, "I have not found such great faith, not even in Israel" (Luke 7:9). Luke mentions nothing of himself in the Gospel he wrote, yet he was described as "the beloved physician" (Colossians 4:14). Paul asked the question of the Corinthians:

> "Do we begin again to commend ourselves?" (2 Corinthians 3:1)

The answer was 'no.' He said:

> "For we do not commend ourselves to you . . ."
> (2 Corinthians 5:12)

And later he said:

> "We dare not class ourselves or compare ourselves with those who commend themselves ... and comparing themselves among themselves, are not wise." (2 Corinthians 10:12)

Our reaction to praise reveals what kind of people we are. In verse 21 we read:

> "A man is valued by what others say of him."

Again our thoughts go to *Jesus* – the greatest person who ever walked on planet earth. He is our example; our standard. He was always giving praise and glory and credit to His Father, God.

Deliberately making Himself of no reputation, "He humbled Himself and became obedient to the point of death, even the death of the cross" (Philippians 2:8). And what is the result of that humility?

> "Therefore God also has highly exalted Him and given Him the name which is above every name, that at the name of Jesus every knee should bow, of those in heaven, and of those on earth, and of those under the earth, and that every tongue should confess that Jesus Christ is Lord, to the glory of God the Father."
>
> (Philippians 2:9–11)

- Do not boast about tomorrow.
- Do not boast about yourself.
- Let's look to Jesus, and say together, "Jesus Christ is Lord."
- Let's look to our tomorrows and say, "If the Lord will." Our times are in His hands. What a wonderfully safe place to be.

Friendship

What a wonderful blessing true friendship is. What would life be like without friends? The greatest friendship of all is friendship with God, and the Lord Jesus Christ. As the old hymn says, "What a friend we have in Jesus!" Abraham had the glorious description of being, "the friend of God" (James 2:23). God spoke to Moses "face to face, as a man speaks to his friend" (Exodus 33:11). Remember what Jesus said to His disciples:

> "You are My friends if you do whatever I command you. No longer do I call you servants, for a servant does not know what his master is doing; but I have called you friends, for all things that I heard from My Father, I have made known to you." (John 15:14–15)

Friendship has to be maintained and developed. We are exhorted in verse 10:

> "Do not forsake your own friend or your father's friend."

A true friend's counsel is so pleasant:

> "Ointment and perfume delight the heart,
> And the sweetness of a man's friend gives delight
>   by hearty counsel."   (v. 9)

There is something which is mutually beneficial when friend is with friend. Solomon describes it:

> "As iron sharpens iron,
> So a man sharpens the countenance of his friend."   (v. 17)

Just as iron sharpening iron puts a keen edge on a knife, so friends sharpen one another's minds, to make them more effective. Sometimes a true friend may expose a need, or weakness, but when done in love, it is a demonstration of the friend's faithfulness:

> "Faithful are the wounds of a friend."   (v. 6)

A true friend will also be sensitive as to what to say, and when to say it. There is this trite warning in verse 14:

> "He who blesses his friend with a loud voice,
>   rising early in the morning,
> It will be counted a curse to him."

Solomon has previously mentioned friends in other chapters:

> "A friend loves at all times."   (17:17)

> "A man who has friends must himself be friendly,
> But there is a friend who sticks closer than a brother."   (18:24)

So let us thank God for friends. Let us be good friends. Do not forsake them. All Christians in one sense are friends because we are all linked with the same greatest of friends. Then there is a circle of friends, and then there are close and intimate friends. All the disciples were Jesus' friends, but He had an intimate friendship with the inner circle of Peter, James and John. This was not favoritism, just friendship. These kinds of friends are always available for us, loving us, praying for us, completely trustworthy and reliable. What a blessing.

Be wise

Again in this chapter Solomon says: "My son be wise ... " (v. 11). This sums up the whole purpose of this book. How much is involved in that simple statement. Remember he said previously:

> "Wisdom is the principal thing,
> Therefore get wisdom."   (4:7)

The manifestations of wisdom

Foreseeing evil

> "A prudent man foresees evil and hides himself."   (v. 12)

That is, he is going to avoid situations which could be harmful. He will take the Lord's prayer to himself, "Lead me not into temptation, but deliver me from evil."

Being diligent
How often this is encouraged. He speaks of the importance of diligence in attending an orchard:

> "Whoever keeps the fig tree will eat its fruit."   (v. 18)

The shepherd must be diligent:

> "Be diligent to know the state of your flocks,
> Attend to your herds."   (v. 23)

Prepare for the future
Prepare for the winter; gather in the hay (vv. 23–27).

Foolishness

Again there is the comparison between wisdom and foolishness.
Avoid the foolishness of:

Wrath, anger, jealousy

> "Wrath is cruel and anger a torrent,
> But who is able to stand before jealousy?"   (v. 4)

> "The wrath of man does not produce the righteousness of God."
>   (James 1:20)

> "Make no friendship with an angry man,
> And with a furious man do not go."   (22:24)

What havoc comes from envy and jealousy. It was for envy the Jews
delivered Jesus to be crucified. It was for envy Cain slew Abel. It was
for envy Joseph's brothers sold him into slavery.

Wandering

> "Like a bird that wanders from its nest
> Is a man who wanders from his place."   (v. 8)

How important it is to know the boundaries God sets for us, and to
be content within these boundaries. There is the saying, "The grass
is always greener in another field." Dinah wandered from her place,
and was seduced by the prince of Shechem, with such tragic results.
Cain became a wanderer and a fugitive. How dangerous to stray
from the place of our security, the will of God.

The story is told of the Scandinavian, Pierre Ghint, who,
dissatisfied with the village where he lived, left to go in to the
world and seek his fortune. He said goodbye to his friends and his
sweetheart. He wandered for many years until he was an old man,
and never fulfilled his dreams. He returned to his home village,
walked up the street and paused at the house where his sweetheart
once lived. He wondered, and knocked on the door. She answered
it, now an old lady. "Where have I been all my life?" he moaned.

The old lady said, "In my heart, Pierre, in my heart." Where have you been all your life? In His heart; in His heart.

How very important it is to apply the Word of God to our hearts and lives.

Things mentioned in this chapter

Again we see in this chapter such a variety of subjects mentioned:

- Our attitude to the future.
- Our attitude to ourselves.
- Our attitude and behavior toward others.
- The blessings of friendships.
- The importance of diligence.
- The foolishness of anger, wrath and jealousy.
- The unpleasantness of contention.
- The rightness of wisdom.

Then there are the warnings:

- The uncertainty of the future.
- The uselessness of being a wanderer.
- The dangers of continual dissatisfaction.
- The folly of foolishness.

There are the instructions – the "do nots"

- Do not boast about tomorrow.
- Do not boast about yourself.
- Do not forsake your friends.
- Do not be fooled by the "kisses of an enemy" (v. 6).
- Do not be fooled by riches; they don't last forever (v. 24).

There are the encouragements:

- The blessings and effects of good friends, and good counsel.
- Wise children make glad parents.
- Diligence brings its rewards.
- All your needs will be supplied.

Let us embrace truth and reject folly

We embrace truth by obedience and personal application.

- The truth about the future. Let us commit our future ways and works to the Lord, saying, "If the Lord will, I will do this or that, go here or there."
- The truth about ourselves. Acknowledge we are but unprofitable servants. All the successes have been His. All the failures ours.
- The truth about our friends. Let us thank God for them, and pray for them, and if necessary contact them and renew fellowship if it has been neglected.
- Let us resolve to be diligent in all that we do. The instruction to the farmer was "to know the state of your flocks" (v. 23).

    It is good to pause and know the state of what we are responsible for: our business; our work; our marriage; our children; our church; our home. What state are they in? Are we, as the farmer was, encouraged and preparing for the future?
- Let us accept and respond to the circumstances that God allows in our lives for our refining.
- Let us reject self-exaltation, anger, jealousy, unfaithfulness, strife, contention, and wanderings.

I suppose we can sum up these thoughts by a very simple but powerful prayer:

Father God, please, by the aid of Your Holy Spirit, make me more like Jesus.

The verses of an old hymn come to my mind, written over a century ago by Eliza E. Hewitt.

More about Jesus would I know,
More of His grace to others show.
More of His saving fullness see,
More of His love who died for me.

More about Jesus let me learn,
More of His holy will discern,
Spirit of God, my teacher be,
Showing the things of Christ to me.

More about Jesus; in His Word,
Holding communion with my Lord,
Hearing His voice in every line,
Making each faithful saying mine.

More about Jesus; on His throne,
Riches in glory all His own.
More of His kingdom's sure increase;
More of His coming, Prince of Peace.

More, more about Jesus,
More, more about Jesus,
More of His saving fullness see,
More of His love who died for me.

If any of you lacks wisdom, let him ask of God, who gives to all liberally
and without reproach, and it **will** *be given to him* (James 1:5).

Chapter 28

1. The wicked flee when no one pursues, but the righteous are bold as a lion.
2. Because of the transgression of a land, many are its princes; but by a man of understanding and knowledge right will be prolonged.
3. A poor man who oppresses the poor is like a driving rain which leaves no food.
4. Those who forsake the law praise the wicked, but such as keep the law contend with them.
5. Evil men do not understand justice, but those who seek the LORD understand all.
6. Better is the poor who walks in his integrity than one perverse in his ways, though he be rich.
7. Whoever keeps the law is a discerning son, but a companion of gluttons shames his father.
8. One who increases his possessions by usury and extortion gathers it for him who will pity the poor.
9. One who turns away his ear from hearing the law, even his prayer is an abomination.
10. Whoever causes the upright to go astray in an evil way, he himself will fall into his own pit; but the blameless will inherit good.
11. The rich man is wise in his own eyes, but the poor who has understanding searches him out.
12. When the righteous rejoice, there is great glory; but when the wicked arise, men hide themselves.
13. He who covers his sins will not prosper, but whoever confesses and forsakes them will have mercy.
14. Happy is the man who is always reverent, but he who hardens his heart will fall into calamity.
15. Like a roaring lion and a charging bear is a wicked ruler over poor people.
16. A ruler who lacks understanding is a great oppressor, but he who hates covetousness will prolong his days.

17. A man burdened with bloodshed will flee into a pit; let no one help him.

18. Whoever walks blamelessly will be saved, but he who is perverse in his ways will suddenly fall.

19. He who tills his land will have plenty of bread, but he who follows frivolity will have poverty enough!

20. A faithful man will abound with blessings, but he who hastens to be rich will not go unpunished.

21. To show partiality is not good, because for a piece of bread a man will transgress.

22. A man with an evil eye hastens after riches, and does not consider that poverty will come upon him.

23. He who rebukes a man will find more favor afterward than he who flatters with the tongue.

24. Whoever robs his father or his mother, and says, "It is no transgression," the same is companion to a destroyer.

25. He who is of a proud heart stirs up strife, but he who trusts in the LORD will be prospered.

26. He who trusts in his own heart is a fool, but whoever walks wisely will be delivered.

27. He who gives to the poor will not lack, but he who hides his eyes will have many curses.

28. When the wicked arise, men hide themselves; but when they perish, the righteous increase.

People can be categorized by many descriptions: by nationality, religion, status, occupation, class, rich and poor, and so on. However, when you come to the book of Proverbs there are two main descriptions: wicked and righteous. In this chapter their character, attitudes, and behavior are described. The purpose of the contrasts is that hearers and readers should see the folly and consequences of unrighteousness, and the wisdom and blessings of righteousness. We have a choice. Moses set before the children of Israel a choice. He had shown them God's ways of blessings, and also the consequences of disobeying God. He said:

> "I have set before you life and death, blessing and cursing; therefore choose life, that both you and your descendants may live." (Deuteronomy 30:19)

His successor Joshua gave the same challenge at the end of his life as he reminded them of their history, which proved that when they followed and obeyed God they were blessed, and when they disobeyed God they suffered. He had made his own decision and called on them to make theirs. He said:

> "As for me and my house, we will serve the LORD."
>
> (Joshua 24:15)

How true, that the choices we make not only affect our own lives, but the lives of so many others. It is always personal when we come to choosing, isn't it? "As for me, I will . . . " To help us decide, let us look at how the wicked are described, those who make wrong choices.

"The wicked flee when no one pursues" (v. 1)
Conscience makes cowards of us all. Wickedness brings fear. Fear of discovery, fear of the consequences.

The wicked have no real peace

> "There is no peace," says the LORD, "for the wicked."
>
> (Isaiah 48:22)

> "Be sure your sin will find you out."   (Numbers 32:23)

Today we hear how those who committed crimes many years ago are being brought to justice because of the great scientific advances in tracing people by their genetic information, known as DNA.

"Those who forsake the law praise the wicked" (v. 4)
In Romans 1, Paul lists sins which bring God's wrath and says of those who practice them that "not only do they do the same but also approve of those who practice them" (Romans 1:32).

What else can they do? If they condemned them they would condemn themselves. By approving them they approve their own conduct, even though it is sinful.

"Evil men do not understand justice" (v. 5)

They rebel against any law that condemns them. They do not understand justice because they do not, or refuse to, understand righteousness. They do not understand the inevitability of the biblical pronouncement, "whatever a man sows, that he will also reap" (Galatians 6:7).

Their prayers are not heard

> "One who turns away his ear from hearing the law,
> Even his prayer is an abomination."   (v. 9)

David said:

> "If I regard iniquity in my heart,
> The Lord will not hear."   (Psalm 66:18)

How tragic for God not to hear us. God will always hear the prayer of the penitent, those who want to acknowledge and turn from wickedness.

Calamity faces the wicked

> "He who hardens his heart will fall into calamity."   (v. 14)

Sin hardens, and sin pays wages: "the wages of sin is death" (Romans 6:23) and in verse 18 of this chapter:

> "He who is perverse in his ways will suddenly fall."

And in verse 13:

> "He who covers his sins will not prosper."

Calamity; fall; not prosper – who wants to choose these consequences?

Thank God there is an answer for the wicked; and all of us were at one time in that category:

> "*All* have sinned and fall short of the glory of God."
>
> (Romans 3:23, emphasis added)

What great news the gospel is. How Paul loved declaring:

> "This is a faithful saying and worthy of all acceptance, that Christ
> Jesus came into the world to save sinners, of whom I am chief."
>
> (1 Timothy 1:15)

Thank God for verse 13 in this chapter of Proverbs:

> "Whoever confesses and forsakes them [his sins] will have mercy."

Oh, the grace of God that transforms wicked people into righteous
people! If you are a Christian, reflect on what you were, and what
you are now. John Newton knew this grace and wrote the hymn:

> "Amazing grace! How sweet the sound
> That saved a wretch like me."

If you are not a Christian, you can be:

> "Whoever calls on the name of the LORD shall be saved."
>
> (Romans 10:13)

I was once preaching in the town hall in a small town in New
Zealand. Half way through the message a Maori man at the back
shouted to me, "I want to be saved now, what can I do?" I said,
"Whoever calls on the name of the LORD shall be saved." He cried,
"Lord, save me," and sat down saved. From that day till the day he
died lived for God.

Yes, when we acknowledge our sins, repent of our sins, turn from
our sins, believe that Jesus died for our sins, rose again from the
dead, and are ready to yield our lives to His Lordship, the great
miracle takes place. All the past is forgiven and forgotten. His Spirit
indwells us to empower us. His Word is available to teach us. His
church ready to receive us. We have a new relationship: God is our
Father, Jesus is our Lord, the Holy Spirit is indwelling our lives.

> "that if you confess with your mouth the Lord Jesus and believe in
> your heart that God has raised Him from the dead, you will be

saved. For with the heart one believes unto righteousness, and with the mouth confession is made unto salvation."

(Romans 10:9–10)

Thank God for such glorious, life-changing news. Amen?

Righteousness

What a contrast between the wicked and the righteous. Here is the description of the righteous in this chapter:

"The righteous are bold as a lion" (v. 1)
They have both courage and confidence. When you do what is right, God is with you:

"If God is for us, who can be against us?"   (Romans 8:31)

There is boldness because of a clear conscience. There is trust and confidence in God to give the strength and ability to stand for that which is right.

Righteous people are reverent and happy

"Happy is the man who is always reverent."   (v. 14)

The key to righteousness is to fear God; that is, to reverence Him. If we truly fear Him we will hate evil and love righteousness. These are two good words: "reverent" and "happy." Verse 12 speaks of the righteous rejoicing:

"When the righteous rejoice, there is great glory."

Righteous people are not sad and morbid, and falsely pious. They have joy in living for God:

"The joy of the LORD is your strength."   (Nehemiah 8:10)

Righteous people hate covetousness

Righteous people will be contented. They are not covetous or envious. They are confident in the promise, that:

> "My God shall supply all your need according to His riches in glory by Christ Jesus."   (Philippians 4:19)

Righteous people can say with Paul:

> "I have learned in whatever state I am, to be content."
> (Philippians 4:11)

When he wrote to Timothy he said:

> "Godliness with contentment is great gain."   (1 Timothy 6:6)

There is also a another wonderful promise in verse 16:

> "He who hates covetousness will prolong his days."

Righteous people know God's deliverance

> "Whoever walks blamelessly will be saved."   (v. 18)

How many times this is illustrated in Scripture. David was delivered from all the murderous plots of King Saul. Daniel was delivered in the lions' den and his friends from the fiery furnace. Paul and Silas were delivered from prison. Many others of course have been martyred for righteousness sake, and are being killed today for standing for righteousness. Death for them is no tragedy, but an immediate entrance into God's presence with the martyrs' crown awaiting them.

Righteous people are faithful

> "A faithful man will abound with blessings."   (v. 20)

They are dependable. They keep their word. Faithfulness is an evidence of righteousness. Solomon speaks elsewhere about faithful people:

> "A faithful ambassador brings health."   (13:17)

> "A faithful witness does not lie."   (14:5)

> "Like the cold of snow in time of harvest
> Is a faithful messenger to those who send him,
> For he refreshes the soul of his masters."   (25:13)

A faithful man would rather be poor and honest, that rich and unrighteous:

> "Better is the poor who walks in his integrity,
> Than one perverse in his ways, though he be rich."   (v. 6)

Righteous people care for the poor

> "He who gives to the poor will not lack."   (v. 27)

We are continually reminded to consider the poor. Righteous people care for them. The majority of people on earth are poor. Jesus knew what it was like to be poor:

> "Though he was rich, yet for your sakes He became poor, that you through His poverty might become rich."   (2 Corinthians 8:9)

A person may be poor, yet if a Christian, possesses the greatest riches anyone can have: eternal life; peace with God; a certain hope for the future; an incorruptible inheritance that never fades away. Paul could say of himself:

> "as poor, yet making many rich; as having nothing, and yet possessing all things."   (2 Corinthians 6:10)

How glaring is the contrast between the righteous and the unrighteous in this chapter. The unrighteous:

- Are wicked.
- Are evil.
- Are gluttons.
- Have hardened hearts.
- Charge excessive interest.
- Forsake the law.
- Cover sin.
- Are murderers and thieves.
- Rob their parents.
- Show partiality.
- Are flatterers.
- Are proud.
- Are foolish

The righteous:

- Keep the law.
- Are diligent.
- Are generous.
- Are faithful,
- Fear God.
- Are blameless.
- Walk wisely.
- Consider the poor.

Surely when presented with the virtues of righteousness, and the vices of unrighteousness, the choice should be easy to make. Let us pray and witness by our lives that we are changed. Only one message can give the answer: the gospel of Jesus Christ. All who receive the message become new creations in Christ Jesus:

> "Old things have passed away; behold, all things have become new."   (2 Corinthians 5:17)

Oh, the transforming power of the grace of God. Paul reminded us:

> "... not having my own righteousness, which is from the law, but that which is through faith in Christ, the righteousness which is from God by faith."   (Philippians 3:9)

As in other chapters, one is amazed at the subjects and people mentioned in twenty-eight verses: princes and rulers; rich and poor; oppressors and murderers; extortion; partiality; generosity and meanness; abominations and blessings. It is always refreshing when our attention is drawn to the Lord, as we will now see.

The Lord is the forgiver of sins

"He who covers his sins will not prosper,
But whoever confesses and forsakes them will have mercy."

(v. 13)

The same truth is proclaimed by John:

"If we confess our sins, He is faithful and just to forgive us our sins and to cleanse us from all unrighteousness." (1 John 1:9)

As we read God's Word we are sometimes convicted of sin. How wonderful is His mercy and grace to forgive when we uncover; that is, confess. That is how sin leaves our lives, by confession and repentance.

The Lord is a rewarder of those who seek him

"Those who seek the LORD understand all." (v. 5)

So much happens in life which we cannot understand, but when we seek the Lord, pray to Him, wait on Him and for Him, then the promise is fulfilled: we get understanding. Remember that was David's experience. He was seeking to live for God and please Him, yet he had so much trouble, while the wicked seemed to prosper and have fewer problems. Then he said:

"When I thought how to understand this,
It was too painful for me –
Until I went into the sanctuary of God;
Then I understood their end."

(Psalm 73:16–17, emphasis added)

He sought the Lord and got understanding. The wicked's prosperity was only temporary, there was an end. God is not obligated to give us a reason for all that happens in our lives, but as we seek Him we are assured:

> "that all things work together for good to those who love God, to those who are called according to His purpose."   (Romans 8:28)

Have you unanswered questions? Are there circumstances you do not understand? Take them to the Lord and do what David exhorted us to do:

> "Commit your way to the LORD,
> Trust also in Him,
> And He shall bring it to pass...
> Rest in the LORD, and wait patiently for Him;
> Do not fret because of him who prospers in his way."
>
> (Psalm 37:5, 7)

Commit; trust; rest; wait ... you will understand.

"He who trusts in the LORD will be prospered" (v. 25)

All who totally commit their lives to the Lord, seeking to live for Him and please Him, will know the truth of His Word:

> "No good thing will He withhold
> From those who walk uprightly."   (Psalm 84:11)

How does one assess prosperity? Is it having riches? They disappear. Real prosperity is having what no money or riches can buy, that which is eternal. No wealth can give true peace and happiness as we have already seen. Look up. "In My Father's house are many mansions" (John 14:2). Thank God for true prosperity, fellowship with God and His beloved Son Jesus; the indwelling presence of the Helper, the Holy Spirit with all His gifts and fruit, the love of God, His abundant mercy, and all His "exceeding great and precious promises."

Conclusion

There is so much in this chapter for which to *praise* Him – so praise Him; truths to *apply* – so let's apply them; matters to *pray* for – so let's pray; things to *commit* to Him – so let's commit; things to *trust* Him for – so let's trust Him. Let's pray for the salvation of people, wicked people to become righteous people.

---

*If any of you lacks wisdom, let him ask of God, who gives to all liberally and without reproach, and it **will** be given to him* (James 1:5).

Chapter 29

1. He who is often rebuked, and hardens his neck, will suddenly be destroyed, and that without remedy.
2. When the righteous are in authority, the people rejoice; but when a wicked man rules, the people groan.
3. Whoever loves wisdom makes his father rejoice, but a companion of harlots wastes his wealth.
4. The king establishes the land by justice, but he who receives bribes overthrows it.
5. A man who flatters his neighbor spreads a net for his feet.
6. By transgression an evil man is snared, but the righteous sings and rejoices.
7. The righteous considers the cause of the poor, but the wicked does not understand such knowledge.
8. Scoffers set a city aflame, but wise men turn away wrath.
9. If a wise man contends with a foolish man, whether the fool rages or laughs, there is no peace.
10. The bloodthirsty hate the blameless, but the upright seek his well-being.
11. A fool vents all his feelings, but a wise man holds them back.
12. If a ruler pays attention to lies, all his servants become wicked.
13. The poor man and the oppressor have this in common: the LORD gives light to the eyes of both.
14. The king who judges the poor with truth, his throne will be established forever.
15. The rod and rebuke give wisdom, but a child left to himself brings shame to his mother.
16. When the wicked are multiplied, transgression increases; but the righteous will see their fall.
17. Correct your son, and he will give you rest; yes, he will give delight to your soul.
18. Where there is no revelation, the people cast off restraint; but happy is he who keeps the law.

19. A servant will not be corrected by mere words; for though he understands, he will not respond.
20. Do you see a man hasty in his words? There is more hope for a fool than for him.
21. He who pampers his servant from childhood will have him as a son in the end.
22. An angry man stirs up strife, and a furious man abounds in transgression.
23. A man's pride will bring him low, but the humble in spirit will retain honor.
24. Whoever is a partner with a thief hates his own life; he swears to tell the truth, but reveals nothing.
25. The fear of man brings a snare, but whoever trusts in the LORD shall be safe.
26. Many seek the ruler's favor, but justice for man comes from the LORD.
27. An unjust man is an abomination to the righteous, and he who is upright in the way is an abomination to the wicked.

When the Bible was written, it was not originally divided into chapters, although chapters are a wonderful help. In this chapter, as in others, there is no introduction, but just a clear statement of facts. Here at the beginning we are shown the folly of ignoring correction.

Ignoring correction

"He who is often rebuked, and hardens his neck,
Will suddenly be destroyed, and that without remedy."　　(v. 1)

Let's face it, most of us don't like to be rebuked. We don't like being shown our faults. People can correct us with a variety of reasons and attitudes: judgmental, condemning, critical, but also some do it out of loving concern, and desiring the best for us. That is how it is with God. When God rebukes and corrects, it is for our blessing. When God does it, it should have our total attention, even though it is uncomfortable. The writer to the Hebrews said:

"My son, do not despise the chastening of the LORD,
Nor be discouraged when you are rebuked by Him."

(Hebrews 12:5)

It is a dangerous thing to ignore God's rebukes. In the very first chapter in Proverbs we are exhorted:

> "Turn at my rebuke;
> Surely I will pour out my spirit on you."   (1:23)

When we do respond we are blessed, when we don't we are in danger, because our hearts get hardened. Sometimes, because of this, some are "suddenly cut off." What is the story behind "some"? Not all, of course, but some sudden deaths. As we continue in Proverbs we may discover things which displease God, things we are doing which are not right. Then the message is, obey God promptly, recognize it is His love for you behind the rebuke, and respond immediately.

Rulers and those in authority

Included in this chapter we are shown the blessing of righteous rulers, and the dangers of wrong ones.

Righteous rulers

> "When the righteous are in authority, the people rejoice;
> But when a wicked man rules, the people groan."   (v. 2)

How true. Rulers affect the whole nation either for good or evil. We have seen plenty of examples of that in our lifetime. That is why we should obey the word:

> "Therefore I exhort first of all that supplications, prayers, intercessions, and giving of thanks be made for all men, for kings and *all* who are in authority, that we may lead a quiet and peaceable life in all godliness and reverence." (1 Timothy 2:1–2, emphasis added)

We should pray that they will be righteous. We should pray that they will be just:

> "The king establishes the land by justice."   (v. 4)

We should pray that leaders will not be affected by lies:

> "If a ruler pays attention to lies,
> All his servants become wicked."   (v. 12)

Rulers should have open hearts to the poor:

> "The king who judges the poor with truth,
> His throne will be established forever."   (v. 14)

Rulers need to discern the characters of people who seek their favor:

> "Many seek the ruler's favor."   (v. 26)

Many times the desire for favor is for personal interest, and not for national interest.

Children and family

In this chapter we go not only to the throne, but also to the family. This has been a recurring theme in Proverbs, and rightly so, because the family is so vitally important. We have previously been encouraged as far as children are concerned:

> "Train up a child in the way he should go,
> And when he is old he will not depart from it."   (22:6)

What a responsibility and privilege for parents to bring up their children in God's ways. What joy it brings to parents when their children live right, and what sorrow when they don't. How true verse 3 is:

> "Whoever loves wisdom makes his father rejoice."

Loving wisdom is loving God and living in reverence of Him, manifested by seeking to obey Him. How good it is for children when their parents have been examples of loving God. Remember when Paul wrote to Timothy he said:

"From childhood you have known the Holy Scriptures, which are able to make you wise for salvation through faith which is in Christ Jesus." (2 Timothy 3:15)

We are also reminded in this chapter of the importance of correction. These days such standards are not only ridiculed, but forbidden by law. But what has it produced? Crime statistics among children and teenagers are staggering. Verse 15 tells us:

"The rod and rebuke give wisdom,
But a child left to himself brings shame to his mother."

Right correction brings wisdom, the wisdom of knowing good and evil, and the consequences of doing wrong. As we have seen, wise children bring joy, children left undisciplined bring shame. Not only does right correction produce wisdom, but it gives rest and joy to the parents:

"Correct your son, and he will give you rest;
Yes, he will give delight to your soul." (v. 17)

The rest given to parents is the freedom from anxiety and worry about their children. There is also the rest and confidence that as you continually pray for them, the Lord will hear and answer your prayers for their protection and wellbeing. Sure, it takes time, but what an investment. I have five children, all of them married, sixteen grandchildren, and two great grandchildren, who are prayed for by name every day. What a joy and privilege, and how faithful God is in answering prayer, bringing us rest and joy and faith for their future. As John wrote:

"I have no greater joy than to hear that my children walk in truth."
(3 John 4)

Proverbs is the book of wisdom, and how profitable it is to read and have your children read its great truths and advice.

Wisdom

We are reminded in this chapter of how wise people act and react.
A wise man will sometimes contend with the foolish:

> "If a wise man contends with a foolish man,
> Whether the fool rages or laughs, there is no peace." (v. 9)

The foolish have sometimes to be confronted with their folly, but if the counsel and advice is rejected by anger or mockery, there is no satisfactory result, but he has been warned. Wise people turn away wrath:

> "Scoffers set a city aflame,
> But wise men turn away wrath." (v. 8)

Scoffing and mockery is destructive but wise people bring wisdom and sense into a situation:

> "An angry man stirs up strife,
> And a furious man abounds in transgression." (v. 22)

Wise people discipline their feelings:

> "A fool vents all his feelings,
> But a wise man holds them back." (v. 11)

A fool does does not control his spirit, but a wise man knows restraint. What warning is given in verse 20:

> "Do you see a man hasty in his words?
> There is more hope for a fool than for him."

The main reason for all strife and contention is pride:

> "By pride comes nothing but strife." (13:10)

How devastating that is, as verse 23 tells us:

> "A man's pride will bring him low,
> But the humble in spirit will retain honor."

May I remind you again of the importance of praying these truths into our lives. Do you have children? Perhaps some are still young and at home, or perhaps they are older and have left home. As we prayed for those in authority, let us pray for our children and grandchildren the things we have seen in this chapter. Pray:

- That we as parents will be a good example.
- That as children they will know the Scriptures.
- For God's wisdom in applying the right rebuke and correction.
- That our children will be wise.
- That they will bring joy and not shame.
- For the salvation of those who do not know the Lord.
- For any who have gone away from the Lord, that they will return to the God of their fathers.
- That they will be kept by the power of God.

We have been continually reminded in this book of how essential it is to have wisdom, the wisdom which God gives. We have seen how much rulers and those in authority need wisdom. We have been also been reminded how much parents need wisdom in bringing up their families, and, also, how much our children need wisdom. How reliant we are on God. Three times in this chapter Solomon mentions God. First:

> "The poor man and the oppressor have this in common;
> The LORD gives light to the eyes of both."   (v. 13)

God makes available to all the capacity to know Him. He "gives light to every man coming into the world" (John 1:9). The important thing is what we do with Jesus. He is the true light. He came to shine in human darkness. He is the Light of the world. The offer of salvation and light is to whoever will respond, whether rich or poor. All stand before God as the same:

> "All have sinned and fall short of the glory of God."
>
> (Romans 6:23)

All are the same, whether oppressors or poor men. We can have the light of life by receiving Him into our lives. He is the giver of light, of eyes to see, the author of salvation. We need not walk in darkness, but walk in the light.

Secondly, there is salvation and safety in the Lord. Verse 25 tells us:

> "The fear of man brings a snare,
> But whoever trusts in the LORD shall be safe."

What a promise! When we trust the Lord for our salvation, and trust Him day by day for His direction, we are safe. Whatever faces us, He will see us through. Safety is of the Lord. He is absolutely righteous. All His ways are just.

The third mention of the Lord in this chapter tells us:

> "Many seek the ruler's favor,
> But justice for man comes from the LORD." (v. 26)

How wonderful is the Lord: He gives light; He is trustworthy; He is just. The choices we make shape our lives, making us the people we are. There are different people mentioned in this chapter. There are:

- The righteous.
- Those who love wisdom.
- Those who trust the Lord.

Others that are mentioned are:

- Fornicators.
- Thieves.
- Flatterers.
- Evil and wicked men.
- Scorners and fools.
- Bloodthirsty, unjust and deceitful men.
- Angry and proud men.

How wonderful is the grace of God, the grace that makes evil men righteous, the grace that makes foolish people wise people, that mercy which makes people change from trusting in themselves to trusting in the Lord. The Lord is the giver of "every good gift and every perfect gift" (James 1:17). He gives us revelation of Himself and His will. He gives joy and happiness in obeying and following Him. Verse 18 tells us:

> "Where there is no revelation, the people cast off restraint;
> But happy is he who keeps the law."

How much we need revelation, insight from the Lord. We need His Word, His teaching, His guidance, His encouragement, His direction, His corrections. We need to know His law, His Word, to be able to keep it. Where people are ignorant of His ways, or refuse to follow them, they cast off restraint. They do their own thing. We read in a previous chapter:

> "There is a way that seems right to a man,
> But its end is the way of death."   (14:12)

What a warning! Again what a choice: my way or God's way. We need constraint and we need restraint. When there is no fear of God, no vision, no obedience to His revelation, people cast off, discard, refuse God's restraint, His protection, with such dire consequences:

> "The wages of sin is death, but the gift of God is eternal life in Christ Jesus our Lord."   (Romans 6:23)

Obeying God brings true happiness. It is not some joyless existence. Solomon encourages us in this throughout Proverbs:

> "Happy is the man who finds wisdom."   (3:13)

> "Happy are all who retain her [wisdom]."   (3:18)

> "He who has mercy on the poor, happy is he."   (14:21)

> "Whoever trusts in the LORD, happy is he."   (16:20)

> "Happy is the man who is always reverent."   (28:14)

> "Happy is he who keeps the law."   (29:18)

There is no joy on earth like the joy of the Lord, the joy and happiness that comes from Him. Nehemiah said: "The joy of the LORD is your strength" (Nehemiah 8:10).

Application

As we come to the end of another chapter in Proverbs let us apply or reconfirm its teachings:

- Let us not ignore the rebukes and corrections God gives us.
- Let us pray for leadership, those in authority in our land.
- Let us seek to be good and godly parents, influencing the lives of our children for God by being examples, praying for them and with them continually.
- Let us continually ask God for His wisdom.
- Let us guard what we say, not merely venting our own feelings, or being hasty with our words.
- Let us choose to be righteous.
- Let our lives be governed by revelation, teaching from His Word, obeying His constraints and restraints.
- Let us trust the Lord, with that guaranteed safety when we do.
- Let us ask Him for His help, make our resolves, and trust Him for His enabling.

If any of you lacks wisdom, let him ask of God, who gives to all liberally and without reproach, and it **will** *be given to him* (James 1:5).

Chapter 30

1. The words of Agur the son of Jakeh, his utterance. This man declared to Ithiel – to Ithiel and Ucal:
2. Surely I am more stupid than any man, and do not have the understanding of a man.
3. I neither learned wisdom nor have knowledge of the Holy One.
4. Who has ascended into heaven, or descended? Who has gathered the wind in His fists? Who has bound the waters in a garment? Who has established all the ends of the earth? What is His name, and what is His Son's name, if you know?
5. Every word of God is pure; He is a shield to those who put their trust in Him.
6. Do not add to His words, lest He rebuke you, and you be found a liar.
7. Two things I request of You (Deprive me not before I die):
8. Remove falsehood and lies far from me; give me neither poverty nor riches – feed me with the food allotted to me;
9. Lest I be full and deny You, and say, "Who is the LORD?" Or lest I be poor and steal, and profane the name of my God.
10. Do not malign a servant to his master, lest he curse you, and you be found guilty.
11. There is a generation that curses its father, and does not bless its mother.
12. There is a generation that is pure in its own eyes, yet is not washed from its filthiness.
13. There is a generation – oh, how lofty are their eyes! And their eyelids are lifted up.
14. There is a generation whose teeth are like swords, and whose fangs are like knives, to devour the poor from off the earth, and the needy from among men.
15. The leech has two daughters – Give and Give! There are three things that are never satisfied, four never say, "Enough!":

16. The grave, the barren womb, the earth that is not satisfied with water – and the fire never says, "Enough!"
17. The eye that mocks his father, and scorns obedience to his mother, the ravens of the valley will pick it out, and the young eagles will eat it.
18. There are three things which are too wonderful for me, yes, four which I do not understand:
19. The way of an eagle in the air, the way of a serpent on a rock, the way of a ship in the midst of the sea, and the way of a man with a virgin.
20. This is the way of an adulterous woman: she eats and wipes her mouth, and says, "I have done no wickedness."
21. For three things the earth is perturbed, yes, for four it cannot bear up:
22. For a servant when he reigns, a fool when he is filled with food,
23. A hateful woman when she is married, and a maidservant who succeeds her mistress.
24. There are four things which are little on the earth, but they are exceedingly wise:
25. The ants are a people not strong, yet they prepare their food in the summer;
26. The rock badgers are a feeble folk, yet they make their homes in the crags;
27. The locusts have no king, yet they all advance in ranks;
28. The spider skillfully grasps with its hands, and it is in kings' palaces.
29. There are three things which are majestic in pace, yes, four which are stately in walk:
30. A lion, which is mighty among beasts and does not turn away from any;
31. A greyhound, a male goat also, and a king whose troops are with him.
32. If you have been foolish in exalting yourself, or if you have devised evil, put your hand on your mouth.
33. For as the churning of milk produces butter, and wringing the nose produces blood, so the forcing of wrath produces strife.

The last two chapters of Proverbs are an appendix. Nothing certain is known of the writers, but enough to know that "holy men of God spoke as they were moved by the Holy Spirit" (2 Peter 1:21). Agur was obviously a wise man, but like all wise people he realized how much he did not know and described himself as stupid. He is sharing his thoughts with two friends, perhaps his students, and humbly confesses before them his lack of understanding and limited knowledge of God, whom he describes as "the Holy One" (v. 3).

Like other wise men before and after him he is conscious of his needs. Jacob declared, "I am not worthy of the least of all [Your] mercies" (Genesis 32:10); Isaiah cries, "Woe is me, for I am undone" (Isaiah 6:5); Paul admits, "I am the least of the apostles" (1 Corinthians 15:9); Peter says to Jesus, "Depart from me, for I am a sinful man" (Luke 5:8). In his contemplations of God, Agur is full of questions. He wonders at creation, and asks: "Who has ascended . . . descended . . . gathered the wind . . . bound the waters . . . established all the ends of the earth? . . . What is His name, and what is His Son's name?" (v. 4).

He knew, as we do, that it was *God*:

> "In the beginning God created the heavens and the earth."
>
> (Genesis 1:1)

We agree with the writer of Hebrews:

> "By faith we understand that the worlds were framed by the word of God."   (Hebrews 11:3)

We know the answer to the question, "What is His Son's name?":

> "You shall call His name JESUS, for He will save His people from their sins."   (Matthew 1:21)

He descended and He ascended and is now at the right hand of the majesty on high, having obtained for us redemption through His precious blood. He not only declares the wonders of God, and His works, but the wonders of His Word.

> "*Every* word of God is pure."   (v. 5, emphasis added)

Don't add to it, and don't subtract from it. That word reveals to us God's protection for us:

> "He is a shield to those who put their trust Him."   (v. 5)

What an introduction to the chapter.

A wise man's prayer

He is a searcher for truth so he asks:

"Remove falsehood and lies far from me."   (v. 8)

He has no desire for material prosperity:

"Give me neither poverty nor riches."   (v. 8)

He trusts God to teach him and asks:

"Feed me with the food allotted to me."   (v. 8)

Would you like to borrow these prayers? Not, "Who wants to be a millionaire?" but, "Who wants to know God and the contentment that comes from Him?"

The generations

He goes on to describe particular generations, which I suppose are descriptive of all generations. They certainly all apply to our present generation. Verses 11–14 describe generations that:

- Disrespect their parents. Unfortunately so many children have not found their parents to be good examples, but the command is constant, "Honor your father and your mother" (Exodus 20:12).
- Are self-righteous. They therefore have no sense of need of God, and no sense of sin.
- Are proud.
- Are violent. They have no pity or concern for the poor and needy.

When the disciples asked Jesus what conditions would be like at the end of the age, all these things were included. Praise God for the gospel of Jesus Christ which can change people, restoring obedience to God and parents, realizing total dependence of God and walking humbly with Him, making people gentle, kind and considerate. The gospel is "the power of God to salvation for everyone who believes" (Romans 1:16). There is complete satisfaction in God.

Things that are never satisfied

The quest of all mankind is satisfaction. Many seek it and never find it, and will never find it apart from Jesus Christ. He refers to a leech which is never satisfied. A leech is a blood-sucking annelid found in Palestine which fastens on to the tongue or nostril of a horse, clings to its victim and is never satisfied. It is all give, give. Verse 16 tells us the following are never satisfied:

- The grave – there is never a time when people cease to die.
- The barren womb – a childless wife is never fulfilled until she has had a baby.
- The earth with water – dry ground will absorb and keep on absorbing.
- Fire – it will keep destroying anything that is available and is flammable.

Thank God again that there is satisfaction in Jesus Christ, as the old chorus puts it:

"Now none but Christ can satisfy,
None other name for me,
There's life and peace and lasting joy.
Lord Jesus, found in Thee."   (Author unknown)

For the Christian the grave has no victory. Whatever our circumstances, we can accept from God, trust Him, believe in Him, rejoice in Him.

Learning from things

How much Agur learned from observation, things that to him were wonderful, although he could not fully understand. He mentions some of these things in verse 19:

"The way of an eagle in the air"

The eagle is fascinating, soaring high, flying so effortless in the heavens. Isaiah said:

> "Those who wait on the LORD
> Shall renew their strength;
> They shall mount up with wings like eagles." (Isaiah 40:31)

It is wonderful that we can seek those things which are above where Christ sits, not being earth-bound, but Christ-centered.

"The way of a serpent on a rock"

On a rock no trace is left. It reminds us that we have an enemy, "the old serpent," but through His death and resurrection Jesus has defeated His power. How wonderful that in Christ we have the ability to resist him steadfastly, so that no trace is left in our lives of his work.

"The way of a ship in the midst of the sea"

The ship plows its way through the waves, driven by the wind taking it to its destination. Thank God for the wind, the power of the Holy Spirit to empower us in our lives and take us to our heavenly harbor.

"The way of a man with a virgin"

Because of the verse that follows, this implies sexual immorality. Agur said it was difficult to understand the folly of it. The girl would lose something she could never regain. How would she explain when she got married? Sin cannot be hidden. Without any pangs of conscience she can say, "I have done no wickedness" (v. 20). Yes, it is truly difficult to understand. Again thank God for His forgiveness. For example, recall Jesus' response when a woman caught in the act of adultery was brought to Him. When she acknowledged Him as Lord, He said, "Neither do I condemn you; go and sin no more" (John 8:11).

As Agur learned from these things let us learn too.

In Agur's observations on life not only has he noticed that there are things which are unsearchable, but there are also things which are intolerable; things which perturb, causing problems. He mentions four in verses 22–23:

"A servant when he reigns"

History has proved that people of lowly birth can rise to places of power and authority. For example Joseph, who became a ruler in Egypt. There are also servants who have come to prominence and become tyrants. They misused power.

"A fool when he is filled with food"

The fool is no doubt filled with drink too, and through his excesses adversely affects others. Remember Belshazzar's feast, given over to appetite and idolatry, which was shattered by God's writing on the wall and pronouncing His verdict on the king's life.

"A hateful woman when she is married"

Such a woman is quarrelsome, bitter and a troublemaker. That sure is perturbing! Remember Herod's wife who was responsible for having John the Baptist beheaded, or Jezebel with all her hatred for God's prophet.

"A maidservant who succeeds her mistress"

This is similar to the first thing mentioned, a servant when he reigns. Our thoughts go to Hagar, who mocked her mistress Sarah when she became pregnant by Abraham. Jane Seymour and Anne Boleyn, who became wives of Henry VIII, were servants before they became queens.

The message is, avoid these things if possible at all costs. They spell trouble.

Four little things

Drawing from his observations from nature, Agur calls on us to learn from insects and animals. During the ministry of Jesus, He often drew attention to nature to teach certain lessons. He mentioned the lily of the field, a mustard seed, a corn of wheat, tares, birds of the air, foxes etc. Agur speaks of things which were not only little but were also wise.

The ants (v. 25)

What wonderful insects. Agur said, "they are a people not strong," but exceedingly wise. The main lesson they teach us is the importance of taking advantage of *now*, and to prepare for the future.

Of ourselves we are not strong. Paul could say:

> "For when I am weak, then I am strong."   (2 Corinthians 12:10)

David said:

> "I am weak today, though anointed king."   (2 Samuel 3:39)
>
> "Have mercy on me, O LORD, for I am weak."   (Psalm 6:2)

We must continually realize that without Him we can do nothing, but that the Lord is our strength. Yet the ants prepare for the future. The greatest preparation is our preparation to meet God, laying up treasure in heaven. Using every opportunity now while there is time. What a lesson. Be wise. Prepare for the future.

The rock badgers (v. 26)

Like the ants, the rock badgers also are not strong, and are described as feeble. What they lack in strength they make up for in wisdom. They make their homes in the rocks. Here they take refuge from attacks. They do not deliberately expose themselves to danger. Thank God we have a Rock, a place and person of protection. As the old hymn describes it:

> "Rock of Ages, cleft for me,
> Let me hide myself in Thee;
> Let the water and the blood,
> From Thy riven side which flowed,
> Be of sin the double cure –
> Cleanse me from its guilt and power."
>
> (Richard Redhead, 1820–1901)

David cried:

> "He only is my *rock* and my salvation;
> He is my defense;
> I shall not be greatly moved."   (Psalm 62:2, emphasis added)

How great is our God. What security. What safety. What salvation.

The locusts (v. 27)

The locusts have no king, yet they advance in ranks. They are disciplined to go forth in unity. It was said of the sons of Zebulun that they were men "who could keep ranks" (1 Chronicles 13:33). Therein was their strength.

> "Behold, how good and how pleasant it is
> For brethren to dwell together in unity!"   (Psalm 133:1)

There is strength in unity.

The spider (v. 28)

Spiders also are exceedingly wise. They have the wisdom of patience and perseverance and untiring labor. They use what they have in their own hands. Remember Moses, sensing his own weakness, was asked of God, "What is that in your hand?" (Exodus 4:2). It was a staff which God used mightily. God help us to use what we have, and like the spider, to be wise, to be diligent, to be patient, to be persistent. He can open doors even to palaces.

What wonderful lessons. No doubt we have heard about these many times before, but the important thing is, how are we *now*? Let's summarise the lessons:

- *The ant*:
  > "Be even more diligent to make your call and election sure."
  >   (2 Peter 1:10)

  > "Redeeming the time, because the days are evil."
  >   (Ephesians 5:16)

- *The rock:*

  "He *only* is my rock and my salvation."

  (Psalm 62:2, emphasis added)

- *The rock badger:*

  "Nor is there salvation in any other, for there is no other name under heaven given among men by which we must be saved."

  (Acts 4:12)

- *The locust:*

  "That they all may be one ... that the world may believe that You sent Me."   (John 17:21)

- *The spider:*

  "See, I have set before you an open door, and no one can shut it."   (Revelation 3:8)

  "And let the beauty of the LORD our God be upon us,
  And establish the work of our hands for us;
  Yes, establish the work of our hands."   (Psalm 90:17)

God's majestic creatures

So far in this chapter we have been considering:

- Things which are never satisfied.
- Things which are too wonderful for Agur, and us.
- Things which perturb the heart.
- Things which are little but wise.

Now we look to God's creatures; things which are majestic in bearing.

The lion (v. 30)

The lion is the king of the animals, "mighty among beasts." The lion is used in Scripture to speak of boldness:

"The righteous are bold as a lion."   (28:1)

It speaks of security. "He [Israel] lies down as a lion" (Numbers 24:9) – unafraid. Jesus is described as "the Lion of the tribe of Judah" (Revelation 5:5) – majestic. There is a dignity about the lion, so there should be a dignity in our Christian living. Not a dignity prompted by pride, but a dignity because of the fact that we are representatives here on earth, of Jesus – King of kings and Lord of lords. We are the sons and daughters of the living God. Paul exhorts us to "walk worthy of the Lord, fully pleasing Him" (Colossians 1:10), and again to "walk worthy of the calling with which you were called" (Ephesians 4:1). The Lord, when here on earth was so dignified; dignified and the friend of sinners. Jesus was so dignified that:

> "when He was reviled, did not revile in return; when He suffered, He did not threaten, but committed Himself to Him who judges righteously."   (1 Peter 2:23)

What an example of majesty and dignity!

The greyhound (v. 31)
This passage is interpreted in different ways in different versions. It is described as "a strutting cock," and "a war horse." However, we will stick to the greyhound. There is also a dignity in its walk. It keeps its head high, it is highly trained, it goes with such speed at its master's instructions. There is a gracefulness about it. So we should be well-trained, and quick to respond to whatever our Master tells us to do, or where He wants us to go. Going with willingness, dignity and graciousness.

The male goat (v. 31)
This is the picture of a male goat at the head of a herd, being their guide and protector. Here, too, there is a dignity about his position. The herd feel safe with him there. What privilege God gives us to help others; sometimes to lead them, sometimes to protect them. The male goat will protect the herd from unlawful intruders. It is watchful and caring.

A king whose troops are with him (v. 31)
Everyone loves a parade! There is something awe-inspiring about

troops in formation, smartly uniformed and disciplined. Here is manifest authority and submission to it. Everyone is in line, no one wanting to be seen, part of a unit, all in step. A display of men and weapons of war, prepared to fight. I was a major in the army in World War II. I remember the thrill of a parade, with the band playing, standards waving, everyone neat, the marching, the shouted orders, the immediate response. We were representatives of His Majesty's forces. Here, too, there was a dignity, with discipline. But the greatest is still to be seen. Here it is:

> "I saw heaven opened, and behold, a white horse. And He who sat on him was called Faithful and True, and in righteousness He judges and makes war. His eyes were like a flame of fire, and on His head were many crowns. He had a name written that no one knew but Himself. He was clothed with a robe dipped in blood, and His name is called The Word of God. And the armies of heaven, clothed in fine linen, white and clean, followed Him on white horses.
>
> Now out of His mouth goes a sharp sword, that with it He should strike the nations. And He Himself will rule them with a rod of iron. He Himself treads the winepress of the fierceness and wrath of Almighty God."
>
> And He has His robe and on His thigh a name written:
>
> KING OF KINGS AND LORD OF LORDS."
>
> (Revelation 19:11–16)

Now that is a parade! Majestic, dignified, awesome.

Conclusion

What a chapter, written by a man who described himself as "more stupid than any man" (v. 2). What a range of subjects; what observations; what lessons. Lessons from people; lessons from insects; lessons from animals; lessons from creation. The greatness of God, the greatness of His creation. What a Word! Every word very pure. What things to avoid and also what things to embrace. Among all the lessons I suppose the most important is for us to be *prepared*. Prepared for the future, and also that we might be found diligent in serving Him.

Prayer

Let us apply these truths to our lives.

*If any of you lacks wisdom, let him ask of God, who gives to all liberally and without reproach, and it **will** be given to him* (James 1:5).

Chapter 31

1. The words of King Lemuel, the utterance which his mother taught him:
2. What, my son? And what, son of my womb? And what, son of my vows?
3. Do not give your strength to women, nor your ways to that which destroys kings.
4. It is not for kings, O Lemuel, it is not for kings to drink wine, nor for princes intoxicating drink;
5. Lest they drink and forget the law, and pervert the justice of all the afflicted.
6. Give strong drink to him who is perishing, and wine to those who are bitter of heart.
7. Let him drink and forget his poverty, and remember his misery no more.
8. Open your mouth for the speechless, in the cause of all who are appointed to die.
9. Open your mouth, judge righteously, and plead the cause of the poor and needy.
10. Who can find a virtuous wife? For her worth is far above rubies.
11. The heart of her husband safely trusts her; so he will have no lack of gain.
12. She does him good and not evil all the days of her life.
13. She seeks wool and flax, and willingly works with her hands.
14. She is like the merchant ships, she brings her food from afar.
15. She also rises while it is yet night, and provides food for her household, and a portion for her maidservants.
16. She considers a field and buys it; from her profits she plants a vineyard.
17. She girds herself with strength, and strengthens her arms.
18. She perceives that her merchandise is good, and her lamp does not go out by night.
19. She stretches out her hands to the distaff, and her hand holds the spindle.

20. She extends her hand to the poor, yes, she reaches out her hands to the needy.

21. She is not afraid of snow for her household, for all her household is clothed with scarlet.

22. She makes tapestry for herself; her clothing is fine linen and purple.

23. Her husband is known in the gates, when he sits among the elders of the land.

24. She makes linen garments and sells them, and supplies sashes for the merchants.

25. Strength and honor are her clothing; she shall rejoice in time to come.

26. She opens her mouth with wisdom, and on her tongue is the law of kindness.

27. She watches over the ways of her household, and does not eat the bread of idleness.

28. Her children rise up and call her blessed; her husband also, and he praises her:

29. "Many daughters have done well, but you excel them all."

30. Charm is deceitful and beauty is passing, but a woman who fears the LORD, she shall be praised.

31. Give her of the fruit of her hands, and let her own works praise her in the gates.

This last chapter in Proverbs was written by someone called Lemuel. Although there is no certain proof, it is assumed by Jewish tradition that Lemuel is Solomon, and the mother of whom he writes is of course Bathsheba. There was a strong bond between Solomon and his mother. In chapter 4 he said he was "tender and the only one in the sight of my mother" (4:4). It was Bathsheba who went in to see a dying David, when Adonijah had proclaimed that he was David's successor, to plead for Solomon whom David had promised would take his place.

The advice of a mother to her son

She speaks to her son: "My son ... son of my womb ... son of my vows" (v. 2). She had obviously made promises to God about bringing up this boy. What a blessing godly mothers are, whose chief ambition for their children is that they may love and serve

God. What examples in Scripture of such mothers: Jochebed, the mother of Moses; Hannah, the mother of Samuel. Someone has said "if there were more Hannahs there would be more Samuels." Other mothers are Elizabeth, the mother of John the Baptist; Mary, the mother of Jesus. When she says, "What, my son?" she is probably thinking, "What is the best advice I can give to my boy?"

A mother's warning

Women

His mother warned him to be careful about women. Solomon himself had spoken in previous chapters of the dangers of strange women, immoral women. He gave warnings, and sadly towards the end of his life did not apply what he had advised others to his own conduct. She warned him that women could destroy kings. So many men have been trapped in spite of the warnings given about the sins of adultery and fornication. In Deuteronomy 17:16–18 God gave clear instructions to the kings of Israel of things they should avoid:

- He shall not multiply horses to himself.
- He shall not multiply wives for himself.
- He shall not multiply silver and gold for himself.

What havoc has been wrought by immorality resulting in broken homes, divorce, children being brought up without a father, because one of God's commandments has been disobeyed, "You shall not commit adultery" (Exodus 20:14).

Wine

His mother also warns him about the danger of drink. Over-indulgence leads them to "forget the law" (v. 5), which is the proper standard for righteous living. "It is not for kings" (v. 4), not for those in authority. The dangers are illustrated in the lives of kings and rulers: Belshazzar, Benhadad, Ahasueres, and Herod, who was responsible for the death of John the Baptist. Solomon himself had warned of the dangers:

"Wine is a mocker,
Strong drink is a brawler,
And whoever is led astray by it is not wise."   (20:1)

It is the abuse that brings the dangers. Paul encouraged Timothy to take "a little wine for your stomach's sake" (1 Timothy 5:23). The psalmist spoke of "wine that makes glad the heart of man" (Psalm 104:15). Paul set us certain character qualifications for spiritual leaders, elders, and includes that they should not be "given [addicted] to wine" (1 Timothy 3:3).

The virtuous woman

This mother, while warning him about women to avoid, encourages him to find the right kind of wife. The question is asked:

"Who can find a virtuous [an excellent] wife?"   (v. 10)

Mothers want their sons to have the best kind of wife. A wife can bless or ruin. The initial necessity is character, not beauty. What a blessing an excellent wife is. Here again this is included by Paul as a qualification for spiritual leaders:

"Their wives must be reverent, not slanderers, temperate, faithful in all things."   (1 Timothy 3:11)

Who can find a virtuous woman? In Proverbs Solomon has described women using a variety of words:

- Strange women.
- Evil women.
- Whorish women.
- Foolish women.
- Brawling women.
- Contentious women.

And also:

- Gracious women.
- Fair women.

- Women who fear God.
- Virtuous women.

This teaching has two obvious purposes:

1. That men will seek the right kind of wives.
2. That ladies will aspire to have the character and virtues which will please God, and to be a blessing to their husband and children.

How true are the words Solomon spoke in chapter 18:

> "He who finds a wife finds a good thing,
> And obtains favor from the LORD."   (18:22)

I personally am so grateful to God for a good wife, Shelagh. We were married for fifty-six years. She was a virtuous woman, and our five children rose up and called her blessed. I am sure so many of you men can say the same. If you are sitting beside your wife, why don't you tell her, and together praise and thank God?

The character of a virtuous woman

The chapter reveals the character of a virtuous woman. How precious and valuable she is. Her worth is "far above rubies" (v. 10). She is a jewel in any man's crown, but money couldn't buy her.

She is trustworty

> "Her husband safely trusts her."   (v. 11)

He has total confidence in her, and what she does. She does him good all the days of her life. She is consistent, and not moody. Both husband and wife appreciate and value their relationship. So much is involved in the simple statement, "she does him good" (v. 12). Her husband appreciates her: "he praises her" (v. 28). We read:

> "Her husband is known in the gates,
> When he sits among the elders of the land."   (v. 23)

He has a position of authority in the city, and his wife's life is a credit to him. He is unashamed. There is no better or higher standard for husband and wife that that which is taught in Scripture. Paul writing to the Ephesians takes up the theme, and says to wives:

> "Wives, submit to your own husbands, as to the Lord."
>
> (Ephesians 5:22)

And to husbands:

> "Husbands, love your wives, just as Christ also loved the church and gave Himself for her."   (Ephesians 5:25)

Peter's advice to wives is:

> "Do not let your adornment be merely outward – arranging the hair, wearing gold, or putting on fine apparel – rather let it be the hidden person of the heart, with the incorruptible beauty of a gentle and quiet spirit, which is very precious in the sight of God."
>
> (1 Peter 3:3–4)

And to husbands:

> "Dwell with them with understanding, giving honor to the wife, as to the weaker vessel, and as being heirs together of the grace of life, that your prayers be not hindered."   (1 Peter 3:7)

She is industrious

> "She seeks wool and flax,
> And willingly works with her hands."   (v. 13)

> "She is like the merchant ships,
> She brings her food from afar."   (v. 14)

> "She also rises while it is still night,
> And provides food for her household."   (v. 15)

> "She is not afraid of snow for her household,
> For all her household is clothed with scarlet."   (v. 21)

She is busy, but then most mothers are. If you listed what a mother did every day and week it would be quite a list!

She considers the poor

> "She extends her hand to the poor,
> Yes, she reaches out her hands to the needy."   (v. 20)

She makes time for her own hobbies

> "She makes tapestry for herself;
> Her clothing is fine linen and purple."   (v. 22)

Different words describe her: discipline and dignity; diligence and dependability; care and compassion; efficiency and effectiveness. There is no sense of drudgery detected.

This particular lady has maidservants, and no doubt delegated a lot of the work, but she was at the helm. It was her household, and one gets the impression it was not a chore but a delight. Like all mothers there would be times when she was tired, needing a rest.

Thank God for mothers. I had a very good mother. I loved her and all my memories of her are great. As one of her five children I rise up and call her blessed. She lived until she was ninety-four, then one night in her sleep slipped into the presence of the Lord whom she loved and served.

What a need there is today for good mothers and good fathers. What disintegration we are seeing in society. What need there is of role models of good parents. Today we see such disobedience to parents, and lack of respect. Sometimes the fault lies with the parents because they have not brought their children up for God. Bible reading and daily prayers have been neglected: too busy; wrong priorities; the children don't like it, so we won't do it. Better to train now than weep later.

To every mother reading, the Lord bless you. Do you realize how valuable you are? How precious you are? What an influence you have, which can affect the lives of your children now and in the future? Bring them up for God. Make it your highest ambition for them that they may love and serve the Lord. Pray for godly spouses for them.

We dedicated each of our five children to the Lord. Though they have all done well, and done well scholastically, our greatest desire for them was that they might know God and make Him known. We have been blessed by evidence of that, but they, like their parents have still a long way to go; so much to learn, so much to do in the glorious Kingdom of our glorious God. No credit can ever be taken. The glory all belongs to the Lord.

Yes, God bless you and your household.

How does a woman become virtuous?

In the description of a virtuous woman in this chapter we have been concentrating mainly on what she does:

- She gives excellent advice to her son, not only warning him of the dangers of wrong women, and the dangers of strong drink, but also encourages the virtues of judging righteously, and pleading for the poor and needy.
- She runs her home efficiently and cares for her household.
- She foresees future needs, and efficiently provides for them.
- She not only has advised her son to care for the poor, but she herself does that.
- She is also a good business woman and makes profitable transactions.
- She is an excellent wife as well as a mother, and is a credit to her husband who trusts in her and relies on her whole-heartedly.

These are things she does or has done, but what is the key or keys in her life which make her what she is? We find the answer in certain verses. She is described as strong, and honorable, and these lovely words are ascribed to her:

"On her tongue is the law of kindness."   (v. 26)

She is a wise woman

She is an example of the teaching of the book of Proverbs:

"She opens her mouth with wisdom."   (v. 26)

We can ask the questions: "Why is she wise?" "Why is she strong?"
"Why is she honorable?" "Why is she such a blessing and example?"
The answer to each of them is:

She fears God

"A woman who fears the LORD, she shall be praised."   (v. 30)

Proverbs 9:10 tells us:

"The fear of the LORD is the beginning of wisdom."

If we have read the book of Proverbs we will know that the main
teaching for us individually is that we will be men and women who
fear God, who reverence Him, respect Him, love Him, obey Him.
   Not only is the fear of the Lord the beginning of wisdom, it is also
the beginning of understanding as we have read:

"The fear of the LORD is the beginning of wisdom;
And the knowledge of the Holy One is understanding."   (9:10)

Here again are the promised blessings to those who fear God:

- A longer life:
   "The fear of the LORD prolongs days."   (10:27)
- A hatred of evil:
   "The fear of the LORD is to hate evil;
   Pride and arrogance and the evil way."   (8:13)
- Strong confidence:
   "In the fear of the LORD there is strong confidence."   (14:26)
- Walking uprightly:
   "He who walks in his uprightness fears the LORD."   (14:2)
- It gives satisfaction:
   "Better is a little with the fear of the LORD,
   Than great treasure with trouble."   (15:16)

- It gives true happiness:

> "Happy is the man who is always reverent."   (28:14)

And how do we get the fear of the Lord? Here is the recipe. It was the recipe for the virtuous woman we have been looking at. It is the recipe for you and me. Listen again to the words of Solomon:

> "My son [my daughter], if you *receive* my words,
> And *treasure* my commands within you,
> So that you incline your ear to wisdom,
> And *apply* your heart to understanding;
> Yes, if you *cry out* for discernment,
> And *lift up your voice* for understanding,
> If you her as silver,
> And *search* for her as for hidden treasures;
> *Then* you will understand the fear of the LORD,
> And find the knowledge of God."   (2:1–5, emphasis added)

In summary if we will obey the Word of God, value the Word of God, hunger and thirst for God and His Word, seek and search, *then* we will know the fear of the Lord and find the knowledge of God. This should be our lifetime's quest.

Then your children will call you blessed, and say about you, mother:

> "Many daughters have done well,
> But you excel them all."   (v. 29)

And who will really get the credit?

> Praise God from whom all blessings flow.
> Praise Him all creatures here below.
> Praise him above you heavenly hosts.
> Praise Father, Son and Holy Ghost.

To God be the glory, great things *He* has done.